2 Litchfield Road
Londonderry, NH 03053
Meetinghouseofnhdems@gmail.com

PRAISE FOR *Obama's Challenge*

"[Kuttner's] thoughtful, hopeful, and apprehensive book is a particularly valuable guide to what the progressive left hopes to see in the Obama presidency."
—*New York Times Sunday Book Review*

"[*Obama's Challenge* will] probably more powerfully transform your understanding of American politics, progressive economics, and the role of leadership in saving a nation than any other book currently in print."
—THOM HARTMANN, from his BuzzFlash review

"*Obama's Challenge* is the fruit of Bob Kuttner's lifetime of *engagé* reporting, analysis, and advocacy . . . it is riveting, brilliant, and persuasive. Kuttner, in concise chapters written with great vigor and clarity, shows what the change could look like if Obama is bold enough to go for it and the gods continue to smile on him."
—HENDRIK HERTZBERG, from his *New Yorker* blog

"Bob Kuttner pulls off the all-but-impossible. He hits the high notes with artful precision, lifting expectations and articulating the steps that can make Barack Obama a great president—while setting forth a strong and highly readable call for comprehensive and essential economic change."
—JOHN SWEENEY, AFL-CIO President Emeritus

"As Kuttner convincingly argues, a President Barack Obama will have an historic opportunity to radically transform America's direction—but only if he rejects the tired centrist policies of the past and inspires his fellow citizens to forge new progressive paths. Kuttner systematically lays out the case for why Obama should give full voice to a robust progressive message at a time when the American people are suffering from years of conservative policy. *Obama's Challenge* is an enlightening road map for all Americans who hunger for a change in direction and priorities in America, and who hope Obama can be our leading agent of change."
—MARKOS MOULITSAS ZÚNIGA, founder of DailyKos.com, author of *Taking on the System* and coauthor of *Crashing the Gate*

"Robert Kuttner has incisively captured the political moment, underscored by the deepening economic crisis. Lucidly and passionately, he lays out the hurdles facing an Obama presidency and challenges him to seize the moment and achieve greatness by redeeming the promise of America."

—ARIANNA HUFFINGTON, cofounder and editor-in-chief, The Huffington Post

"A manifesto, forceful but fair, by a leading political economist who lays out a bold but solid program if Obama is elected. As current as the morning's newspaper, this book should be read by all activists—especially Barack Obama."   —JAMES MACGREGOR BURNS, author of *Leadership*

A PRESIDENCY
IN PERIL

**THE INSIDE STORY OF OBAMA'S PROMISE,
WALL STREET'S POWER, AND THE STRUGGLE
TO CONTROL OUR ECONOMIC FUTURE**

ROBERT KUTTNER

CHELSEA GREEN PUBLISHING
WHITE RIVER JUNCTION, VERMONT

Project Manager: Patricia Stone
Developmental Editor: Joni Praded
Copy Editor: Laura Jorstad
Proofreader: Nancy Ringer
Indexer: Peggy Holloway
Designer: Peter Holm, Sterling Hill Productions

Printed in the United States of America
First printing March, 2010
10 9 8 7 6 5 4 3 2 1   10 11 12 13 14

Our Commitment to Green Publishing
Chelsea Green sees publishing as a tool for cultural change and ecological stewardship. We strive to align
our book manufacturing practices with our editorial mission and to reduce the impact of our business
enterprise in the environment. We print our books and catalogs on chlorine-free recycled paper, using
vegetable-based inks whenever possible. This book may cost slightly more because we use recycled paper,
and we hope you'll agree that it's worth it. Chelsea Green is a member of the Green Press Initiative
(www.greenpressinitiative.org), a nonprofit coalition of publishers, manufacturers, and authors working
to protect the world's endangered forests and conserve natural resources. *A Presidency in Peril* was printed
on Natures Book Natural, a 30-percent postconsumer recycled paper supplied by Thomson-Shore.

Library of Congress Cataloging-in-Publication Data is available upon request.

Chelsea Green Publishing Company
Post Office Box 428
White River Junction, VT 05001
(802) 295-6300
www.chelseagreen.com

DEDICATION

For Owen, James, Eli,
Amaryah, and Alex

ALSO BY ROBERT KUTTNER

---

*Obama's Challenge: America's Economic Crisis and the Power of
a Transformative Presidency* (2008)

*The Squandering of America: How the Failure of Our Politics
Undermines Our Prosperity* (2007)

*Family Re-Union: Reconnecting Parents and Children in
Adulthood* (with Sharland Trotter, 2002)

Everything for Sale: The Virtues and Limits of Markets (1997)

*The End of Laissez-Faire: National Purpose and the Global
Economy After the Cold War* (1991)

The Life of the Party: Democratic Prospects in 1988 and Beyond
(1987)

*The Economic Illusion: False Choices Between Prosperity and
Social Justice* (1984)

Revolt of the Haves: Tax Rebellions and Hard Times (1980)

CONTENTS

I have spent my entire adult life trying to bridge the gap between different kinds of people. That's in my DNA.

—Barack Obama, April 2008

I did not run for office to be helping out a bunch of fat-cat bankers on Wall Street.

—Barack Obama, December 2009

You can always count on Americans to do the right thing—after they've tried everything else.

—Winston Churchill

The Man and the Moment

We will need to remind ourselves, despite all our differences, just
how much we share.

— Barack Obama, *The Audacity of Hope*

In the spring of his second year in the White House, Barack Obama is at risk of
being a failed president. What would failure mean? Economically, not quite a
second Great Depression, but very possibly a great stagnation with prolonged
suffering for ordinary people—an intensification of trends that were intoler-
able before the crash began. Politically, it would mean the lost promise of an
age of reform anchored in a durable progressive governing coalition. Failure
would leave 2008–12 as merely a brief interregnum in a long Republican era,
with the far right more dominant and more extreme with each election cycle.

Events were not supposed to turn out this way. As the financial crash of
2007 and 2008 deepened, Barack Obama's appearance on the political scene
seemed an almost providential rendezvous of man and moment. Wall Street
was in shambles. Its excesses had brought the economy to the brink of depression. The great collapse was also the practical failure of an ideology and the
ruling elite that embraced it. The claim that the banking system operated
most efficiently with the least government interference was suddenly ludi-
crous. The high priests of that worldview were coming hat-in-hand to the
same government for help.

The failure of the old order was pervasive. The public officials of both
parties who had assured us that financial deregulation would deliver broad
prosperity were shown to be catastrophically wrong. The Wall Street moguls
who insisted that their own grotesque enrichment was merely a by-product of
their vital service to capital markets were revealed as frauds. The free-market

economists who had given intellectual cover to the deregulators in government and the scoundrels in the banks were now intellectually bankrupt.

For progressives, it was the ultimate teachable moment, and here was a leader with unusual gifts as a teacher. As an outsider, Obama owed few debts to the political establishment. His idealistic call for transformative change roused a fearful electorate to vote its hopes. George W. Bush, meanwhile, was leaving office as the most unpopular incumbent since Richard Nixon's resignation in disgrace, adding to the impetus for a clean break.

The early signs were encouraging. In a powerful speech on the financial collapse, in March 2008, Obama declared, "Instead of establishing a twenty-first-century regulatory framework, we simply dismantled the old one, aided by a legal but corrupt bargain in which campaign money all too often shaped policy and watered down oversight. In doing so we encouraged a winner-take-all, anything-goes environment that helped foster devastating dislocations in our economy."

Obama displayed a superb facility for framing boldly progressive ideals as reassuringly patriotic. In his keynote address to the 2004 Democratic National Convention, which instantly established him as a national contender, Obama declared:

> If there's a child on the south side of Chicago who can't read, that matters to me, even if it's not my child. If there's a senior citizen somewhere who can't pay for her prescription and has to choose between medicine and the rent, that makes my life poorer, even if it's not my grandmother. If there's an Arab American family being rounded up without benefit of an attorney or due process, that threatens my civil liberties. It's that fundamental belief—I am my brother's keeper, I am my sister's keeper—that makes this country work. It's what allows us to pursue our individual dreams, yet still come together as a single American family.

If Obama heartened liberals, it was also because here was a black man who had lived the American dream, a man whose own life experience was exemplary as husband, father, scholar, and community leader—a genuinely idealistic politician who once again could inspire. When the extended

Obama family was introduced at the 2008 Democratic National Convention, this was a family of strivers far more evocative of the American dream than the McCain family. It was an all-American family that just happened to be African American. The possibility that the Obamas could be America's First Family suggested a degree of racial healing that most of us thought we'd never see in our lifetimes.

In the 2008 elections, the Democrats gained twenty-four seats in the House and eight in the Senate. Soon their Senate margin would grow to sixty, the largest Democratic governing majority in more than three decades. Young people who knew John Kennedy only from history books had their first experience of being deeply moved by a believable new leader. Voters casting ballots for the first time favored Obama by an astonishing 71 percent. Obama carried states that Democrats had long given up for lost, such as Indiana and North Carolina; he won nearly all the important swing states, like Ohio and Florida. His campaign strategy eventually enlisted an army of 3,000 full-time organizers and an unprecedented 1.5 million volunteers, while more than 13 million people signed up for his e-mail list.

Obama's inspirational eloquence, his call for transforming change, and his skill at the mechanics of retail politics suggested a president who could mobilize citizens as a necessary counterweight to the concentrated power of financial elites. This was not just posturing. His voting record was one of the most liberal in the Senate. So the stage was set, seemingly, for a great ideological and political reversal, comparable to the Roosevelt revolution of 1933. Obama was poised to create a new majority coalition, built on the premise that rapacious private finance had to be contained so that the rest of America could thrive.

But history has a way of playing tricks, and this hopeful scenario is not the way Barack Obama's first year unfolded. Instead of making a radical break with Wall Street, he delivered a startling continuity with the ad hoc bank rescues of the Bush administration. As these policies averted a second Great Depression, the economy has bifurcated. Wall Street has recovered and its executives are once again collecting tens of billions in bonuses, but Main Street is not sharing in the prosperity.

Indeed, the economic pain of ordinary Americans is far more serious than it was before the crash, when economic unease was already a prime concern.

Real unemployment is stubbornly high. Mortgage foreclosures continue to rise. Small businesses are starved for credit. State and local budgets are in free fall. Secure health care remains a distant ideal.

By the time Republican Scott Brown won an upset victory for the Massachusetts Senate seat once held by Ted Kennedy, on the very eve of the anniversary of Obama's inauguration, the administration was already in deep trouble. The Massachusetts debacle was an accident waiting to happen. President Obama has been steadily losing the voters who took a chance on him in 2008. As populist anger rises, and the real economic pain of regular Americans contrasts with lavish Wall Street paydays, Obama and the Democrats are becoming targets of the rage rather than instruments of its remediation.

One man who voted for Obama, a former steelworker now driving a taxi in Pittsburgh, told me, "He's taking over the auto industry, the mortgages, and health care, and the banks. The deficit is going through the roof. And what's it doing for me?" When I appeared on a talk show the morning after the Massachusetts election, one caller told me that he had worked his heart out for Obama in 2008, "and now I'm sitting on my hands." In a Hart Research poll taken in September 2009, 76 percent of respondents said that the government's economic policies had helped large banks, while just 24 percent felt that the policies had helped them or their families. By a margin of 54 to 38, January polls showed that a majority of Americans didn't support Obama's health reform. Pollster Peter Hart described the prevailing attitude as "total disgust" with Washington. But "Washington" now means a Democratic administration and a Democratic Congress.

So the stakes are immense. A rare opportunity for realignment and reform is being missed. A loss of either house of Congress in the 2010 elections would create legislative deadlock, making it that much more difficult for Obama to deliver anything of substance in 2011 and 2012. Obama himself could be a one-term president. Though conservative dominance of economic policy caused the collapse, the Republican far right rather than the reformist left is increasingly supplying the narrative of economic distress, and could pick up the pieces.

During the campaign of 2008, we saw glimmers of a very different Barack Obama and a very different political future. For progressives like me, Obama represented a chance to reclaim a tradition of enriched democracy, affirmative government, and social justice. If Obama does fail, he takes down our hopes with him.

The Enigma of Obama

This book is an exploration of why Obama did not rise to seize a Roosevelt moment. What happened to the audacity? What stunted the promise of sweeping reform? The book also asks: Was the path that Obama chose the only politically possible one? And what would it take for Obama to redeem his promise? Is there still time for him to recoup? The chapters that follow offer not just reportage, analysis, and criticism but some strategic ideas and a basis for hope.

The reasons for Obama's failure, thus far, to deliver transforming change are both personal and structural. One is his own character as a conciliatory consensus builder. A second is that economics was never Obama's strong suit. A third is the residual power of Wall Street; without a president personally committed to Roosevelt-scale change, even a national financial collapse has not been able to shake the hegemony of finance. And a fourth is that the social movements that were so prevalent during other eras of crisis and great presidential leadership are largely absent today.

Obama was also a victim of timing and of the dysfunction of American democracy. At first blush, it appeared that his accession to the presidency was perfectly timed. There was no doubt that the collapse had happened on George W. Bush's watch, and Obama had the public support for a clean break. But where Franklin Roosevelt took office after three and a half years of Depression and Republican failure, Obama became president while the crisis was still deepening. In March 1933, with unemployment at 25 percent and thousands of banks closing their doors, the public was truly ready for radical change. In January 2009, with unemployment still under 8 percent and the banking system seemingly pulled back from the brink, transformative change was still a big political stretch that required exceptional presidential leadership.

In addition, Obama had to contend with the Republicans' relentless use of the filibuster. An effective president needs to drive congressional politics as well as popular politics. Until the health showdown of March 2010, Obama did not frontally challenge the premise that Republicans in the Senate had an absolute right to block any major bill with just 41 votes. In fact, that use of the filibuster dates only to the mid 1970s. Prior to 1975, filibusters had been used mainly by racists to block civil rights legislation, and there was no general premise that all major legislation required a supermajority. The filibuster rule can be changed by a simple majority Senate vote. George W. Bush repeatedly used the budget-reconciliation process to pass bills with only 51 votes. Not since the 1920s have Republicans had as many as the fifty-nine senators that the Democrats have now, yet they have managed to pass major legislation under Reagan and both Presidents Bush. The dysfunctional use of the filibuster was something Obama inherited. But assuming that it should not be contested was his choice.

As the son of a black Kenyan and a white Kansan, Obama has spent his entire life seeking common ground. Obama on occasion could give a speech that made him sound like Franklin Roosevelt. But his desire for consensus has usually trumped his New Deal impulses. His book *The Audacity of Hope* is filled with warnings against excessive partisanship. Despite the Republican "stridency and hardball tactics," he writes, "I believe any attempt by Democrats to pursue a more sharply partisan and ideological strategy misapprehends the moment we're in . . . For it's precisely the pursuit of ideological purity, the rigid orthodoxy and sheer predictability of our current political debate, that keeps us from finding new ways to meet the challenges we face as a country."

Many progressive Democrats at first took Obama's post-ideological stance as merely an astute tactic and were a little surprised to find that Obama was evidently in earnest. "A lot us thought this was just politics," a slightly alarmed Barney Frank told me early in 2009. "But I think maybe he means it." Obama's view of politics and human nature remains a deep part of who he is, even as Republicans block him at every turn and trillion-dollar banks rescued by taxpayers resist reform with impunity.

On the eve of the 2008 election, Barack Obama's friend and University of Chicago colleague Cass Sunstein aptly characterized Obama as a "visionary minimalist." Sunstein, who took a post as a senior White House official in charge of regulatory reform, wrote:

Barack Obama is widely regarded as a visionary because of his emphasis on "change" and his soaring rhetoric, but he also has strong minimalist tendencies. In his victory speech in Iowa, Obama went out of his way to say that it is time for a president who will "listen to" those who disagree, and also "learn from" them. In *The Audacity of Hope,* he asks for a politics that accepts "the possibility that the other side might sometimes have a point" . . . Like all minimalists, Obama believes that real change usually requires consensus, learning, and accommodation—a belief directly reflected in many of his policies. ·

In ordinary times, a post-ideological "visionary minimalist" might be sufficient to coax new areas of common ground. But in a severe crisis created and prolonged by the hegemony of Wall Street, minimalism is capitulation. And with a Republican Party determined to destroy Obama no matter how much he listens, a politics of accommodation is a fool's errand. The moment required transformative leadership, not visionary minimalism. Another distinguished social scientist, James MacGregor Burns, contrasted two kinds of presidential leadership: "transactional leaders who thrive on bargaining, accommodating, and manipulating within a given system" versus "transforming leaders who respond to fundamental human needs and wants, hopes and expectations, and who may transcend and even seek to reconstruct the political system rather than simply to operate within it."

Obama has turned out to be the epitome of a transactional leader, and a fairly hands-off one at that. Obama's desire to be a conciliator, bridge builder, and post-ideological leader might have fit the moment, if only the prime challenges of this era had been those that he anticipated when he began his campaign in early 2007—expanding tolerance, restoring and broadening constitutional government, and redefining a constructive role for America in the world. These were more or less the issues that faced the young John F. Kennedy, at a time when Wall Street was well regulated, America's economy was basically sound, and liberal Republicans still existed. Had Obama been president in such an era, his mix of temperament, conviction, and governing style might have made him a great progressive president. But that cluster of issues, though important, was not the grenade that history tossed Barack Obama.

Even Obama's splendid role as a healer on race has been, to some extent, at odds with what he needs to do on the economy. In the campaign, Obama's advisers were determined that he not trigger images of the angry black man. His style was cool, competent, managerial, and very buttoned up. But sometimes, at a moment of crisis, it is necessary to express passion on behalf of the average person against heedless elites. Obama in office has been diffident to a fault. For most of 2009, his political advisers discouraged any talk that might evoke anger, while his economic aides have resisted anything that smacks of class warfare directed against Wall Street. The result: "Change we can believe in" is blocked, the administration looks like more of a friend to elites than to ordinary people, and Republican obstruction makes Obama look weak. To succeed, Obama, who has reinvented himself more than once, will need to drastically revise his view of how to bring about durable change.

As noted, a related reason for his temporizing on financial reform is that economics was never Obama's passion or personal forte. On pocketbook issues, he was the most centrist and cautious of the three leading Democratic contenders. Obama, rather, won the hearts of progressives through his opposition to the Iraq War, his promise to restore rights and liberties, his artistry as a racial healer, and his capacity to inspire. Those who were skeptical of his views on the economy were willing to cut him some slack because they saw in him the potential for greatness. But when the financial collapse turned out to be his defining challenge, Obama lacked either the self-confidence or the radicalism to appoint insurgents. Instead, he sent for the old guard. As a consummate outsider short on Washington experience, he sought the trust and counsel of the financial establishment.

And financial elites were only too happy to oblige. For, even at the hour of its disgrace, Wall Street continues to have a persistent lock on national politics. This hold is all the more remarkable given that the excesses of Wall Street crashed the economy. The sway of finance is not limitless. But neutralizing the financial industry's pervasive power requires a president far more committed to radical change and hands-on leadership than Obama was in his first year.

The Imperative of Leadership

In August 2008, after Obama had become the Democrats' certain nominee but before the general election, I published a book expressing my own audacious hopes titled *Obama's Challenge: America's Economic Crisis and the Power of a Transformative Presidency.* Because of the deepening financial collapse, I wrote, Obama was very likely to be elected. And because of the scale of change required to surmount the crisis, he would be either a transformational president or a failed one. I noted the undertow of deeply conservative forces that he would need to overcome. Still, I was optimistic that Obama's boldness, intellect, and independence combined with the imperatives of the crisis gave him a real chance to be one of America's great presidents. To put it mildly, these hopes have not yet been realized.

As I wrote in *Obama's Challenge*, at other moments of great crisis and change, progressive presidents had social movements pushing them from the left. Sometimes the president encouraged the movement and used it as a prod; other times the movements pushed them harder than they were comfortable being pushed. Though the particulars were very different, this complex dance of presidential leadership and mass protest describes Lincoln and the abolitionists, Roosevelt and the industrial labor movement, and Lyndon Johnson and the civil rights movement.

Today, by contrast, there is a gross political imbalance in which elites are mobilized and ordinary people are frightened and sullen, but mostly passive. Despite deep economic pain, the streets are eerily quiet, except for right-wingers on the march. There is restive complaint in the progressive blogosphere, but it hasn't yet translated into a coherent movement. Obama mobilized millions of activists for his own campaign, but the Obama White House neutered that operation as soon as he was elected. When there is no mass movement, the president must lead if he is to be an agent of radical change—or the people somehow need to get themselves mobilized to demand the change.

To give Obama some benefit of the doubt, let's acknowledge that resolving this economic crisis was never going to be easy. But getting America out of the Great Depression and winning World War II was not easy. Nor was holding together the Union and freeing the slaves, or finally overturning the system of racial privilege a century later. To invoke these comparisons with Roosevelt, Lincoln, and the Lyndon Johnson of the civil rights era is to measure Barack Obama against American history's greatest feats of leadership. Yet the current crisis is of such a magnitude—and Obama's admirers have compared him to the greatest of presidents.

The challenges he faced entering office, to be sure, were not just financial. He inherited two wars, and the prior administration had played fast and loose with the constitutional rights of Americans. While Obama's policies on national security and constitutional liberties are beyond the scope of this book, he has often disappointed his admirers on these fronts as well. The same syndrome seemed at work—an outsider president seeking the validation of the old order. But if Obama fails as a president, it will not be the result of his policies on Afghanistan or on Guantanamo. His defining challenge was and is the economy.

We should be sympathetic to Obama, given the scale of the disaster that he inherited and the political obstacles to profound change—but not excessively sympathetic. A crisis requires a leader to look beyond the short-term obstructions and to mobilize the people. Instead, Obama appointed an economic team headed by Larry Summers and Tim Geithner, both with close ties to Wall Street. To chair the Federal Reserve, he reappointed Ben Bernanke, who had stood idly by as the crash unfolded and then offered relief without reform. And he named Rahm Emanuel, the epitome of a Beltway corporate Democrat, as his chief of staff. Emanuel, in turn, designed a health reform that was a series of backroom deals with industry interest groups; it soon became justifiably unpopular with the voters. These figures bridged the Clinton era's deregulatory zeal with the even deeper conservatism of the Bush presidency. They represented the opposite of fundamental change.

Events posed obstacles, but events did not require Obama to name these advisers, nor to play an inside game with powerful industries instead of taking a case for radical reform directly to the people. Obama, as his own transition director and admirer John Podesta declared in February, has "lost the narrative" to rightwing populists. In many respects, the most severe constraint Obama faced was the limit of his own imagination.

It is too easy to conclude, cynically, that presidents who sound transformative on the campaign trail invariably become more cautious and accommodative once in office. In fact, however, our greatest progressive presidents have been those who surmounted a national crisis by becoming more radical.

Lyndon Johnson, for example, made his reputation as a southwestern moderate—a bridge between the northern liberals and the Dixiecrats. Once he succeeded the murdered John Kennedy, however, Johnson resolved that his legacy would be to redeem the promise of Lincoln. To a much greater degree than the Kennedy brothers, he encouraged Dr. Martin Luther King Jr. to step up the activism in the streets. He used the prestige of the presidency to affirm and animate the most radical social movement of our era. Before Johnson ruined it all in the jungles of Vietnam, he combined his own persuasive powers with the bravery of movement activists on the ground to get Congress to enact three landmark civil rights laws that overturned once and for all the racist social order in the South.

Franklin Roosevelt, as a candidate, campaigned for budget balance. He was against large-scale public works spending, supportive of the straitjacket of the gold standard, and resistant to federal deposit insurance. He even repeatedly criticized Herbert Hoover as a big spender! But once FDR arrived in office, he sized up the situation he faced and became a presidential radical. He not only used the federal government to deliver relief but faced down the money moguls and remade the financial system. Roosevelt carried Wall Street's hatred of him as a badge of honor. To ordinary voters who elected him four times, there was no doubt that Roosevelt was on their side.

At a moment of great crisis requiring fundamental change, there are basically two available paths. A leader can accept the limitations of conventional politics and try to work with available legislative and interest-group coalitions—the politics of the currently possible. Or the leader can take his case to the people, define the old order as the obstacle to what reform demands, and create whole new possibilities—the politics of the aspirational. Despite his exceptional gifts as a leader and the disgrace of the old power structure, for the most part Obama has chosen the conventional path. And unlike the greatest of presidents, he has been oddly aloof—almost above the fray instead of playing a dominant, defining role.

In this environment, crony capitalism persisted; the best-connected Wall Street firms were showered with government money while smaller banks, other businesses, and ordinary Americans were left to fend for themselves. Our story charts the stages of this business-as-usual political path—from Obama's appointment of an economic team filled with Wall Street insiders and their allies, to his seamless continuation of Bush's financial policies, to the systematic sidelining of fundamental financial reform, to the resulting weakness of the rest of the economy—and the increasing risk of a lost progressive era.

A Road Not Yet Taken

Dare we still hope that Obama may yet deliver change we can believe in? The quiet desperation of millions of Americans is not being remedied by either party. But for now, the economic unease is increasingly being defined and narrated by the Republican right. The crucial question is whether Obama himself has been so totally captured by the financial elite that his path is now irreversible.

It has become a cliché among pundits that the Democratic Party is hamstrung by interest groups. Commentators usually have in mind groups that are actually fairly weak politically—blacks, Hispanics, gays, feminists, schoolteachers, trade unionists. Politicians who propitiate these groups are accused of pandering. The fact that the most powerful interest group of them all, the financial industry, seldom makes the list is testament to its quiet power. Princeton University political scientist Larry Bartels observes, "In the New Deal era, the Democratic Party was about as liberal as it could be without alienating southern racists. In the contemporary era, the Democratic Party is about as liberal as it can be without alienating Wall Street bankers." That power structure needs to be dislodged before real reform can proceed.

In principle, Obama is free to toss out his top aides and bring in a new team. Bill Clinton repeatedly shuffled his advisers. So did Lincoln. But, as we shall see, the threads that link Obama's political aides to his Wall Street–dominated group of top economic advisers will not be easily sundered. The addiction of this administration to flows of Wall Street's political money reinforces the impulse to go easy on the financial industry. Obama's style is to delegate and to proceed with extreme caution. To shift course and lead a different economic team with drastically different views and goals, Obama would have to grow immensely in office.

There is, however, an outside chance that the Massachusetts Senate race will be remembered as a salutary wake-up call, even as a turning point in Obama's presidency. In the days that followed, a stunned Obama tacked in opposite directions. On health care, he tried to sound conciliatory. His initial public comment, in an interview with ABC News, was that the Democrats should not defy the verdict of the voters of Massachusetts, and that a much more modest health reform might be salvaged with bipartisan support. "I would advise that we try to move quickly around those elements of the package that people agree on," he said. But judging by the scornful Republican reaction, this was the empty sound of one hand clapping. After a year of pummeling by a Republican Party determined to take no prisoners, Obama, almost pitiably, was still seeking an elusive bipartisan consensus.

Yet during that same week, he began sounding far more populist when it came to the banks. He inserted himself for the first time directly into legislative battles, pressing for much tougher regulation, and declaring that if the bankers "want a fight, it's a fight I'm ready to have." During his first year, economic populism was treated by the Obama administration as something to be kept in a glass case, for use only in emergencies. It was more rhetorical than real. But the Massachusetts defeat got the president's attention. It may yet dawn on Obama and his political advisers that he needs to deliver more for Main Street, or at least fight harder against Wall Street even if he loses some battles. And on March 3, as this book was going to press, Obama belatedly decided to wage a partisan battle for health reform. It remains to be seen how much collateral damage was done by his earlier missteps.

It is, of course, too early for a definitive judgment on Barack Obama. History reminds us that Lincoln, in mid-1862, was facing a bleak military and political landscape. His peers considered him a failure. His greatness came later. John Kennedy, judged a year and a half into his term, looked like a pretty disappointing president, too. Often, wisdom ripens with experience—and Obama is nothing if not a learner.

Sometimes, however, leaders fail to seize moments pregnant with possibility. Sometimes, to invert a much loved verse of the poet Seamus Heaney, hope and history don't rhyme. The British historian A. J. P. Taylor, referring to the revolutionary year 1848, when nationalist revolutions in central Europe seeking self-determination and liberal democracy were all aborted, memorably characterized the events as a turning point of history on which history failed to turn. We will soon learn whether our own era is such a time.

In Obama's fateful first year, there was a road not taken, a possible road to radical financial reform, broadened prosperity, and the mobilization of an appreciative citizenry. This book explains how the key decisions unfolded, the stakes, and the alternatives, as we look forward to the second half of Obama's term. There is still time for him to redeem his presidency. But that time is fast running out.

CHAPTER ONE

The Politics of Capture

Increasingly, I found myself spending time with people of means—law firm partners and investment bankers, hedge fund managers and venture capitalists. As a rule, they were smart, interesting people, knowledgeable about public policy, liberal in their politics, expecting nothing more than a hearing of their opinions in exchange for checks. But they reflected, almost uniformly, the perspectives of their class; the top 1 percent or so of the income scale that can afford to write a $2,000 check to a political candidate. They believed in the free market and an educational meritocracy; they found it hard to imagine that there might be any social ill that could not be cured with a high SAT score. They had no patience with protectionism, found unions troublesome, and were not particularly sympathetic to those whose lives were upended by movements of global capital . . .

I know that as a consequence of my fund-raising I became more like the wealthy donors I met, in the very particular sense that I spent more and more of my time above the fray, outside the world of immediate hunger, disappointment, fear, irrationality, and frequent hardship of the other 99 percent of the population—that is, the people I'd entered public life to serve.

—Barack Obama, *The Audacity of Hope*

In many respects, the path Obama chose was determined by the people he appointed. Early in the campaign, his advisers were an eclectic bunch, true to the team-of-rivals model that Obama often invoked. He impressed his aides by inviting discussion and disagreement, and then weighing in with his own considered view. But by the time he clinched the Democratic nomination, his advisers had become a much narrower group, as the aides oriented toward Wall Street had efficiently elbowed out the progressives on Obama's team.

Earlier in 2008, however, candidate Obama was sounding like a more radical reformer. In a major address at the Economic Club of New York on March 27, as he was running neck and neck with Hillary Clinton, Obama called for a sweeping restructuring of the nation's financial system. The speech, delivered at Cooper Union, was a gem. It was Obama's bid to be taken seriously as a thoughtful critic of the unfolding calamity, and a jab at the culpability of Clinton-era policies.

The symbolism of the moment was potent. The financial crisis was deepening. The venerable investment banking house Bear Stearns had just collapsed. The Obama campaign deliberately went to New York, carefully choosing a venue near, but not in, the Wall Street financial district. Cooper Union was also chosen to evoke echoes of the greatest presidents. At Cooper Union in February 1860, Lincoln had established himself as a serious presidential contender with a celebrated address on slavery. And Cooper Union was the site where George Washington took the oath of office as the nation's first president.

Obama's basic message was surprisingly populist, and he began by linking the presidency of Hillary Clinton's husband to that of George W. Bush. "Under Republican and Democratic administrations," he pointedly declared, "we've failed to guard against practices that all too often rewarded financial manipulation instead of productivity and sound business practice. We let the special interests put their thumbs on the economic scales. The result has been a distorted market that creates bubbles instead of steady, sustainable growth; a market that favors Wall Street over Main Street, but ends up hurting both."

The speech wasn't just rhetoric. It was a highly detailed blueprint of reform based on an analysis of the crisis that departed from the bipartisan orthodoxy. Obama had one core point. The crisis had been caused by the ability of financial engineers to dupe regulators by creating new corporate forms or products that evaded existing regulatory categories. But no corner of the financial system with the capacity to create risk should be unregulated. "We need to regulate institutions for what they do, not what they are," Obama said. "Capital requirements should be strengthened, particularly for complex financial instruments like some of the mortgage securities that led to our current crisis . . . Transparency requirements must demand full disclosure by financial institutions to shareholders and counter-parties."

In his review of why the system had failed, Obama pointed squarely to the political power of the financial industry: "This was not the invisible hand at work. Instead, it was the hand of industry lobbyists tilting the playing field in Washington."

It was, sadly, an all-too-prophetic description of his own administration.

At the time, however, Obama's Cooper Union address was the most sophisticated and interventionist of any speech on the financial crisis by any candidate up to that point in the campaign. Obama was not an expert on finance; observers wondered where it came from. Obama had been reaching out to a number of critics of the administration, including former Federal Reserve chairman Paul Volcker and Nobel Prize–winning economist Joseph Stiglitz, who helped influence his views. Volcker, who had recently endorsed Obama, was conspicuously seated in the first row.

The speech, though, was actually drafted by Daniel Tarullo, a Georgetown law professor and critic of financial deregulation, who was one of Obama's earliest and closest senior economic advisers. Tarullo had served in the Clinton administration as an assistant secretary for international economic affairs. As a financial scholar based at Georgetown Law School, he had written a definitive and scathing book-length critique, *Banking on Basel,* on the failure of international financial regulation. Along with then Labor Secretary Robert Reich, Tarullo had been one of the Clinton presidency's most liberal officials.

Obama had met Tarullo in 2005, inviting him to talk about financial issues over a sandwich, and the two hit it off. Tarullo enlisted in the campaign as soon as Obama declared. At the time of the Cooper Union speech, Tarullo was also the sole member of Obama's inner circle with a serious grasp of how financial markets worked. The speech was the result of a brainstorming session at Obama's Chicago campaign headquarters, in which several campaign aides argued about what position the candidate should take. Listening to the various viewpoints, Obama concluded that he agreed most closely with Tarullo, whom he designated to draft the speech. Unlike many of Obama's campaign speeches, this one emerged fairly unscathed from the speechwriting team's puree machine, since many of the details were too complex for the speechwriters to grasp.

In retrospect, however, that Cooper Union address was the high-water mark of Obama's financial radicalism. It was a one-off. For there were huge counterweights to Obama's sometime populist instincts and to the thinking of people like Tarullo. One was Obama's desire to reassure America's corporate elite. Another was the related allure of campaign finance. Still another was the influence of the Robert Rubin faction of the Democratic Party. The place where all three pressures converged was Wall Street.

Within two months, as he was locking up the Democratic nomination, Obama had turned to a familiar team of corporate Democrats, most of whom were Clinton administration veterans and protégés of the financier Rubin, the Clinton-era Treasury secretary who has been a senior executive of both Goldman Sachs and Citigroup. By November, this same team would be ensconced as the top officials in charge of economic policy, closely allied with Chief of Staff Rahm Emanuel, whose own history and political strategy reflected intimate personal, financial, and policy links with Wall Street. There would be no broad spectrum of senior advisers, as there had been under both Lincoln and Roosevelt. The reigning policy would be Rubinism.

Larry Summers, Obama's chief economic policy maker, had been Rubin's deputy in the Clinton years and had succeeded Rubin as Treasury secretary. The ubiquitous Rubin was also Summers's patron at Harvard, where Summers was appointed university president in 2002. When Summers was tossed out as president of Harvard in 2006 after a series of missteps, Rubin was the last holdout on the Harvard governing board urging Summers's retention. Subsequently, Rubin successfully promoted Summers to be Obama's economic policy chief. Tim Geithner, a former deputy to both Rubin and Summers at the Clinton Treasury, became Treasury secretary. Geithner's more recent post had been head of the New York Federal Reserve Bank, in effect the deputy to Fed chairman Ben Bernanke, whom Obama reappointed. Geithner bridged the Clinton, Bush, and Obama eras.

Another close Rubin protégé, Peter Orszag, director of Rubin's lobby for budget balance, the Hamilton Project, got the powerful post of director of management and budget. Bob Hormats, another Goldman Sachs alum, was awarded the top economic policy job at the State Department. Michael Froman, Rubin's chief of staff at Treasury and protégé at Citi, got the senior White House staff position in charge of international economic policy. It was a sweep. All of these people, and several more, owe Robert Rubin. One can safely assume that he gets his phone calls returned.

The Kingmaker

Robert Rubin is the apotheosis of a type—the Wall Street Democrat—and he personifies the capture of much of the Democratic Party by Wall Street. This capture is systemic, reflecting the interplay of campaign finance and conservative ideology coupled with the relative weakness of counterweights such as the labor movement. There are others like Rubin, but he epitomizes the way a corporate Democrat can cross-promote business and political interests, and place close allies in key power positions.

Rubin dodged scandals and palpable failures in both his public and corporate life that would have sunk a lesser figure; yet he remained the Democratic Party's éminence grise on matters economic. A man of nimble intellect, self-effacing charm, and professed concern for America's downtrodden, Rubin functions as what in the old days would have been called a power broker, an influence peddler, or a fixer. But those labels don't attach to Rubin, because he is so seemingly public-minded, so socially liberal, and so personally nice. Rubin's rise reflects, and reinforces, the increasing influence of finance on the American economy and polity, through both deregulated financial markets and campaign money.

Until recently Rubin enjoyed a worshipful press. In the 1990s, along with Warren Buffett and Alan Greenspan, Rubin became almost a cult figure. A 1999 *Time* magazine cover lionized Rubin, Summers, and Greenspan as "The Committee to Save the World." In the economic boom of the 1990s, "Rubinomics" supposedly achieved the holy grail of low interest, low inflation, high GDP growth, high job growth, and a blazing stock market. It later turned out that much of this growth was illusory, built on financial bubbles. When I wrote an unflattering profile of Rubin for *The American Prospect* in 2007, I first reviewed every feature article that had ever been written on the man. I was stunned to realize that there had never been a major critique.

After leaving the Clinton administration, Rubin became chairman of

Citi's executive committee in 1999. In the fall of 2008, after the collapse of Citigroup's business model, its dependence on massive federal bailouts, and a sickening slide in its share price, Rubin infuriated other Citi senior executives by disclaiming detailed knowledge of the high-risk trading strategies that had brought Citi low. He was paid upward of $126 million in cash and stock over a decade (and he cashed out before the stock tanked), but Rubin's posture was that of the piano player in the whorehouse. He insisted that his actual responsibilities were amorphous. When reporters asked Rubin about Citi's policy of guaranteeing investors to buy back certain high-risk securities sold by Citi—this was known as a liquidity put—Rubin disarmingly insisted that he wasn't familiar with the concept. In fact, Rubin, earlier in the decade, had been a key architect of Citi's strategy of moving aggressively into high-risk securities. He counseled the new CEO, Chuck Prince, to make riskier plays and persuaded him to recruit senior traders from Goldman and Morgan Stanley.

So when Citi crashed and burned, senior executives who had lost fortunes in the plunge in Citi's stock were enraged at both Rubin's legacy and his disingenuous posture. According to Citi insiders, there was pressure on Rubin to resign. Yet a still-friendly press took at face value Rubin's story that he had voluntarily decided to retire. The *New York Times* version of events informed its readers:

> Mr. Rubin, whose contract specifically absolved him from daily operational responsibilities, has maintained that he could not have foreseen the current mess. "This is not a decision that I have come to lightly," Mr. Rubin said in a statement released by the bank. "But as I enter my 70s and with all that is now in place at Citi, I believe the time has come for me to make these changes."

All that is now in place at Citi! What was in place at Citi when Rubin exited was a financial disaster—a company that survived only thanks to almost unlimited government aid.

Given the abject failure of the financial deregulation that Rubin championed as Clinton's top economic adviser, followed by the collapse of the business model that he promoted as a senior executive at Citigroup, it is remarkable that a consummate outsider like Barack Obama did not view Rubin (or his protégé Summers) as fatally damaged goods. On the contrary, Obama felt he needed men like Rubin and Summers for tutelage, access, and validation. That itself speaks volumes about where power reposes in America.

How Wall Street Neuters the Democrats

Rubin rose through the ranks of Goldman Sachs as a risk-arbitrageur, becoming a partner in 1971 and Goldman co-chairman in 1990. The other co-chair was Steve Friedman, a Republican who would later serve as head of the Bush National Economic Council, the same position that Rubin held in the first Clinton administration. Completing the incestuous symmetry, Rubin's successor, Hank Paulson, went on to be Bush's Treasury secretary—the job Rubin held in the second Clinton term. It's hardly accidental that Goldman has populated the government with scores of sub-cabinet officials, that it helped write the rules of the Bush-Obama bailout program, and that the firm repeatedly received preferential treatment.

But what exactly is a risk-arbitrageur? It is someone who bets on prospective financial takeover deals, buying and selling stocks of companies that might be in play, and sometimes promoting takeover deals to create opportunities for some action. In the takeover mania of the early 1980s, Rubin ran a billion-dollar portfolio. Goldman is well positioned to capitalize on insider knowledge since one side of the firm works on mergers and acquisitions, while the other profits from trades. In principle, there is a "Chinese Wall" between underwriting and trading, since information about pending deals is supposed to be confidential. Insider trading is a criminal offense. Rubin's top assistant and protégé, Robert Freeman, was led out of Goldman Sachs in handcuffs in 1986 and served prison time for using confidential information to profit from trades for both Goldman's arbitrage account and his personal account.

On the other hand, there is a huge gray area about what constitutes privileged knowledge and plenty of ways to exploit the conflict of interest in a firm like Goldman that is both banker and trader on the same deal, and to stay just within the law. For instance, you can legally take positions in a stock and then promote the takeover. Despite the supposed wall between the investment banking side and the trading side, executives from both sides talk strategy all the time. After the Freeman affair, Goldman invested massively in legal talent to make sure it could both exploit its privileged position and stay within the law. As he moved up at Goldman, this balancing act was Rubin's trademark. His other signature move was investing in politicians.

As a major fund-raiser for Democrats, Rubin invariably used his entrée as a moneyman to offer his services as counselor. He emerged as a top campaign solicitor for Walter Mondale in 1984, which in turn positioned Rubin as a key Mondale policy adviser. When Mondale occasionally struck a populist note, Rubin cautioned him to tune it down. At one meeting of fund-raisers in St. Paul in August 1984, Mondale, at Rubin's urging, literally apologized for sounding too much like Roosevelt, according to one participant whom I interviewed. "Oh my goodness," he told his moneymen, "I'm so sorry. There's nothing wrong with wanting to be rich. I want to be rich." It was Rubin who persuaded Mondale to make his politically disastrous call for tax increases to balance the budget the centerpiece of his 1984 convention address.

The Wall Street Democrat is a familiar species, as fund-raiser, policy maker, and cross-fertilizer of business and politics. Democratic presidents typically appoint relative conservatives to the post of Treasury secretary, to reassure the financial markets that they are not Bolsheviks. There is a long tradition of Democrats who pursue second careers as lawyer-lobbyists or fund-raisers. These include even liberal former legislators such as Dick Gephardt and Tom Daschle, and ex–New Dealers reborn as lobbyists such as Tommy "the Cork" Corcoran. But looking back on a century of Wall Street Democrats, Rubin stands alone. None has combined the extraordinary power reflected in the synergy of Rubin's multiple roles—as fund-raiser, gatekeeper, banker, policy guru, certifier of fiscal soundness, and the man reputedly responsible for the artificially inflated boom of the 1990s.

Rubin's unparalleled reach into the overlapping worlds of corporate and Wall Street boardrooms, nonprofits, party organs, and senior Democratic politicians systematically pushes the party to the right, leaving it with less to offer its latent base of ordinary working Americans. The leading center-left Democratic-oriented think tank on budget issues is the Center on Budget and Policy Priorities. Rubin was the dinner speaker at its 2006 fund-raiser. He has also worked closely with Washington's premier center-left think tank, the Center for American Progress, headed by Obama's transition director and

Clinton's former chief of staff John Podesta. The Hamilton Project, founded by Rubin, based at the Brookings Institution, and initially headed by Peter Orszag, promotes free capital movements, light regulation, fiscal balance, cuts in social insurance, and small, market-friendly gestures toward greater equality. When Orszag left that position to become head of the Congressional Budget Office, he was succeeded by another Rubin protégé, Jason Furman, who subsequently became Obama's economic policy director.

The ideology that Rubin is selling is one part deregulation, one part globalization, and one part budget balance, with verbal solicitude but only modest social outlay for the less fortunate. He is passionate about capping the cost of Social Security and Medicare and spent much of the Bush era trying to broker a grand bargain of budget balance, in which Democrats would cut Social Security and Medicare and in exchange Republicans would agree to tax increases. The intransigence of George W. Bush saved the Democrats from sacrificing their crown jewels. This is an ideology that Bill Clinton, not exactly a radical, once disparaged as "Eisenhower Republican."

In the Obama era, Rubin has been a relentless behind-the-scenes advocate for a commission that would create a formula to put automatic caps on public spending, particularly of Social Security and Medicare, if deficits exceeded a set amount. His influence and that of his protégés inside the administration has helped make deficit reduction the test of sound policy (in a deep recession!) and has undercut Obama's ability to deliver for economically stressed voters. Until 2009, Rubin valued his role as a public spokesman. But since Obama took office, with Rubin's own reputation somewhat tarnished, Citigroup a financial basket case, and Wall Street something of a lightning rod, Rubin has preferred to exercise his still-potent influence from behind the scenes.

Citi would have collapsed in 2008 without massive government aid, because of its speculative strategies creating and trading in high-risk securities. Citi's grand design to become a financial supermarket would not have been possible without repeal of the 1933 Glass-Steagall Act. Glass-Steagall had separated largely unregulated and more speculative investment banks like Goldman Sachs from government-supervised and government-insured commercial banks like Citi, which play a key role in the nation's monetary policy. Glass-Steagall was designed to prevent the kinds of speculative conflicts of interest that pervaded

Wall Street in the 1920s and helped bring about the Great Depression (and that reappeared in the 1990s and helped cause the crash of 2007). The Clinton administration's prime architect of the Glass-Steagall repeal was Robert Rubin. On Capitol Hill, the law repealing Glass-Steagall was nicknamed "the Citigroup Enabling Act." Four months after leaving the White House, Rubin joined Citi as chairman of its executive committee.

Abritrage as Politics

Rubin spotted Barack Obama as a comer early on, generously offered his services, and influenced both Obama's thinking and his hiring. Michael Froman, Obama's former Harvard classmate and Rubin's aide both in the Clinton Treasury and later at Citigroup, introduced Rubin to Obama. By 2005, Obama's first year as a senator, Rubin was meeting periodically with Obama and offering himself as a tutor on economic issues.

Obama has repeatedly cited Rubin as a major influence on his own thinking. Writing in early 2006, in *The Audacity of Hope*, Obama affectionately called Rubin "one of the more thoughtful and unassuming people I know." The context for the comment was Obama's concern about what to do for workers in places like Galesburg, Illinois, who have lost their manufacturing jobs at iconic American manufacturers such as Maytag. Obama quotes extensively from a conversation with Rubin in 2005 on how to deal with the dislocations of globalization. Obama approvingly quotes Rubin: "I tend to be cautiously optimistic that if we get our fiscal house in order and improve our educational system, their children will be just fine. Anyway, there is one thing that I would tell the people in Galesburg *is* certain. Any efforts at protectionism will be counterproductive—and it will make their children worse off in the bargain." This is classic Rubin. A broad range of possible policies—on how to regulate global capital, whether to have social standards in trade, whether to make an issue of other nations' industrial policies, and whether to seek to revive US manufacturing—all get conflated and damned as "protectionism."

It's a testament to his political nimbleness that Rubin, a close confidant and official supporter of Hillary Clinton, insinuated himself into the Obama team early on without alienating the Clinton camp. The Clinton strategy was to make her the inevitable nominee. At a time when the Clinton machine warned Democrats that playing footsie with other candidates would not be forgiven and sinners would be denied access to a Clinton administration, this admonition somehow did not apply to Rubin.

Like a good arbitrageur, Rubin covered his bets. While nominally supporting Clinton, he cultivated close ties to Obama. Early in 2007, Rubin encouraged his son Jamie Rubin, a private equity fund manager, as well as his protégé Michael Froman, to offer their services as principal fund-raisers for Obama. Yet as late as May, Rubin still was officially part of the Clinton camp.

On the eve of the March 4 Texas primary, with the race virtually tied, Hillary Clinton spoke at a fund-raising event at the vacation home of one of her strongest supporters, Susie Buell, in Bolinas, California. Senator Clinton excused herself to take a call from Robert Rubin, and she reported back some juicy insider tidbits to this group of elite donors. Her adviser Rubin, she confided, was recommending his former deputy Roger Altman to be her Treasury secretary and Larry Summers for head of the National Economic Council. A conversation about the pros and cons ensued. It was clear that Clinton was relying heavily on Rubin's advice. Had she won the nomination, there is little doubt that Rubin would have been a senior counselor. Meanwhile, Rubin was playing the same role with Obama, promoting several of his closest associates into key positions in the Obama campaign.

In the run-up to the 2008 election, Rubin went to great lengths to try to reposition himself as more of a liberal. In 2006, he gave an extended interview to *The Nation* magazine's senior economic writer, William Greider. Rubin was so persuasive on the need to address poverty and inequality that even the radical Greider was convinced that Rubin had moved with the times. "Rubin now freely acknowledges what the American establishment for many years denied or dismissed as inconsequential—globalization's role in generating the thirty-year stagnation of U.S. wages, squeezing middle-class families and below, while directing income growth mainly to the upper brackets," Greider wrote. However, in the actual interview transcript, published by *The Nation* online, Greider asked Rubin lots of tough questions, but Rubin declined to embrace the policies that might logically flow from his liberal-sounding rhetoric.

In the Obama campaign, seeking to reassure liberals who were increasingly alarmed at his influence, Rubin composed a very peculiar op-ed piece, jointly written with Jared Bernstein. At the time, Bernstein was senior economist at the liberal Economic Policy Institute and was serving as the rare left-liberal economic adviser to the campaign. The idea of joint op-ed, according to sources at EPI (where I serve on the board), was threefold. The campaign hoped it would demonstrate unity and signal Obama's appeal to the entire spectrum of the Democratic Party. Rubin hoped it would help redeem him with liberals. And EPI hoped that Rubin, no friend of the labor movement, could be induced as part of the bargain to lend his support to labor's top legislative priority, the Employee Free Choice Act, which would make it much more difficult for a company to illegally block formation of a union once a majority of its workers signed union cards. Barack Obama himself endorsed EFCA—but in the end, Rubin as a good capitalist refused to.

After tortuous bargaining over language, the op-ed appeared in *The New York Times* on the eve of the election, reading like a diplomatic communiqué in which some items are "bracketed," as they say at the State Department, indicating an agreement to disagree. No fewer than three major points of disagreement were noted—in an op-ed intended to signal unity! On trade, the two wrote, "[O]ne of us (Mr. Bernstein) would advocate provisions in trade agreements that are intended to protect workers, both here and abroad, and the other would have considerable skepticism about the likely effectiveness of those provisions for our workers." Not surprisingly, Obama's actual trade policies were those of Rubin, not Bernstein.

More than anyone else, Robert Rubin determined the direction and composition of Obama's economic team—one charged with repairing a crisis for which the same Robert Rubin could take substantial credit. It is hard to imagine someone other than a senior figure from the financial industry exercising this kind of economic influence on a novice presidential candidate. And the Wall Street connection was reinforced by the Obama campaign's need for money.

Wall Street Falls in Love

To be credible among the commentators and to underwrite the costs of a campaign, a candidate needs to win not just voter affections but the money primary. Within a few weeks of his announcement for president in February 2007, Obama stunned observers with the strength of his prodigious fundraising machine. Some of it tapped small donors, using the networking techniques of the Internet. Obama was popular in Silicon Valley, where software executives with their technical brilliance and love of viral marketing blended perfectly with legions of Web-savvy young volunteers. He also piggybacked on then Democratic Party chairman Howard's Dean's strategy of building a fifty-state campaign. The campaign enjoyed huge, favorable press publicity thanks to Obama's unprecedented success with small donors.

By June 2008, the campaign had enlisted nearly 2 million e-mail contributors who had donated $200 million in donations averaging $100. That impressive feat disarmed the criticism of Obama's decision to reject public financing in favor of private funds. The campaign's story line was that the cure for the corrosive influence of big money was plenty of small money. Obama's success with small donors was sold as a different brand of campaign finance reform. In rationalizing the decision to go back on his pledge to take public funding, Obama declared, "The public financing of presidential elections as it exists today is broken, and we face opponents who have become masters at gaming this broken system."

But despite the success in raising small money, Obama in fact got most of his funds from big, self-interested donors. He was a huge and early hit on Wall Street. From the start, a large network of financial bigwigs decided they liked both the man and his message. Wall Street Democrats are characteristically liberal on issues like foreign policy, race, and human rights, centrist on many pocketbook issues such as alleviating poverty and school reform, and deeply conservative on financial regulation and taxation. Obama, a social, constitutional, and foreign policy liberal running a shade to the right of Hillary Clinton and well to the right of John Edwards on his economic message, seemed like their kind of guy. The star quality didn't hurt, either. Younger people on Wall Street, like the young everywhere, particularly warmed to this remarkable novice.

On February 6, 2007, Hillary Rodham Clinton, deliberately upstaging Obama's declaration of his candidacy scheduled for February 10, rolled out her fund-raising team. It was part of a strategy that her advisers called "shock and awe"—create a juggernaut of early endorsements and fund-raising supremacy that would create a politics of inevitability, create an unstoppable bandwagon, and lock up the nomination. At a dinner at her house in Washington, seventy of the top fund-raisers from around the country pledged to raise at least $250,000 each.

For weeks, Clinton's people had been aiming to roll up Wall Street. They had the loyalty of some of the top fund-raisers from the Bill Clinton era—financier Steve Rattner, private equity eminence Alan Patricof, Wall Street veterans Roger Altman, Fred Hochberg, Stanley Shuman, Carl Spielvogel, and dozens more. Clinton bragged that she would raise $15 million just in the first quarter. Supermarket magnate John Catsimatidis boasted, "She's going to raise more money than all the other candidates put together." It was intended to create an unstoppable bandwagon. The Clintons had long memories, and they played hardball; Wall Street people who backed someone else would not be forgiven.

But like many other Americans, some on Wall Street did not want a replay of the Clinton era. They were either weary of the family soap opera or worried that Hillary could not win the general election. Obama soon managed to poach one large Wall Street donor after another. The legendary Wall Street billionaire and philanthropist George Soros was one of his first big catches, and within just two months Obama had a New York money machine that rivaled Clinton's. Its steering committee, in addition to Jamie Rubin and Michael Froman, included Robert Wolf, chief executive of UBS Americas; fund manager Jim Torrey; hedge fund executive and longtime Democratic operative Orin Kramer; and Provident Group partner Brian Mathis. *The Washington Post* quoted Jim Torrey, chief executive of the $1.3 billion hedge fund that bears his name: "I've never had a higher hit ratio in terms of asking people for money and them saying yes."

When her first-quarter 2007 fund-raising totals were announced on April 1, Hillary Clinton reported raising a prodigious $23 million. Of that, $19.1 million could be spent on the primary. The rest was money for the general election, which the Clinton campaign had solicited early in order to inflate its totals (and bragging rights). The Obama campaign waited two days until April 3, "to build suspense," according to Obama campaign manager David Plouffe. Obama, it turned out, pulled in $26 million in primary money—$7 million more than the supposedly inevitable nominee Hillary Clinton did.

Despite the carefully cultivated buzz about Obama's small-money base, his biggest donor source was Wall Street. As the year wore on, large donors were instructed to break up their contributions into small checks over time, in order to reinforce the campaign's small-donor myth. By the first quarter of 2008, when the primaries finally began, Obama had raised more money on Wall Street than either New Yorker in the race—Hillary Rodham Clinton on the Democratic side or Republican Rudy Giuliani, who was then viewed as a major contender. Obama was a particular favorite at Goldman Sachs, whose employees provided the biggest single bundle, $571,330 for the year 2007. Obama's small donations accounted for 32 percent of his total, more than Hillary Clinton's 14 percent, but less than John Edwards's 36 percent.

The A-Team

As of Obama's March 27, 2008, speech in New York, his group of economic advisers was still something of a pickup team. Obama and Clinton had split the early contests in Iowa and New Hampshire and roughly divided the Super Tuesday primaries, but then Obama faltered in Ohio and Pennsylvania. The race promised to go all the way to the convention. By April, it was increasingly clear that the next chief executive would face a severe economic crisis. During this period, Obama's Democratic rivals and his critics in the press and in the Republican camp were ramping up the rhetoric that Obama was untested; that he had radical friends; that he might be a secret Muslim; and that his true views were unknown. It was the period of repeated eruptions on the part of his pastor, the Reverend Jeremiah Wright. At that point in the campaign, Obama still had just two part-time economic experts on his inner campaign team—a University of Chicago economist colleague, Austan Goolsbee, who was a complete newcomer to national politics, plus Tarullo—along with a floating group of other volunteer advisers. On all counts, the Obama campaign decided that it needed to bring in some economic heavyweights.

On June 9, shortly after topping Hillary Clinton in the delegate count, Obama unveiled a very familiar-looking team. Most were veterans of the Clinton administration. The nominal economic policy director would be thirty-seven-year-old Jason Furman, the director of Robert Rubin's Hamilton Project. The heavy hitters were Rubin, Summers, former Clinton chief economic adviser Laura Tyson, and former Federal Reserve chairman Paul Volcker, plus Obama's longtime campaign advisers Goolsbee and Tarullo. Furman told reporters, "My key mandate, which came directly from the senator, is to bring him a diverse set of voices and ideas, because that's the kind of debate he likes to hear to make up his mind about his economic agenda." He added that he'd be relying on Rubin, Summers, former Federal Reserve vice chairman Alan Blinder, and liberals Jared Bernstein of EPI and James Galbraith of the University of Texas, a former staff director of the Congressional Joint Economic Committee. Robert Reich was also a some-time adviser, and Obama was fond of saying that he listened to both Bobs, Reich and Rubin.

But when the dust settled, it was evident that the Rubinistas had taken control of the economics team, and the liberals were the outer planets. Instead of the team-of-rivals model that Obama had often invoked, Obama hired a team of Rubins. Summers quickly assumed control of the campaign's weekly telephone meetings on economics. The more junior Furman, ostensibly the economic policy director, functioned more like the team's executive secretary, staying in e-mail communication with a broader community of advisers and hangers-on, and facilitating discussions. Rubin had direct access to the candidate whenever he wanted. After Obama wrapped up the nomination, Summers, sometimes accompanied by Laura Tyson, represented the campaign in meetings with congressional leaders.

I was present at one meeting in Speaker Nancy Pelosi's office in October, prior to the election, when the subject was how to structure the financial bailout. Pelosi had assembled eight outside economic experts, and the Obama campaign was represented by Summers and Tyson. By far, the most conservative person in the room was Summers, who kept insisting government should treat the banks gently and not undercut their profits, because "we want private capital to come in." In other words, the leverage for reform created by the banks' massive dependence on government aid should not be used. At one point, a question was raised about the terms that should be exacted from banks receiving government assistance. With supreme confidence, Summers grandly responded, "Let's leave that to the next Treasury secretary."

A Well-Timed Collapse

Wall Street's financial collapse, which turned critical in mid-September 2008, was a gift to the Obama campaign. How ironic that the Obama administration reciprocated by showering financial aid at Wall Street.

With John McCain's selection of Sarah Palin as his running mate on September 4, the Republican base was reenergized; Obama seemed blindsided and off his game. Palin had not yet self-destructed, and John McCain had opened a lead in the polls. I vividly remember those days because I had my fifteen minutes of televised fame on September 11, on the eve of the collapse, in a dustup with Sean Hannity of Fox News. My book *Obama's Challenge* had just been published. A producer from Fox phoned my publisher and asked if my first TV interview could be with Fox's food-fight show, *Hannity & Colmes* (Alan Colmes, Hannity's punching-bag "liberal" sidekick, has since left the show). I did not want to appear with the thuggish Hannity, but the producer promised that the low-key Colmes would do a straight book interview. I reluctantly agreed. The interview began well enough, with Colmes asking neutral and civil questions about my book and me laying out its argument: that Obama, as the likely next president, would face a severe economic crisis.

About two minutes in, Hannity could no longer contain himself. "Oh, stop it, stop it. This is garbage you're spewing here," he bellowed contemptuously from off camera. The camera panned over to Hannity's side of the set. Astoundingly, just four days before the Lehman Brothers collapse, Hannity insisted that the economy was in great shape. "Unemployment in this country has been lower than the last four decades. Economic growth in the last quarter was 3.3 percent. Interest rates and inflation have been lower in the Bush years than they've been in the last three decades and you are trying to convince the people of America that something is wrong." When Hannity deigned to let me get a word in, I responded, "If you can persuade the

American people that the average family is doing great, your guy deserves to win the election. But I don't think the American people are that stupid."

This turned out to be the very week that one storied financial house after another faced either total collapse or government bailout. September 14 began a week when the Treasury and the Fed mounted frantic, serial rescues and the stock market was in free fall. It is a mark of the sheer panic and incompetence that the trio of Bernanke, Paulson, and Geithner handled the imminent insolvency of the Federal National Mortgage Association (Fannie Mae), American International Group (AIG), Lehman Brothers, and Merrill Lynch in four entirely distinct ways, even though the systemic threats were quite similar. Fannie Mae was taken over by the government. Lehman was allowed to collapse. AIG was given almost unlimited government funding with majority government ownership, and Merrill was pushed into a shotgun merger guaranteed by the government.

None of this reflected well on the Bush administration, the Republican incumbency, the conservative story about how the world worked, or the candidacy of John McCain. As the financial economy spun deeper out of control, Bush's Treasury secretary, Hank Paulson, concluded that he was out of ad hoc tricks. After more than a year of working with the Fed on emergency weekend rescues and essentially winging it using the Fed's capacity to create money, Paulson now needed two things from Congress—explicit authority and a lot of taxpayer dollars. On Thursday, September 18, Paulson met with congressional leaders of both parties and warned of a complete financial meltdown if Congress did not act over the weekend. Paulson requested $700 billion in public funds to operate an emergency program to purchase the toxic securities that were clogging the balance sheets of banks, and he asked Congress to rush through the legislation with no legislative hearings and few questions asked. The plan was named the Troubled Asset Relief Program, or TARP. The bill authorizing the program ran just two and a half pages. Its core was just one sentence: "The Secretary is authorized to purchase, and to make and fund commitments to purchase, on such terms and conditions as determined by the Secretary, mortgage-related assets from any financial institution having its headquarters in the United States."

The idea that legislative action was required by the following Monday was preposterous. As I and other critics wrote at the time, if Congress took several weeks to hold hearings and solicit a variety of views on the best way to recapitalize and restructure the banks, it would have far better served the public interest. Paulson and Bernanke would have simply continued their emergency loans and loan guarantees, as they had been doing for nearly a year. But so fearful was the congressional leadership of denying this emergency request and taking responsibility for a possible complete collapse that Congress delivered only a slight variation on the Paulson bill, though it took nearly three weeks. Among the minor embellishments were the creation of a congressional oversight panel and an independent special inspector general to review how Treasury was spending the money, as well as the authority, which Paulson had not sought, to pump public capital into the banks directly rather than just buying up their distressed securities.

Paulson's bailout was deservedly unpopular—and still is. As House Speaker Nancy Pelosi prepared to take the bill to the House floor, House members of both parties were being bombarded with phone calls, e-mails, and letters from constituents who detested the Paulson plan. The backlash transcended party. Liberals objected that public funds were going to be used to bail out the very financial engineers who had caused the collapse. Conservatives resented the huge use of taxpayer dollars, the interference with the free market, and the extraordinary power to be given to "King Henry," as angry Republican back-benchers termed Paulson. Some Republican members told their leaders that their calls were running 100 to 1 against the plan. A revolt was brewing among rank-and-file members of both parties.

Because of the unpopularity of the bill, House Speaker Nancy Pelosi insisted that the Republican leadership had to produce at least 100 votes in support. In return, the Democrats would provide at least 120, enough for a bare majority. But on September 30, only 65 Republicans (and 140 Democrats) voted aye, and the bill failed, 228–205. The Dow Jones average dropped 777.68 points.

Five days later, the House did pass a revised bill, and the Senate concurred. It was the Democrats, with Barack Obama urging them on, who delivered the key votes for a rescue designed by and for a Republican administration to serve Wall Street. It was not an auspicious portent for a new Obama administration. For McCain, who looked inept and equivocal, the fatal damage was done: This was the decisive turning point when swing voters concluded that Barack Obama was the more trustworthy leader in a crisis. The race basically locked at a 6- to 8-point lead for Obama, and scarcely budged in the campaign's remaining six weeks. And Barack Hussein Obama set about preparing to govern.

The Strange Selection of Larry Summers

As President-elect Obama named his top economic team, it became clear just how sweeping was the victory of the Rubin faction. Summers emerged as chairman of the National Economic Council—the president's overall chief of economic policy. There had been talk of making him Treasury secretary. But questions quickly emerged about whether Summers could get through a bruising confirmation hearing.

Summers had legions of detractors from his multiple battles with the Harvard faculty. In a confirmation hearing, women's groups would surely deplore his comments about the possibly innate inferiority of women in math and science. But that controversy was only the most visible of Summers's problems. He had made windfall profits on Wall Street in 2006, 2007, and 2008, some of them courtesy of very generous speaking and consulting fees from the same firms that were getting government bailout aid. The particulars were belatedly made public by the White House only in April 2009, and raised eyebrows, but they were known to the transition team in November. D. E. Shaw, a hedge fund, had paid Summers $5.2 million for about a day a week of work. Goldman Sachs, a regular seeker of favors from government, paid Summers $135,000 for a single speech. A *Wall Street Journal* editorial acidly commented, "That must have been some stemwinder."

The awkward revelations did not end there. Summers's close friend, colleague, and protégé, Andrei Schleifer, was embroiled in a lawsuit under the False Claims Act whose settlement ended up costing Harvard $26.5 million plus millions more in legal fees. Schleifer, who ran the Russia project for the Harvard Institute of International Development, which received contracts from the US Agency for International Development (USAID), had used his privileged knowledge to make investments in Russian companies and funds on which he was advising the Russian government, despite both government and Harvard University policies expressly prohibiting such conflicts. Sworn depositions in the trial suggested that Summers had protected his friend. Shleifer continues to hold a chair in the Harvard economics department. It was a lengthy investigative piece in the financial magazine *Institutional Investor* on Summers's role in the Shleifer affair, widely circulated on the eve of a key faculty meeting, that turned key faculty members against Summers and ultimately forced the Harvard Corporation to oust him. Further digging, likely at a Senate confirmation hearing, would have also produced more awkward details. This was not the kind of material that would reflect well on Obama at an extended confirmation battle.

Summers was very much a free-market sort of economist, having served in the early 1980s on the senior staff of Ronald Reagan's Council of Economic Advisers. He was a proponent of deregulation, both domestic and global. He often waded into subjects where he had little expertise, and his style was to humiliate adversaries. He had repeatedly worked to overcome a deficit of interpersonal skills based on the supposed power of his intellect. He had the tragic flaw of certitude, but also an endearing capacity to acknowledge old mistakes. Old patterns kept repeating themselves in new contexts.

There are hundreds of stories about his bull-in-a-china-shop style at Harvard. Here is just one. In 2004, a young and highly regarded professor at the Harvard Business School, Rawi Abdelal, was going through the rite of passage of presenting his first case. Abdelal is an expert on international currency movements. In the late 1990s, currency speculation, the fruit of the deregulation applauded by Summers and Rubin, had destabilized the economies of several Asian nations. An exception was Malaysia, which had resorted to currency controls, a perfectly legal emergency action under International Monetary Fund and World Trade Organization rules, and one periodically used by other nations. Abdelal concluded, based on his research, that Malaysia had pursued the right course.

Summers invited himself to sit in on Abdelal's presentation. During the question period, Summers excoriated Abdelal for being a total fool. How could the business school be so ill advised as to have a professor who believed in currency controls? Abdelal, at the time, was not yet tenured, his first case was a very big deal, and this amounted to a public humiliation by the university's president. As the discussion continued, it became clear to the audience that Abdelal knew a great deal more about the subject than Summers, but that did not stop the Harvard president's tirade. Not long afterward, Summers mentioned Abdelal's idiocy to University of Chicago economist Robert Barro, a free-market conservative.

"Larry," Barro said, "he's right." Later, Summers phoned Abdelal to apologize—and Abdelal became one of the youngest people granted tenure at Harvard Business School.

Even more important for his credentials as the president's economic policy czar, Summers pursued a set of reckless fiscal policies at Harvard that might lead one to question his economic brilliance. Summers ordered a spending spree, based on the premise that Harvard's endowment would continue to inflate at several times GDP growth. Harvard's endowment, pursuing highly risky strategies, regularly beat the market, which itself was becoming a dangerous bubble. But rather than recognizing that stocks rise with the economy over the long term but are subject to periodic downturns, and putting some of the windfall into a rainy-day fund, Summers dramatically increased the university's operating budget, which grew by 67 percent in a decade. And he put the operating budget—Harvard's checkbook account for current expenses—into the same fund with the endowment. Historically, Harvard had strictly avoided this kind of risky commingling of funds.

Astoundingly, between 2000 through 2008, Harvard added 6.2 million square feet of building space, about the size of the Pentagon. It was nearly twice the amount of space added in the previous two decades. Summers's strategy was to keep building, based not on money actually raised, but on the wildly improbable assumption that the endowment could keep beating the market and that the market would keep beating the economy. Summers directed that ground be broken for a new science center that alone cost $1.2 billion. In 2008, after the crash, work abruptly was halted, leaving nothing but a giant hole in a once vibrant neighborhood—a monument to Summers's grandiose economic misjudgment.

Over the objections of many senior law faculty, he and his ally Elena Kagan, whom he had appointed law school dean, ordered the school to build an enormous new building that many felt it didn't need. Summers told a very skeptical faculty planning group at one key meeting that he would be "breaching my fiduciary duty to the university" if he didn't order construction of the new building. When the stock market collapsed and the Harvard endowment lost a third of its value, the well-heeled law school was directed to absorb $20 million in annual budget cuts—most of it the result of the costs of the unwanted new building. The larger faculty of arts and sciences was told that it had to make up a deficit of $220 million. By the fall semester of 2009, Harvard's ongoing programs were in severe austerity mode. Hiring was frozen, and Harvard undergraduates were no longer being served hot breakfasts. Over the winter break in 2009–10, all dormitories were shut down and students not planning to spend the five-week break with families were left with no place to live.

Other Ivy League universities with large endowments lost big in the stock market crash. But no other one had pre-committed so much money to a vast unfunded building campaign based on extrapolations of non-stop double-digit endowment growth. And none had commingled its operating budget— the university's checking account—with speculative long-term investment funds.

This gambling was pure Summers, who repeatedly overruled the warnings of Harvard's financial advisers and insisted on placing nearly all of the operating budget in the highly risky endowment portfolio, with its reliance on volatile hedge funds, private equity, and other "alternative" investments. This blunder reflected Summers's familiar flaw: His self-confidence about areas where he was expert extended to those where he was ignorant.

Summers annoyed the hugely talented professional management team responsible for investing the endowment, second-guessing their strategy and in one case personally directing the investment experts to make a bet on interest rate movements that cost the university more than $1 billion. He made life so uncomfortable for Jack Meyer, the talented and respected chief money manager for Harvard's endowment, that he finally drove Meyer out. At an early meeting with Meyer, Summers had advised the money manager that Bob Rubin, now at Citi, would be "calling the shots" on new investment plays. Summers's behavior, betting the financial health of America's premier university on perpetually rising asset values, was reminiscent of nothing so much as the giddy euphoria of the subprime industry (heavily backed by Citi), which bet the ranch on the improbable premise that housing prices would keep rising much faster than the growth of the economy.

In December 2004, according to an investigative report by Bloomberg

News, Harvard locked in future interest costs on $2.3 billion of bonds. Summers was planning to use the proceeds to underwrite his expansion of the university across the Charles River in Allston. At that time, the overnight interest rate target set by Federal Reserve was 2.25 percent. Summers was convinced that rates would rise, and he used complex swaps to bet that he was right. This was not a necessary hedge against rising rates—the bonds were already sold—it was a speculative gamble. He expected that Harvard would profit from the bet. But Summers bet wrong, and when the Fed lowered interest rates to near zero after the crisis, Harvard had to scramble to come up with just under $1 billion to extricate itself from its swaps contracts. As it happens, the swaps contracts were written by JPMorgan, Goldman Sachs, and Citigroup. Rubin was in a familiar conflicted role, as both a top executive of Citi and Summers's closest ally on the small Harvard governing body.

Summers's checkered past was more than sufficient to persuade the political team and the official vetters that he was not an acceptable risk for Senate confirmation. But evidently it did not give much pause to the premise that Obama should put Summers in charge of America's economic policy.

Rubin, in promoting Summers for president of Harvard, assured people time and again that "Larry has changed." After Summers flamed out at Harvard, Rubin used the same pitch in persuading Obama to take the man on as his chief economist. His remarriage, to Harvard English professor Elisa New, had given him a gentler manner. He had learned how to listen. His setbacks had taught him humility. In auditioning with Obama, Summers kept his bullying in check and also went on a charm offensive to persuade skeptical Democrats that he had really become almost a liberal. He had changed, evidently—not just temperamentally but ideologically.

In a series of op-ed commentaries in the influential *Financial Times*, Summers wrote article after article contending that inequality had reached unacceptable levels, that financial markets needed to be re-regulated and laissez-faire trade reconsidered—articles that read like audition pieces for a post in a liberal administration. Addressing trade and the national interest in a piece on April 27, 2008, Summers wrote, "The growth in the global economy encourages the development of stateless elites whose allegiance is to global economic success and their own prosperity rather than the interest of the nation where they are headquartered." Larry, we hardly knew ye! But when he became Obama's top economic official, it was clear that Summers's views had scarcely changed at all.

In late October and early November 2008, when it seemed increasingly clear that Obama would win, his senior political team went back and forth on whether Summers could survive Senate confirmation as Treasury secretary. But either way, it was already clear that Summers would be top dog. In the end, the jobs were reconfigured so that the top power position would be chairman of the National Economic Council. That post had been invented for Bob Rubin by Bill Clinton, in 1993.

Far from representing a radical break with the deregulation common to the Clinton and Bush presidencies and the badly flawed crisis management of Bush's last year, Summers bridged these two failed sets of policies. He became personally close to Hank Paulson, whom he repeatedly defended against criticism. The two had a similar reading of the financial crisis and enjoyed a cordial working relationship during the transition. It annoyed Summers that some felt that Paulson, former head of Goldman Sachs, epitomized crony capitalism. When Harvard Law School professor Elizabeth Warren was appointed to chair the Congressional Oversight Panel for the TARP bailouts, her Harvard colleague Hal Scott, a proponent of deregulation who had advised the Bush administration, quipped to a colleague, "Elizabeth Warren gets up every day and can't imagine an America without the middle class. Hank Paulson gets up every day and can't imagine an America without Goldman Sachs." The one-liner was widely repeated. When Summers heard it, his irritated reaction to colleagues was that Paulson was wrongly being accused of practicing corrupt favoritism on behalf of his former employer.

Geithner Redux

If Summers was the link to the deregulation crowd of the Clinton era, Tim Geithner epitomized the politics of continuity with Bush. In many respects, Geithner seemed the perfect man for the job. As the Federal Reserve's point man in New York, he knew Wall Street intimately but he had not grown up on Wall Street. You could not appoint a banker to this job after the disgrace that had just befallen the banks; Geithner, though, was both close enough, and just distant enough. He was also a Democrat. Except for a brief stint working for Henry Kissinger's consulting firm, Geithner's whole career had been in government—at the US Treasury and later the International Monetary Fund. And he had been playing a hands-on role in the crisis since it first broke in spring 2007, so he would need no on-the-job training.

Across the political spectrum, Geithner was viewed as competent and honorable. The consensus was that when financial markets were collapsing his interventions were imperfect, but he had saved the economy from the worst. His fans ran the ideological gamut from Barney Frank, the liberal chair of the House Financial Services Committee, to the archconservative Republican private equity billionaire Peter G. Peterson, who had headed the search committee that recommended Geithner to head the New York Federal Reserve Bank in 2002. Geithner's appointment was also viewed as a way of reassuring money markets. And when his nomination was announced, the Dow obligingly rose more than 500 points.

So high was Geithner's personal stock that when his confirmation hearings ran into an embarrassing snag, just enough Republicans were willing to wave him through. Geithner, it turned out, had failed to pay his Social Security taxes for three years while serving at the IMF. To make matters worse, when an audit discovered the discrepancy for 2003 and 2004, Geithner paid up, but he did not go back and pay taxes owed for 2001 and 2002—until he knew the matter would be raised at his confirmation.

Of all people who should know better than to chisel on taxes owed, the Treasury secretary—the nation's top tax collector—should be above reproach. But so palpable was the sense of crisis and so popular was Geithner with the financial elite that key conservative senators—who had destroyed Obama's first nominee for health and human services secretary, Tom Daschle, for much more minor financial lapses—decided to give Geithner a pass. His nomination was confirmed with no attempted filibuster, but with thirty-four dissenting votes. Until he was confirmed, Geithner continued in his position as president of the New York Federal Reserve Bank, working hand-in-glove with Paulson.

Rahmbo

If the Obama administration needed one more key official to discourage economic change we can believe in, it was the president-elect's choice for chief of staff, Rahm Emanuel. The appointment initially won wide praise. Obama, the idealistic novice outsider, was hiring the consummate legislative insider, who in turn brought in a team of congressional veterans. But Emanuel was not just a legislative tactician. Early in his political career, Emanuel came to national prominence as a fund-raiser for the Chicago Daley machine. Next, he went to work as one of Bill Clinton's chief moneymen in the 1992 campaign. President-elect Clinton then named him White House political director. Emanuel specialized in raising money from the financial elite. He also worked closely with William Daley, the brother of the Chicago mayor and Clinton's secretary of commerce, in helping to sell the North American Free Trade Act.

In late 1998, when the Clinton White House was embroiled in the Monica Lewinsky mess, Emanuel decided to leave government to seek his own fortune on Wall Street. As one senior Clinton administration veteran told me, "Rahm was no financial genius. He was set up politically with deals in Chicago to make him wealthy." Bruce Wasserstein, former CEO of Lehman Brothers and later head of his own boutique investment banking firm, Wasserstein Perella & Company, was a major donor who knew the Clinton White House well. Chief of staff Erskine Bowles vouched for Emanuel, and Wasserstein offered him a job.

At the Chicago office of Wasserstein Perella, Emanuel brokered several deals, all of which drew on political contacts. He helped a private equity firm buy a home alarm company called SecurityLink from SBC Communications, the telecom giant then headed by Bill Daley. The $500 million deal was facilitated by Bowles. His other clients included Loral, a major defense contractor headed by major Democratic donor Bernard L. Schwartz, and the Chicago Board Options Exchange, which Emanuel knew well from his days working for Mayor Daley.

His most lucrative deal was the $8.2 billion merger of two utility companies to create the energy conglomerate Exelon. John W. Rowe, CEO of Exelon, was introduced to Emanuel by Chicago billionaire Lester Crown, according to *The New York Times*. The *Times* quotes Crown as saying that he valued Emanuel for his political insights and connections: "You can't understand utility transactions without thinking about whether they'll play or not play in legal and political circles." Emanuel's short career as an investment banker was based entirely in his political access to key power brokers in Chicago and Washington.

By the time Emanuel left the firm to run for Congress after just two and a half years, he had made better than $18 million. During his three terms in the House after his election in 2002, Emanuel was the single largest recipient of funds from the financial industry. The Daley machine threw its support to Emanuel for the seat formerly held by Rod Blagojevich, later the disgraced Illinois governor. Emanuel, not a natural at retail politics, won a close primary mainly because party ward heelers worked his campaign. His talent as a moneyman was recognized by his elders, and in 2005, with less than two terms under his belt, he was named to chair the Democratic Congressional Campaign Committee, the House body that recruits Democratic candidates to run for Congress and helps raise money for them.

As head of the DCCC, Emanuel displayed the strategic patterns that would continue into his tenure as White House chief of staff. His strategy was pure "New Democrat." Emanuel's ideal candidate for Congress was a corporate Democrat who could raise lots of money from Wall Street. In some politically moderate suburban districts, this made tactical sense. But as one senior member of the House Democratic leadership told me, "Rahm recruited a lot of candidates who were more center-right than they needed to be." In several districts, a more progressive candidate defeated the Emanuel-approved and Emanuel-funded candidate in the 2006 Democratic primary and went on to win the general election in November.

In Kentucky's Third District, John Yarmuth, founder of the state's first alternative newspaper, took back a Republican seat. He was Emanuel's fourth choice. In California, Jerry McNerney won without Emanuel's help. Carolyn Shea-Porter in New Hampshire, a social worker and grassroots activist, beat the DCCC-financed primary candidate, Jim Craig, by 20 points. After her primary victory, the DCCC denied Shea-Porter funds for the general election, which she won easily. Progressive John Hall, an anti-nuclear and environmental activist from New York's Nineteenth District, got no help from

Emanuel but won anyway. Liberal Chris Carney, who won Pennsylvania's Tenth District, had trouble getting Emanuel to take his phone calls.

In a very high-profile race in Emanuel's home state of Illinois, Emanuel elbowed aside an effective grassroots progressive, Christine Cegelis, who had come out of nowhere to make a strong showing in 2004 against Representative Henry Hyde in a supposedly safe Republican district. Cegelis was one of the "Dean Dozen," actively promoted by then Democratic Party chair Howard Dean. She was preparing to run again in 2006. Emanuel, however, favored a wounded Iraq War vet, Tammy Duckworth, who was not a resident of the district. Breaking the DCCC's usual norm of not playing favorites in primaries, he gave Duckworth extensive financial support for the primary. But Duckworth barely beat Cegelis in the primary and went on to lose the general election.

According to one candidate who did get Emanuel's funding in 2006, he relied heavily on the economically centrist group Third Way to provide campaign materials and talking points. Third Way downplayed the economic beating that ordinary Americans were taking in favor of bland messaging that rejected any talk of class or criticism of financial elites. This was also pure Emanuel.

Emanuel had targeted thirty-four races, in the hope of flipping at least sixteen seats and giving the Democrats control. But six weeks before the election, the DCCC's polls showed that he was likely to fall short. Many of his favored candidates were behind. When the Democrats did take back the House, it was on the strength of more than a dozen other wins by candidates that either were not on the DCCC's radar or whom Emanuel helped only grudgingly in the campaign's final weeks.

Some commentators have argued that as Democrats win House and Senate seats in Republican territory, their party necessarily becomes more centrist. But the evidence simply does not bear out that claim. Some successful Democrats from conservative states did run as moderate conservatives on social issues such as gun control, abortion, and school prayer. But several of the congressmen and senators who took Republican-held seats in 2006 and 2008 ran and won as *economic* progressives.

In the Senate, where Emanuel was not in charge of the strategy, the vast majority of Democrats who picked up Republican seats were fervent economic progressives, including from the class of 2006 Sherrod Brown (Ohio), Jon Tester (Montana), Claire McCaskill (Missouri), Amy Klobuchar (Minnesota), Bernie Sanders (Vermont), and Jim Webb (Virginia). Similarly, most of the 2008 freshmen senators who took Republican seats won as pocketbook progressives. They included Mark Udall (Colorado), Al Franken (Minnesota), Jeanne Shaheen (New Hampshire), Tom Udall (New Mexico), and Jeff Merkley (Oregon), plus the more moderate Mark Warner (Virginia). In House races in 2008, progressives such as Alan Grayson in Orlando, Florida, and Tom Perriello of Charlottesville, Virginia, picked up Republican seats in highly unlikely places precisely because they were not in Wall Street's pocket and could clearly articulate citizens' economic grievances.

Party chairman Howard Dean, who served from 2004 through 2008, worked very closely with netroots groups like FireDogLake.com, OpenLeft .com, and DailyKos.com. Dean's strategy of building a fifty-state party, even in states that Republicans dominated, laid the groundwork for Obama's own victory. Obama's winning margin in primaries and caucus states was in heavily Republican states, where Dean over the objection of many traditionalists had invested in rebuilding a Democratic Party. The netroots Democrats energized by Dean's strategy were overwhelmingly pro-Obama. Working the red states also produced upset victories in the general election in places like North Carolina and Indiana. Emanuel, however, could not abide the liberal Dean, whom he could not control. He rewarded Dean's effective party building—which had helped lay the basis for Obama's victory—by freezing Dean out for either a political job or any post in the Obama administration.

Emanuel's legacy of Wall Street–friendly House Democrats was one possible game plan, but not the only one. Their disproportionate representation in the classes of 2006 and 2008 would make it much more difficult to get financial reform legislation through the House in 2009 and 2010. Emanuel arranged to place more than a dozen members of the New Democrat Coalition on the crucial House Financial Services Committee as a congenial spot to raise special-interest money, where they would later hobble the efforts of Chairman Barney Frank to get tough regulatory reform. Emanuel, now in the even more powerful post of White House chief of staff, would be another voice against tough regulatory reform of Wall Street, often putting fund-raising goals ahead of effective policy to serve working Americans. He would also side with the deficit hawks, undercutting adequate funding for economic stimulus, jobs, and mortgage relief. Thus, a senior White House position that might have served as a counterweight to the financial conservatism and close Wall Street alignment of the Summers-Geithner-Bernanke team only reinforced it.

Two signature aspects of Emanuel's operating style provided short-term tactical gains but long-term strategic losses for Obama. First, his instinct was to cut expedient deals with business lobbies, whatever the effect on the resulting policy. He did this out of his own economic centrism, his desire to channel special-interest money into the pockets of Democrats, and his zeal for legislative victories, however hollow in substance. Second, Emanuel's operating style was viciously partisan. The political press seemed to find it roguishly endearing that he played partisan hardball and said "fuck" a lot. The street-smart Emanuel was said to provide just the kind of real-world political grounding to balance the gentler Obama. But Emanuel's blend of partisanship and interest-group politics had costs.

In the battle for health-care reform, Emanuel warned the drug, hospital, and insurance industries that if they wanted a bill that served their interests, they had better not donate money to Republicans. Emanuel's crass operating methods, at a time when President Obama was preaching a high-minded rhetoric of building bipartisan bridges, left Republicans feeling that Obama's own gestures of bipartisanship were hypocritical and fake, thus reinforcing their own obstructionist instincts. So Obama got the worst of both worlds. Backstage, there was fierce partisan infighting. But because the president so fervently believed in his own call for greater civility, he seldom made a public issue of the Republicans' obstructionism.

Among Obama's inner circle, the two potential counterweights to Emanuel and the fatal Wall Street orientation of the economic team are Vice President Joe Biden and White House political director David Axelrod. However, Axelrod and Emanuel have a relationship that dates back to 1982, and Axelrod considers Emanuel one of his dearest friends. Thus a very tight web links Emanuel to the Summers-Geithner group on the one side, and to Axelrod and the political team on the other. But after the political earthquake of January 19, Axelrod and Biden began breaking through, at least on the level of Obama's rhetoric.

Internal Exile

Also significant was who did *not* get senior administration posts, and where the relative liberals ended up. During the campaign, an early member of Obama's kitchen cabinet on economic issues was Paul Volcker. As an elder statesman of finance, Volcker has been more of a regulatory interventionist than his career path might suggest. Though he was the bête noire of liberals for his decision in the late 1970s to break the back of inflation by raising short-term interest rates as high as 21.5 percent, deliberately creating what was then the worst recession of the postwar era, Volcker was never comfortable with the extreme financial deregulation that followed. Often, in the senior councils of the Democratic Party, the most "progressive" voice on regulation would be this former chairman of the Federal Reserve—a reality that speaks volumes on how far the center has shifted to the right.

Volcker was a career public servant. Though he knew financial markets as well as anyone, he had never been a big-time financier, before or after his Fed service. And Volcker was very much a defender of the Glass-Steagall Act. When James Baker, Treasury secretary under George H. W. Bush, decided to oust Volcker in June 1987 in favor of Alan Greenspan, one prime reason was Greenspan's support for repeal of Glass-Steagall and Volcker's preference for keeping Glass-Steagall on the books. As the financial scandal unfolded, Volcker was one of the voices calling for much tougher regulation, a posture much more interventionist than that of either the Paulson team under Bush or the Summers-Geithner team under Obama.

Volcker had been introduced to Obama in June 2007 by Mark Gallogly, co-founder of Centerbridge Partners, a New York private investment firm and one of Obama's early Wall Street fund-raisers. Gallogly put together a lunch for Obama to meet Volcker and a dozen other senior financiers, including Gary Cohn of Goldman Sachs, and Merrill Lynch president Greg Flemming. As background, Volcker read Obama's two books and several of his speeches, and he came away from the meeting "genuinely impressed," according to a *Wall Street Journal* account.

Beginning in the summer of 2007, Obama started having regular conversations with the then eighty-year-old Volcker, who gave Obama, still the underdog, his formal endorsement in January 2008. Volcker became a regular participant in the campaign's conference calls on economic issues, and he and Obama frequently spoke one-on-one by cell phone. In October, Obama relied heavily on Volcker's advice on the financial bailout. Volcker even began joining Obama on the campaign trail.

At the point when Obama was seeking to enhance his credibility on economic issues, the press was led to expect that Volcker would play a major role in an Obama administration. One widely floated plan was for Volcker to be named Treasury secretary, with a strong deputy who would succeed him in a year or two. But Volcker's views were far more interventionist than those of Summers, and he would also be difficult to control. Summers, relying on help from Rubin, the political team, and transition chief John Podesta, succeeded in killing the idea.

Volcker told close associates that he wanted to be offered the Treasury secretary job and was wounded when he didn't get it. In the end, he was named to chair an advisory panel that was pure window dressing. The membership of the outreach panel that Volcker chaired, called the President's Economic Recovery Advisory Board (PERAB), was, if anything, to the right of the Summers team. It was part of Obama's early effort to demonstrate that he was receptive to the entire range of viewpoints on economic issues, and to make constituencies feel they were being listened to.

The panel did not even meet as a whole body until late May 2009. Its work was divided into subcommittees, and several members, after busying themselves with policy deliberation and the drafting of position papers, soon concluded that the exercise was a waste of time. Because of the absurdly broad spectrum of views, no pointed positions could emerge. The panel's position papers had no influence on the formulation of the administration's financial reform plan, a closely held process orchestrated by Summers, Geithner, and a few trusted deputies. A proud man, Volcker was unwilling to foist his views on the president, and for the most part his phone didn't ring.

It was only after a full year, when Obama was on the ropes politically from the debacle over health insurance and in desperate need of a more populist message, that the president began listening to Volcker. In January 2010, the space of less than a week, Obama proposed a surtax on bank profits, a tougher financial product safety commission, and a restoration of the Glass-Steagall Act, which Obama pointedly termed "the Volcker Plan." Volcker, in more than a dozen speeches, had been campaigning for such a move. At the urging of Vice President Biden, Axelrod, and White House economic adviser Austan Goolsbee, Obama began meeting with Volcker in late December, and overruled Geithner and Summers. This story is told in full in chapter 4.

Few others to the left of Summers ended up in power positions. Karen Kornbluh, the liberal policy director of Obama's Senate staff, was not a member of the Wall Street club. She was dispatched by the campaign to take charge of writing the Democratic Party platform. While on that assignment, Kornbluh was squeezed out of any White House job or other senior domestic policy post. As a consolation prize, she was named to serve as US ambassador to the Organization for Economic Cooperation and Development (OECD) in Paris. Dan Tarullo, one of Obama's earliest and closest advisers, had served in the Clinton administration and had a decent personal relationship with Summers. Yet his views were rather more interventionist, and there would be no senior spot for him at the White House, either. Tarullo, however, was too personally close to Obama to just be discarded. He wound up getting an open seat on the Federal Reserve. At the Fed, Tarullo chaired the committee responsible for bank regulation. From this perch, he was a circumspect voice in favor of tougher regulatory standards, but he also became a close ally and defender of Chairman Ben Bernanke.

Of the progressive voices prominently displayed during the campaign to reassure the liberal/labor wing of the party, none got a power position. Economic policy coordinator Jason Furman had gone out of his way to declare that the campaign was speaking regularly to James Galbraith, Robert Reich, and Jared Bernstein. But when the appointments were announced, Galbraith and Reich were nowhere to be seen, and Bernstein was named economic adviser to the vice president. Admirers of Bernstein heard the news and groaned. The hard-to-restrain Biden, added to the ticket to signal both working-class roots and foreign policy expertise, would end up playing a more minor role than had been advertised. And if the vice presidency, in the oft-quoted phrase of Roosevelt's VP John Nance Garner, was just "a bucket of warm spit" (Garner had actually used a more pungent word), what did that make the vice president's economic adviser?

Despite this lowly-sounding title, however, Bernstein emerged as a player. He was a regular part of the policy discussions of the senior economic team, and Summers used him as a sounding board to hear out positions to his own left. Biden was named to head an important-sounding task force on middle-class working families, with Bernstein as its staff director. Even the name of the task force was hotly disputed. "Working families" sounded a little too left-wing, while "middle class" always tested well in the polls. As a compromise, the task force, somewhat inelegantly, carried both names. At the White House rollout of the task force on January 29, 2009, with several trade union presidents in attendance, Obama offered brave words about the importance of the labor movement. "I do not view the labor movement as part of the problem. To me, it's part of the solution," he said, to a round of jubilant applause. "You cannot have a strong middle class without a strong labor movement."

Trade union leaders repeatedly urged the White House to elevate the task force to a presidential initiative, and to have it coordinate government-wide initiatives to enforce labor laws already on the books and to use government's latent power as a contractor to insist on minimally decent standards in all companies that bid for federal contracts. Some modest executive orders were issued, but the effort stopped well short of a major Obama initiative. The task force itself had no real staff, and none of the operational links to cabinet departments that would signal a serious initiative to use the leverage of the federal government as a contractor or regulator to raise wages. It was reduced to holding media events.

The Fall and Rise of Ben Bernanke

A certain amount of continuity in economic policy was preordained, since Obama would have Ben Bernanke as Federal Reserve chairman until Bernanke's term expired in January 2010. Yet, to the extent that Bernanke hoped for reappointment, the new president and his economic team enjoyed some leverage. A recent role model was President Bill Clinton, who assiduously courted then Federal Reserve chairman Alan Greenspan. Clinton wanted a quick economic recovery, and Greenspan wanted reappointment. So the two cut a deal in which Clinton would shrink the federal deficit and Greenspan would ease interest rates. Clinton got his recovery and Greenspan kept his job.

However, for the most part Obama's policy leverage on Bernanke was not used, since Summers and Bernanke saw eye-to-eye on the big issues. Bernanke is often mistaken for an economic interventionist, because of his aggressive use of Federal Reserve loans, guarantees, and advances in 2008 and 2009 to prevent total financial collapse. But Bernanke is deeply anti-regulation. During Obama's early months, Bernanke's reappointment was considered a foregone conclusion. As the populist revolt against the banks gathered force in late 2009 and early 2010, Bernanke became the lightning rod.

Bernanke had been appointed by President Bush to the Fed in 2002; he did a stint at the White House Council of Economic Advisers and then was named Fed chairman in February 2006 when Alan Greenspan retired. A Princeton economics professor, Bernanke was a more collegial and seemingly less dogmatic sort than his predecessor. The appointment surprised some—Bernanke was not exactly a movement conservative. Unlike Greenspan, a disciple of Ayn Rand who wore his conservative views on his sleeve, Bernanke was more circumspect about where he stood ideologically. His partisan sympathies were not evident. When Bernanke was named to the Fed, Robert Frank, a moderately liberal Cornell economist and co-author of a textbook with Bernanke, was surprised to learn that he was a Republican. But the Bush White House did not name Bernanke to the second most powerful post in government because Bernanke was anything other than deeply conservative on the issues that mattered to Wall Street.

Bernanke made his academic reputation as an expert on the Great Depression. Yet if you read his collected scholarly works on the 1920s and 1930s, you will find mainly technical monetary economics, disparagement of regulation, and almost no intellectual curiosity or historical knowledge of actual financial abuses other than to discount their effect. In one charming and revealing paragraph in a Bernanke paper written in 1983, titled "Non-Monetary Effects of the Financial Crisis in the Propagation of the Great Depression," Bernanke finds it a little odd that other prominent scholars, with a broader historical view, would think that financial markets are vulnerable to instability or manipulation. He writes, "Hyman Minsky (1977) and Charles Kindleberger (1978) have in several places argued for the inherent instability of the financial system, but in doing so, have had to depart from the assumption of rational economic behavior." Well, yes!

Today Kindleberger and Minsky are widely considered prophetic, and hardly anyone today would argue that financial markets behaved rationally in the crash. Bernanke added in a footnote to that piece, "I do not deny the possible importance of irrationality in economic life; however it seems that the best research strategy is to push the rationality postulate as far as it will go." This is not only his research strategy, but his broad ideology of nonregulation.

The collapse of 2007–09 had parallels in the earlier Great Crash of 1929, but it was potentially even more serious because the financial casino that preceded the recent collapse was that much more opaque, convoluted, and interconnected. In the 1920s, there were no hedge funds and only the most limited of derivatives or securitized loans. There were no pension funds to speak of, and only 1.5 percent of Americans held stock. The classic speculative abuse was playing the stock market on margin, which is a model of transparency compared with, say, credit default swaps.

Even so, the abuses that crashed the stock market in October 1929 had the same core characteristics as the one that produced the collapse that began in the summer of 2007: too much speculation with borrowed money; too many securities that were opaque either to investors or to regulators (who were scarcely existent in the 1920s); and too many conflicts of interest on the part of insiders at the expense of customers. These were precisely the abuses that the reforms of the New Deal addressed. And though there were breaches, for the most part the New Deal prevented their repetition until financial engineers commenced end runs around regulation beginning in the 1970s.

Intervention without Regulation

As a student of the Great Depression, Bernanke was determined not to repeat the mistakes of his predecessors. Bernanke, however, was of the school that believed the Depression was caused not by the speculative excesses of the 1920s, but by the failure of the Fed of that era to respond aggressively to the stock market crash by increasing the money supply. You could hold those beliefs and still cling to the premise that markets mostly worked. Financial panics, in this view, were rare, one-off irrational spasms that justified dramatic but very infrequent interventions when the Fed had to waive the usual rules. The rest of the time, financial markets could be largely unregulated.

The intellectual father of that view was the late conservative guru and economic historian Milton Friedman. With his co-author Anna Schwartz, Friedman contended that if the Fed had only lowered interest rates and flooded the system with liquidity, 1929 would have been merely a normal stock market correction, followed by a swift recovery. Bernanke, speaking in 2002, summarized his agreement with Friedman's view:

> The correct interpretation of the 1920s, then, is not the popular one—that the stock market got overvalued, crashed, and caused a Great Depression. The true story is that monetary policy tried over-zealously to stop the rise in stock prices. But the main effect of the tight monetary policy . . . was to slow the economy—both domesti-cally, and, through the workings of the gold standard, abroad. The slowing economy, together with rising interest rates, was in turn a major factor in precipitating the stock market crash.

No wonder the people around George W. Bush were fully confident of Bernanke's conservatism. It's worth pausing to savor his statement, which is breathtaking in both its extreme free-market conservatism and its studied disinterest in the financial history of the 1920s. For Bernanke, the corrupt stock pools, the extreme speculation on margin, the creation of bogus securities, the watering of public utility stocks, and the other forms of manipulation that pushed the stock market to absurd heights by the late 1920s *were of no consequence.* The crash had occurred only because the Fed raised interest rates. This is a bit like concluding that the straw fully explains the camel's broken back, and that all the weight piled on before was not a factor.

This view put the supposedly moderate Bernanke well to the right of his ultra-conservative predecessor Alan Greenspan, who allowed the possibility that financial bubbles could exist and expressed alarm about a stock market bubble in his "irrational exuberance" speech as early as 1996. Bernanke's understanding of the crash of 1929 and the Great Depression also illustrates his deep aversion to financial regulation. If the abuses of the 1920s were not a cause of the collapse, then there was no reason to regulate them.

Drawing his rather narrow and idiosyncratic lesson from history, Bernanke concluded that the system needed massive infusions of money during a dire crisis—but not preventive regulation. As financial dominoes began falling in 2008 beginning with the collapse of Bear Stearns, he stretched his legal powers to their limits and beyond, cutting rates, creating money, extending guarantees to the shadow banking system, brokering mergers to head off systemic failures, exchanging dubious securities for sound ones, and waiting for the real economy to rebound. By August 2009, when Obama ended the speculation about whether Bernanke would be named to a second term as Fed chairman, Bernanke's reappointment was universally anticipated. It was one more proof that there would be no fundamental break with the Bush-Paulson policies or the existing financial regime.

In the weeks prior to the final Senate vote on his confirmation, Bernanke increasingly became the target of the popular backlash against Wall Street. He annoyed a number of legislators with his lobbying against provisions in the Senate's draft legislation that would have reduced the Fed's regulatory responsibilities and the language in the House-passed bill requiring an audit of the Fed.

It is remarkable that neither the Fed's board of governors nor the New York Fed has offered any public explanation as to the nature of its regulatory failure prior to the collapse. The contrast with the Securities and Exchange Commission's public soul-searching and reform efforts after its failure to detect the Madoff fraud is striking. The Fed had jurisdiction over Citi, Bank of America, Wells Fargo, and Wachovia as bank holding companies throughout the runup to the crisis.

Vermont senator Bernie Sanders spent several days agonizing over whether to slow down the rush to confirmation. Then on November 29, 2009, Sanders, rejecting White House entreaties, announced that he was putting a hold on the nomination, meaning that Bernanke would require sixty votes in the Senate to win confirmation. In his testimony before the Senate Committee on Banking, Housing, and Urban Affairs on December 3, Bernanke managed to express only the most minimal acceptance of responsibility for his failure to crack down on the abuses of the big banks. "In the area where we had responsibility, the bank holding companies, we should have done more," he said. "That is a mistake we won't make again."

But rather than accepting Bernanke's assurances, Congress was more inclined to guarantee that the mistake would not be repeated—by transferring the authority to another agency. And to the surprise of many observers, the Senate Banking Committee approved the nomination only by a vote of 16–7, with a majority of committee Republicans voting no. Freshman Oregon senator Jeff Merkley, who had defeated Republican incumbent Gordon Smith in 2008 by just 4 points, was the only Democratic member of the Senate Banking Committee to vote against Bernanke's confirmation. "Dr. Bernanke failed to recognize or remedy the factors that paved the road to this dark and difficult recession," Merkley declared. "Following our economic collapse, it is also apparent that he has not changed his overall approach to prioritizing Wall Street over American families." Merkley's vote played well with Oregon voters and demonstrated that elected officials had nothing to fear by siding with Main Street.

In early January 2010, Senator Byron Dorgan of North Dakota added his dissent. The Fed had been resisting a Freedom of Information Act request suit filed by Bloomberg News to disclose details of its aid to large banks. A district court judge had ordered the Fed to comply, but in an awkwardly timed case of stonewalling, the Fed appealed the ruling to the Second Circuit Court of Appeals. Bernanke had also fended off similar requests by congressional committees. The special inspector general of the TARP program got confidential information from the Fed, only on the condition that it not be shared with Congress.

"For the first time in history they said to the big investment banks, you can come and get direct lending from the Federal Reserve Board," Dorgan said. "We're trying to find out from the Fed, who'd you give the money to, how much money did you give? . . . And the Federal Reserve Board says 'none of your business.' Well, I tell you what, it is our business, and I'm not going to let the Bernanke nomination to head the Fed for another term go through until he tells, what did he do with our money, the American people's money."

As one more scandal broke, with the revelation that the Federal Reserve Bank of New York has requested that the failed insurance giant AIG not divulge some sensitive details of the Fed-Treasury bailout in its annual filings with the Securities and Exchange Commission, Bernanke attempted a rare form of damage control. He requested a full audit of the matter by the Government Accountability Office, a form of outside scrutiny that Bernanke

had fiercely resisted in the past. This shift, which had the potential to seriously damage Tim Geithner, who was president of the New York Fed at the
time, was less a change of philosophy on Bernanke's part than an effort to
save his own job.

Democratic senators again found themselves on the wrong side of a backlash against Wall Street. Once more, they were being asked to walk the
plank because of a dubious decision of their president. In the end, the White
House used all of its leverage on wavering Democrats, and Bernanke won
confirmation by a vote of 70–30.

Thus the Wall Street colonization of the Obama administration. The 2008
election was treated as a fundamental contest between two competing world-
views. The public was disgusted with politics as usual, and the election was
all about believable change. Increasingly, the test of Obama's presidency was
how effectively it would limit the economic damage to ordinary Americans.
On that front Barack Obama is failing.

Seldom were there two back-to-back presidents more different than George
W. Bush and Barack Obama. Seldom was there a crisis that more thoroughly
discredited a failed economic order. But remarkably, when it came to financial policy and extreme deference to Wall Street, seldom has there been more
policy continuity between the outgoing administration and its successor.

CHAPTER TWO

Continuity and Collusion

My Administration is the only thing between you and the pitchforks.
—BARACK OBAMA, to a group of financial
executives, March 27, 2009

We had to struggle with the old enemies of peace—business and
financial monopoly, speculation, reckless banking class antagonism,
sectionalism, war profiteering. They had begun to consider the
Government of the United States as a mere appendage to their own
affairs. We know now that Government by organized money is just
as dangerous as Government by organized mob . . . They are unani-
mous in their hate for me—and I welcome their hatred.
—FRANKLIN D. ROOSEVELT, Madison Square
Garden, October 31, 1936

When Barack Obama took the oath of office on January 20, 2009, the Bush
administration's ad hoc infusions of money to banks had managed only
to avert a complete financial collapse. These policies had neither restored
normal credit markets nor slowed the steep economic slide. Unemployment
was 7.6 percent and heading toward double digits. GDP was declining at an
annual rate of 6.4 percent. Mortgage foreclosures were surging at the rate of
250,000 a month. Because of the collapse in confidence, credit markets were
frozen except to the extent that they were wards of the government.

The outgoing Bush administration handed Obama a template for financial
crisis management. One part entailed rescuing insolvent banks with direct
transfers of government money. A second element used government guarantees to thaw other financial markets. A third strand was the Federal Reserve's

policy of cutting short-term interest rates to zero. This overall approach, fashioned by the team of Paulson, Geithner, and Bernanke during the frantic week in September 2008 when storied financial houses were tumbling, kept capital markets on life support. But it set the government on a path of propping up rather than cleaning out zombie banks or the system that bred them.

With only minor variations, the formula was continued by the new Obama administration. The main embellishment added by Tim Geithner was a plan that Paulson briefly tried and then abandoned as unworkable—a series of incentives and guarantees intended to encourage speculators to buy toxic assets from banks. A year later, most of these depressed securities were still clogging bank balance sheets, and ordinary business remained starved for credit.

Fateful Choices, Feeble Policies

As 2009 dawned, Obama and his incoming team had several urgent tasks: stemming the deepening economic recession; getting the financial system back in working order; reversing the tide of mortgage foreclosures; and preventing a repeat of the speculative abuses that had caused the bubble economy. These challenges were economically interconnected, since a robust recovery depended on a healthy financial system. They were also connected politically, because the prime legislative obstacle was the financial industry's residual power to block reform.

Wall Street, however, was disgraced but far from disempowered. Bankers were pleased to take the taxpayer money and guarantees from the Federal Reserve but fiercely resisted changing their business models. Industry moguls opposed mandatory mortgage refinancing, which would force accurate valuation of the toxic securities on their books and compel them to acknowledge concealed losses. They resisted any government interference with the speculative trading strategies that had become their main profit centers during the boom years. Some were uneasy about a large fiscal stimulus, fretting that substantial government borrowing would destabilize the bond market once the recovery came. So in order to pursue a successful program of recovery and reform, Obama would first need to shrink Wall Street's influence, both inside and outside his own administration.

But in stark contrast with Roosevelt, who made a clean break with the old political and financial regime, Obama and his economic aides chose instead to work in concert with the Wall Street elite. The government's immense sums of emergency aid were not used as leverage to compel more fundamental reforms. Even when continuing abuses were disclosed—exorbitant bonuses, new speculative schemes, conflicts of interest, refusals to supply needed credit to small businesses and homeowners—Obama seldom criticized the banks except on occasions when he needed a quick dose of symbolic populism. His administration's goal was to restore trust in capital markets, even if confidence in the existing order was far from justified. All of this would prolong recession and favor Wall Street over Main Street. It was dubious economics, and worse politics.

Two Cheers

By late 2009, the conventional verdict on the bipartisan Wall Street team that spanned the Bush and Obama administrations was that they deserved a lot of credit for pulling the economy back from the brink of depression. Despite much carping and second-guessing, the economy was finally on the mend, albeit very slowly. The story line of much of the mainstream press might be summed up as Two Cheers for Muddling Through.

Wall Street Journal writer David Wessel's authoritative book on the financial crisis of 2008, *In Fed We Trust,* had many small criticisms of the way that Fed chairman Ben Bernanke and colleagues had managed the crisis. They were late to realize the gravity of the affair, wrote Wessel, and they bungled some specific key decisions such as letting Lehman Brothers go bust. But on balance, Wessel concluded that Bernanke deserved our gratitude for heading off the worst. "What if Ben Bernanke had not been a student of the Great Depression?" Wessel wrote. "What if he had not resolved to do *whatever it takes* to prevent a second Great Depression?" [italics in the original] In December 2009, *Time* magazine named Bernanke Person of the Year.

In much the same spirit, when the Bureau of Labor Statistics reported that unemployment numbers for July 2009 had actually improved by a tenth of a percentage point (in what turned out to be a statistical fluke), *New York Times* economic analyst David Leonhardt wrote in a front-page piece titled "As Economy Turns, Washington Looks Better":

What if, amid all their missteps and all the harsh criticism, the people in charge of battling the worst financial crisis since the Great Depression—Ben Bernanke, Timothy Geithner, Lawrence Summers, Henry Paulson and the rest—basically succeeded?

It is clearly too soon to know for sure. But the evidence is now pointing pretty strongly in one direction: history books may conclude that the financial crisis of 2008 turned out to be far less bad than it could have been and that Washington deserved much of the credit.

Perhaps, but that appraisal was politically and economically premature. "Less bad" was not good enough. Unemployment continued rising. Despite Leonhardt's sanguine view, too few voters were concluding that "Washington deserved much of the credit." Their condition was too precarious—and Washington was getting the blame. While the policies begun late in the Bush era by Bernanke, Geithner, and Paulson, and continued by the overlapping team of Bernanke, Geithner, and Summers under Barack Obama, did avert a depression, they did not produce an economy of broad prosperity. More ambitious policies could have yielded quicker results. Instead, we are still in for a long, hard slog.

The Mortgage Mess

The protracted mortgage crisis is a good place to pick up the details of this story of Obama's feeble response to the crisis, because the financial meltdown began with the collapse of mortgage securities, and because housing is so central to the economic health of the middle class. By 2007, retail mortgage companies, largely unregulated, had made millions of deceptive, high-interest home loans with almost no meaningful underwriting standards. In plain English, that meant almost anyone could qualify for such a loan. Often these subprime loans required no credit history or income verification. These were known in the trade as liar loans. Many applicants misstated their incomes or capacity to repay. At the same time, about half of all subprime borrowers actually qualified for less costly conventional fixed-rate loans. But they were manipulated into taking out subprime loans, lured by very low, initial "teaser" monthly payments that would "reset" after a year or two and then rise rapidly. Though fraudulent borrowers have gotten most of the publicity, at least half were pure victims.

Borrower and lender were both betting that rising housing prices would rescue them, allowing a refinancing or profitable sale. All of these marginal loans helped bid up housing prices. Even so, lending to liars was a gamble that few sensible bankers would take, if they were planning to keep the mortgages in their own portfolios. But here was the essence of the scheme: These loans were made only to be packaged into bonds and sold off to someone else. Loan originators made their money on fees, and the key to large profits was sheer volume. Investment bankers made their money both in packaging the loans and in trading the securities.

Investors were reassured because most of these securities, though backed by sketchy mortgages, were blessed with triple-A status by a bond-rating agency. Why would a prudent credit rating agency engage in this alchemy? Because housing prices were rising. In normal times, mortgages seldom defaulted; increasing home values only added a cushion of equity. More to the point, the rating agency was paid by the issuer of the securities to deliver the investment-grade rating.

The subprime loans were turned into bonds by big commercial banks and investment houses with names like Lehman Brothers, Bear Stearns, Goldman Sachs, and JPMorgan Chase—the same investment banks that provided financing to retail mortgage companies to originate the loans. There are no centralized records of who bought the bonds, but we know from the subsequent crash that the securities went to a far-flung array of purchasers around the world, ranging from pension funds and small investors to hedge funds and off-balance-sheet affiliates of some of the very banks that created them. Ironically enough, the big banks began by making money on the fees and trading profits for creating products that they knew to be high risk. But eventually, some of these same banks began drinking their own Kool-Aid and buying the stuff for its high yield. It is always a sign of impending doom when a drug dealer gets hooked on his own product.

Adding to the potential for a crash was a second layer of financial leverage—so-called credit default swaps. These were insurance policies against the mortgage bonds going bad, and many were issued or purchased by the same group of investment banks—using even more borrowed money. In some cases, investment banks created swaps purely for the purpose of gambling that the underlying security would go bust, often betting against their own customers. As Phil Angelides, the chair of the Financial Crisis Inquiry Commission, memorably put it, this is like "selling a car with faulty brakes and then buying an insurance policy on the buyer of those cars." In the case of so-called naked credit default swaps, third parties with no interest in the bonds used swaps to make side bets. The whole affair was a house of cards. When Bear Stearns, and later Lehman Brothers and Merrill Lynch, went broke, the failure of bonds backed by subprime loans was the biggest hole in their balance sheets.

The aftermath of this collapse was both retail and wholesale. The worth of homes and mortgage securities led each other downward. At the retail level, housing prices collapsed at just about the time that these adjustable-rate subprime mortgages began to reset. Millions of homeowners could no longer afford their monthly payments, driving down housing values in a self-deepening spiral. Tens of millions found that their homes were suddenly worth less than the mortgages.

Most of these homeowners were innocent bystanders. They had neither taken out mortgages beyond their means nor lied on their applications. They were simply caught in a general downdraft of declining housing prices—something unknown since the Great Depression. With repayment in doubt, banks, hedge funds, pension funds, and other investors were left with hundreds of billions of dollars of bonds worth a fraction of their face value. The Bush administration made the fateful decision to give primary relief to banks, not to homeowners. Obama continued the basic policy.

A housing collapse tends to be geographically concentrated. If several properties in a neighborhood are vacant, the community will be blighted and there will be a disproportionate impact on the value of surrounding properties. The effect was especially concentrated among African American homeowners, for whom the steady gains in homeownership rates over three decades were wiped out.

By the end of 2009, fully one home in four was worth less than the mortgage on it. The collapse in housing prices had wiped out at least $7 trillion of net worth of American families. Almost 15 percent of mortgage loans were in delinquency, default, or foreclosure, putting some ten million homeowners at risk. According to Professor Alan White of the Valparaiso University School of Law, about two million homeowners have already suffered foreclosure. Another six million foreclosures are in process and at least five million more mortgages are considered delinquent.

The downward spiral of declining prices and increasing foreclosures fed back into the financial system. As more mortgages failed to perform, more banks found themselves both losing anticipated mortgage income and stuck with mortgage-backed securities that could not be sold. Economists call this condition a debt-deflation, meaning that debts are fixed but the value of their collateral is declining. A debt-deflation is potentially catastrophic when it causes a fire-sale mentality. People are compelled to sell assets into a declining market, depressing asset prices even further. In the classic statement of the malady, economist Irving Fisher's 1933 paper "The Debt-Deflation Theory of Great Depressions," a debt-deflation is what distinguishes a depression from an ordinary business-cycle recession in which surplus inventory is quickly worked off and prices rebalance.

In its own "stress test" exercise, the Treasury Department in April 2009 predicted a sickening total decline of housing prices of 41 percent between 2006 and 2010, of which the mortgage foreclosure crisis was both a cause and a consequence. Subprime, and only slightly less risky "Alt-A" (poor documentation or credit history) and "option-ARM" (borrower is free to pay less than the minimum interest owed) mortgages made at the peak of the bubble in 2006 and 2007, were resetting in 2009 and 2010, portending worsening defaults. At this writing, 61 percent of securitized subprime loans made in 2006 are in default, followed by 49 percent of option-ARMs and 39 percent of Alt-A loans.

An increasing percentage of distressed homeowners were not subprime borrowers who had gambled on future increases in housing values, but homeowners with good credit ratings who had lost their jobs and could not afford to meet the monthly payments. In mid-2009, Moody's Economy.com projected that 60 percent of mortgage defaults in 2009 would be the result of unemployment, up from 29 percent in 2008. An extensive report by analysts at Deutsche Bank estimated that by the first quarter of 2011, 48 percent of all US homeowners will owe more than their houses are worth.

Weak Medicine

This crisis required very strong remedies. Government needed to use a mix of public funds and concessions on the part of the bankers and investors, who held the mortgage paper, to reduce the principal and interest to a monthly payment low enough to allow distressed borrowers to keep their homes. Otherwise, the foreclosure crisis would keep feeding on itself, glutting the market with vacant homes, driving housing values still lower, and triggering still more foreclosures. But this course would require banks and holders of mortgage-backed securities to take losses, and it was rejected by both the Bush and Obama administrations. Instead, both Bush and Obama relied on a series of voluntary programs, jawboning bankers to reduce monthly payments. Not surprisingly, this approach failed.

Back in 2007, looking over the brink of this precipice, the Bush administration had worked with the banking industry to develop the first voluntary program, called the HOPE NOW Alliance. The group claimed that member banks participated in 2,911,609 "workouts" (reductions of monthly payments) between July 2007 and November 2008, but that number turned out to be grossly inflated. Only 37 percent of the workouts resulted in modification of the loan terms, and of these only 49 percent actually cut monthly payments. Most of the reductions were modest. According to the definitive study of the program by Professor Alan White, 34 percent of the modifications actually *increased* costs to the borrower. Lenders discovered that in restructuring a loan, they could profit by charging up-front fees. Since 2007, under Bush and Obama alike, the pace of new foreclosures has far outstripped the number of loan modifications.

In July 2008, Congress attempted stronger legislative medicine. A program called HOPE for Homeowners authorized the Federal Housing Administration to insure distressed mortgages if private lenders would provide refinancing. But subprime loans are deliberately structured to extract a large prepayment penalty if the borrower refinances. Many of these loans now had negative equity—the loan was worth more than the property—and lenders balked at refinancing even with the FHA insurance. When the HOPE for Homeowners program was enacted, its sponsors predicted that it would help 400,000 homeowners—not nearly enough compared with the millions of defaults. But by February 2009, the scheme had processed exactly 373 applications and closed just 13 refinancings. Hardly any of the distressed properties fit the terms of the program. "HOPE for Homeowners has been a failure by virtually every metric," declared Representative Spencer Bachus of Alabama, the ranking Republican on the House Financial Services Committee—describing a program signed by a Republican president.

By the time Obama took office, serious defaults and foreclosures were on track to reach more than 8 million during the new president's first term. This was a moment for a radical break, yet Obama's plan basically continued the Bush administration's voluntary approach, lubricated by $75 billion in government incentive payments to banks. The Obama variation has also been a complete failure, adding to the general economic downdraft.

Obama's program, called Making Home Affordable, was announced February 18, just four weeks into the new administration. The plan had four major parts. One, a more liberal variant of the old Bush program, allowed homeowners with mortgages to refinance their loans with FHA insurance, even if the outstanding loan was worth 5 percent more than the current value of the house. In July 2009, this ceiling was increased to a premium of 25 percent, meaning that a borrower with a $200,000 home could qualify for a $250,000 mortgage—something inconceivable in ordinary circumstances. This unprecedented remedy of encouraging a homeowner to borrow more than the value of the house was itself very risky, since a homeowner with negative equity loses nothing by just walking away if a better housing option becomes available. Millions did, leaving banks stuck with vacant homes.

A second part of the plan, known as the Home Affordable Modification Program (HAMP), offered lenders incentive payments of up to $4,500 per loan modification, if they reduced a borrower's monthly payment to 31 percent of gross monthly income. A third element increased government capital infusions to the housing finance market, to keep mortgage interest rates low generally. Finally, as a last resort the administration nominally supported a bill authorizing bankruptcy judges to compel the lender to modify the terms of the loan, if the judge concluded that this was on balance preferable to a foreclosure.

The plan had several fatal flaws. Except for the bankruptcy-judge provision, the whole program was voluntary to the banks. Even with the bonus payment from the government, bankers had little motivation to shave the principal and interest on a loan, since this would typically reduce their income by far more than the $4,500 bonus payment. It also turned out that banks relied heavily on fee income that would be undermined by loan refinancings or modifications.

Further complicating the mess, something like half of the distressed loans had been turned into packages of bonds; they were now owned by an investor other than the original lender. Typically, that lender was now merely the "servicer," meaning that it was paid a fee for collecting the monthly payment and forwarding the money to the trust that held the securitized package of loans on behalf of the investor, often a hedge fund, a pension fund, or another bank. "The rules by which servicers are reimbursed for expenses may provide a perverse incentive to foreclose rather than modify," according to a 2009 research paper by experts at the Federal Reserve Bank of Boston.

If the modification seemed unreasonable to the investor, the servicer could get sued for altering the terms. The one provision of the bill with some teeth— the proposed new authority for bankruptcy judges—was fiercely opposed by the financial industry as a threat to its ability to collect debts, and voted down by the Senate. In this key battle, the White House did not lift a finger to urge wavering legislators to support their president. I was told by Tim Geithner that the industry experts he relied upon counseled against this bankruptcy authority, and he did nothing to promote it. Word was quickly passed on Capitol Hill that this was not a provision that mattered to the White House. Twelve Senate Democrats looking for an easy pro-industry vote ended up voting against the administration's proposed bankruptcy measure.

Indulging the Banks

At bottom, the failure of the voluntary mortgage modification program suffered from the same core deficiency as the rest of the Obama financial strategy. If lenders or holders of securitized loans expected that the government would eventually make them whole through one of Geithner's innumerable schemes to levitate the value of depressed financial assets, then they had no incentive to modify the terms and book an immediate loss.

One further flaw: The Obama program was for people whose ability to meet monthly payments was only marginally impaired. It offered nothing for millions of the hardest-hit homeowners in places such as much of Florida,

Arizona, Nevada, central California, and inner-city America, where housing values had dropped 30 to 50 percent since the 2006 peak and negative equity far exceeded the program's limits.

Congressman Alan Grayson, whose district is centered in Orlando, Florida, one of the hardest-hit centers of the mortgage collapse, gives the following example. A constituent has a $250,000 mortgage on a house that is now worth only $150,000. She is in default and heading for foreclosure. She could afford to make payments on a $100,000 mortgage, which would enable her to keep the house. If her house is foreclosed, it becomes one more vacant property, dragging down the value of other homes in the neighborhood. But the bank would rather foreclose—and eventually take an even bigger loss—than give this woman such a large break on her mortgage. Only government, Grayson notes, can act to compel a refinancing.

An investigative piece by *The New York Times* concluded that "data on delinquencies reinforces the notion that servicers are inclined to let problem loans float in purgatory—neither taking control of houses and selling them, nor modifying loans to give homeowners a break." Reporter Peter Goodman added, "As a home slides toward foreclosure, mortgage companies pay for many services required to take control of the property and resell it. They typically funnel orders for title searches, insurance policies, appraisals and legal filings to companies they own or share revenue with."

So there is a direct conflict between the public interest in keeping distressed borrowers in their homes, the mortgage company's interest in reaping fees, and the investor's interest in not acknowledging a loss. This is yet another hidden cost of what was touted as a great innovation—the fragmentation of mortgage origination, servicing, and ownership of the debt through the genius of securitization. In fact, the conversion of home loans into abstract securities created a doomsday machine.

Banks have also been loath to allow what's known in the business as a "short sale," in which the house is sold for less than the amount of the mortgage owed. They resist both because they don't want to book the accounting loss and because they collect hidden fees by maintaining the status quo. *The New York Times* reported on the efforts of Alfred Crawford of Los Angeles to sell a house on which he owes about $800,000, far more than its present market value. Bank of America, which holds the mortgage, blocked sales three times, the highest offer of which was $620,000. Each time, its subsidiary, Land Safe, booked an appraisal fee.

This is the same Bank of America that has received $45 billion in taxpayer largesse, and which supposedly operates under close supervision of the Treasury. But that supervision doesn't extend to its mortgage practices. As of December 2009, despite all of the administration's jawboning, this giant bank had permanently modified exactly 98 mortgages. Citi had modified 271. JPMorgan Chase led the pack with 4,302. Compared with the 8 million projected foreclosures, it was a drop in the bucket.

Because of the incoherence of the government's overall approach, the Treasury Department is caught between two opposite and incompatible goals. One is to prevent the downward spiral of mortgage foreclosures, vacancies, and collapsing housing prices. But the other goal is to maximize bank earnings, the better to shore up bank balance sheets. That, in turn, means regulatory indulgence for rapacious bank practices and little pressure for the banks to refinance mortgages and eat losses.

Meanwhile, a whole new industry of bottom-feeders—many of them veteran perpetrators of the subprime disaster—organized syndicates to buy up bank-owned real estate at a few cents on the dollar. Representative Marcy Kaptur of Toledo, Ohio, where entire neighborhoods are littered with vacant, bank-owned homes, complained bitterly that bankers preferred to sell packages of properties to absentee speculators, rather than selling to a city-run program that was working to purchase empty houses, rehabilitate them, and quickly convert them to affordable rentals or owner-occupied homes. The vacant and boarded-up house next door to her own home in Toledo turned out to be owned by a bottom-feeding company based in North Carolina.

There was a further practical weakness in the design of the administration program. Like so much else sponsored by Tim Geithner, it was run by the banking industry, on the familiar (if lately discredited) premise that private industry operates better than government. Typically, however, loan origination offices are assembly-line, paint-by-the-numbers operations. Everything is done according to formula. A loan applicant qualifies for a loan (or not) based on a credit score and a property appraisal. Computers do all the work, with relatively few human employees, and the humans need only a fairly rudimentary level of training.

But a loan modification or refinancing, in circumstances of general distress, is exactly the opposite kind of exercise. It requires labor-intensive, customized analysis, since everyone's situation is different and there is no one-size-fits-all formula. For a lender, human employees are expensive cost centers. They are under immense pressure to close loans fast. The more human effort an employee spends on a good-faith effort to do a workout, the more money he or she costs the company. So, beyond the problem of a purely voluntary approach not delivering modifications, loan servicing offices were exactly the wrong institutions to do these workouts.

In 2009, as the administration attempted to put the new mortgage relief program into operation, story after story appeared in the financial press and the general newspapers about borrowers who could not get phone calls returned or who finally were offered modification packages that turned out to provide only trivial relief or actually raised costs. The *Times* recounted the story of a woman named Eileen Ulery. Facing default, she tried to get Bank of America to modify the terms of her mortgage. Instead, the bank tried to persuade her take out a new loan with a slightly lower monthly payment, but up-front charges of $13,000 in principal reduction and $5,000 in new fees.

In another case, a Lakeland, Florida, woman named Jaime Smith persuaded Chase to lower her monthly payments from $1,250 to $1,033.63 on a trial basis, in April. She made three payments on time, as required by the program, and then applied to make the modification permanent, telephoning weekly to inquire about the status. In October, she received a letter advising that her house had been foreclosed and sold at auction for $100. The buyer was Chase. Eventually, she hired a lawyer who persuaded a judge to vacate the sale.

In these circumstances, it was not surprising that defaults and foreclosures continued to outpace refinancings and loan modifications. When the administration reported to Congress in December 2009, the Treasury claimed that about 756,000 homeowners had qualified for "trial modifications," in which their lenders provisionally reduced their monthly costs—provided that they stayed current on their payments for several months, after which the new terms would be made permanent. However, Treasury quietly admitted that fewer than 32,000 homeowners had been given permanent modifications. As this book went to press, the number had risen to 116,000.

Jawboning the Bankers

Faced with the failure of its program to produce more than token mortgage relief, the administration resorted to public displays of arm-twisting. In July 2009, Treasury Secretary Geithner and Housing and Urban Development Secretary Shaun Donovan summoned executives of the twenty-five largest mortgage-lending and mortgage-servicing companies to a meeting to demand that they do more. But the shell game continued, with temporary "trial modifications" but precious few permanent cuts in monthly payments. In November, Michael Barr, the assistant Treasury secretary for financial institutions, flatly declared that "the banks are not doing a good enough job." In a blunt criticism of Wall Street rare for the Obama administration, Barr added, "Some of the firms ought to be embarrassed, and they will be," vowing to pressure and shame the banks into increasing trial modifications and making them permanent.

According to my sources, Barr got into some trouble with his supervisors for his populist attack on the banks, which had not been cleared with the White House. But the story played well; and two weeks later, in an interview on the CBS program *60 Minutes,* President Obama himself went Barr one better, declaring that he didn't run for president in order to help a lot of "fat-cat bankers." In one of his earliest explicit attacks on the banks, Obama noted that some big banks had sought to exit TARP early, in order to escape its limits on executive pay, adding: "which I think tells me that the people on Wall Street still don't get it."

The following Monday, December 14, the president called top bankers to the White House for a photo opportunity and a meeting in which he personally pressed them to do more to help struggling homeowners. But three of the bank CEOs stood the president up. They had not bothered to fly in the night before for the morning meeting, and bad weather grounded their flights. When they participated by speakerphone, it was Obama who sounded almost apologetic, and those present at the meeting reported that there was none of the tough talk that the president had used on TV.

Given the flawed structure of the whole approach, banks have no real incentive to provide deep and permanent reductions in mortgage costs, and foreclosures are on track to increase faster than loan modifications or refinancings, needlessly prolonging the great stagnation. Despite this ramping up of rhetoric, the Obama administration has remained in a bubble of denial about the failure of its program of mortgage relief. Geithner, testifying before the Congressional Oversight Panel, said, in a moment of uncharacteristic candor, "We do not have a mortgage market today except for that directly supported by the Government."

Mortgage Relief: The Roosevelt Alternative

There is a straightforward alternative to the administration's approach to foreclosure prevention, but it would require much more direct government involvement. And it would take a nervy battle rather than a friendly collusion with Wall Street. In the case of unaffordable mortgage loans still held by banks, a "public option" of direct government financing could reduce borrower costs without relying on largely futile incentive payments to bankers. And in cases where mortgage loans have been sliced, diced, and packaged into bonds, the simple solution is to turn the securities back into loans and pay off the investors at the prevailing, depressed market value—and use the savings to give homeowners new mortgages that they can afford.

Once again, the comparison with the New Deal is instructive—and depressing, when one contrasts the boldness of Roosevelt with the timidity of Obama. Faced with an epidemic of mortgage foreclosures, the New Deal created four new institutions. First, the government invented the long-term, self-amortizing mortgage. Until the Roosevelt era, the typical mortgage loan was a short-term "balloon note," usually of five years. The borrower paid interest only until the note was due and payable, then had to either come up with the whole amount or persuade the bank to roll over the loan—or lose the house. (The nineteenth-century melodramas about farmers not being able to come up with money to pay "the mortgage" refer not to a monthly payment but to the entire principal.)

At Roosevelt's request, Congress created a Federal Housing Administration to insure these modern mortgages, so that debilitated banks could resume making loans with reasonable confidence of being paid back. Roosevelt's people also created the Federal National Mortgage Association—Fannie Mae—as a secondary market to buy mortgages from banks and thrift institutions and replenish their working capital. But the most audacious intervention of all was the Home Owners Loan Corporation.

The HOLC, created in 1933, used the government's own borrowing rate—then a very low 2.5 percent—to refinance mortgage loans directly. It sold some $2 billion worth of bonds to finance its operations and then purchased nonperforming loans from banks, often with the bank taking a partial loss. Through HOLC, a creditworthy borrower facing economic hardship could get a low-interest-rate, long-term loan directly from the government. By 1937, HOLC owned about 14 percent of the dollar value of all US residential mortgages—today that would be $1.3 trillion. At one point, HOLC held one mortgage in five, and it saved at least a million homeowners from foreclosure. Even more impressively, HOLC was a retail agency, with more than 1,000 local offices and some 20,000 employees. It performed far more effectively than its private-sector counterparts. And when it finally shut down in 1951 for lack of business, after the HOLC's heroic work had returned housing markets to normal, it returned a small operating profit of $12 million to the Treasury.

Something like a new HOLC would be a far more effective remedy for the current mortgage crisis than the voluntary incentive schemes that rely on the financial self-interest and the impaired institutional capacity of the private mortgage industry. But Messrs. Summers and Geithner are utterly allergic to the idea of direct government operation of such programs.

In Roosevelt's day, the HOLC did not face the added complication of securitized loans. But there is a fairly straightforward remedy to that problem. A new HOLC, armed with a revolving fund, could use the power of eminent domain to require the investor to sell pools of securitized subprime mortgages to the government at their fair market value—currently something like 40 cents on the dollar. The HOLC could then convert the security back into a mortgage, using the savings to reduce the principal and the monthly payment by an average of at least half, and further subsidizing the mortgage, where necessary, with TARP money. The overarching goal should be to keep the homeowner in the house. According to Professor Howell Jackson of the Harvard Law School, one of the leading experts on eminent domain, this process is both feasible and constitutional. The obstacle is political.

It is also instructive to consider who would actually bear the loss. While there is no centralized public registry of who holds securitized mortgages, it is known that a lot of this depressed mortgage paper is now held by hedge funds that bought the securities for a fraction of their book value, hoping to make gains if government succeeded in restoring a trading market. We should not weep if hedge funds are made to sacrifice these imagined gains. The other major holder of distressed subprime paper is banks themselves. Some shrewd investment banks, notably Goldman Sachs and JPMorgan Chase, created securities but did not load up on the risky paper themselves. They cynically sold it to their clients, and then when the whole market started going south, they helpfully shorted the paper they themselves had created, profiting a second time. But the dumber banks like Citi, Bear, and Merrill, having created the high-risk securities, then turned around and purchased them, seduced by their own promise of high returns. So they are still sitting on a lot of distressed paper—the same junk that Secretary Geithner keeps haplessly trying to get off their books.

By late 2009, some hedge funds, such as the Fortress Investment Group, were operating a lucrative business buying underwater mortgages from banks at deep discounts and arranging reduced monthly payments for borrowers—while pocketing fat fees for themselves. If the Obama administration truly believed in affirmative government, this process could be accomplished by a public, HOLC-style agency. More of the savings could go to homeowners and less to financial middlemen. The government agency could buy the nonperforming mortgage directly from the bank at its current discounted value. Where the bank did not want to sell, government could use eminent domain. This would translate into a steep reduction of principal and interest to the homeowner, which could be topped up as necessary with TARP funds. The agency would need a hands-on process to sort out innocent-victim homeowners deserving of aid from speculators and people trying to game the system.

A milder alternative was put forth by Sheila Bair of the Federal Deposit Insurance Corporation. She proposed that instead of spending $75 billion on incentive payments to banks, the government should use $50 billion to reduce the costs directly to homeowners. Bair calculated that $50 billion would be sufficient to cut in half the monthly payments on some 3 million distressed mortgages. This would also be an indirect subsidy to the banks, but it would work bottom-up—via the homeowners—rather than top-down. The idea, proposed in the waning days of the Bush administration, was flatly rejected by Paulson and later shot down again when Tim Geithner became

Treasury secretary. Ultimately, under prodding from Democrats in Congress and a threat by the Congressional Black Caucus to vote against the entire administration economic program, the Treasury agreed to a provision allocating $3 billion in TARP money for direct mortgage relief. The contrast was all too vivid—several *trillions* in loans and loan guarantees for the banks, and a grudging $3 billion for the homeowners who had been the banks' victims.

As a consequence of the administration's half measures and failure to move boldly, the mortgage foreclosure crisis is continuing to drive millions of Americans from their homes, depress housing prices, weaken bank earnings, and retard the recovery. Some of what needs to be done to repair the banking system is technically daunting. Refinancing underwater retail mortgages is comparatively easy. It just requires political will.

Looking Under the TARP

The failure of the Bush-Obama strategy for dealing with the mortgage crisis closely parallels the government's feeble approach to restoring the banking system generally. The policy that Tim Geithner inherited from Hank Paulson (and from his own earlier incarnation as president of the New York Fed) had two basic parts. One element put money directly into failing banks, using funds appropriated by Congress under the emergency TARP program. The other part was a series of complex loan guarantees and purchase programs reliant on both the Treasury and the Federal Reserve. This second bundle of programs was intended to restore confidence in other credit markets, such as money market mutual funds, securitized consumer loans, and overnight lending between banks.

By mid-2009, the second part of the policy had more or less worked. Credit flows within the financial sector had resumed. What was not occurring, however, was an adequate outflow of credit *from* the banks to the rest of the economy. This failure was the direct result of a deliberate effort to restore confidence in the banks by concealing the extent of their losses rather than going in, demanding an honest accounting, and cleaning them out.

When the financial world seemed to be coming apart the week of September 15, 2008, the big banks had met with Paulson and jointly came up with the TARP scheme. Something similar had been proposed by Paulson's thirty-five-year-old aide, former Goldman executive Neel Kashkari, back in February 2008, as an emergency fallback. Paulson hoped that a combination of federal incentives, guarantees, and direct purchases could reignite a private market in these distressed securities. If government was buying, private buyers would return to the markets. As the bill was going through Congress, Paulson accepted a Democratic amendment, giving him the option to put government equity capital into the banks directly, but only with reluctance and disdain.

The TARP legislation signed into law by President Bush on October 3, 2008, empowered Paulson either to buy assets directly or to work with private investment firms to purchase the assets from banks at a discount, using taxpayer money as protection against losses. But by the time Bush signed the law, it had become apparent to Paulson that his approach was unworkable. An auction to establish a market price was not feasible because Treasury feared that the low prices would have a devastating effect on bank balance sheets. As long as the bank carried the security on its balance sheet at book value, it could delay acknowledging the loss. Selling it at a deep discount would yield some cash but immediately trigger the accounting loss.

By mid-October, Paulson had changed the game plan and was putting money into banks directly. Ironically, he was using authority that he had not sought, which had been added to the legislation by Congress. On Monday, October 13, the Columbus Day holiday, the chief executives of the nine largest banks were ordered to a meeting at the Treasury and told to take a direct infusion of funds from the Treasury. Banks that didn't really need the money were requested to take it anyway, to provide some camouflage to insolvent banks such as Citi. The terms were remarkably generous. Unlike the auto rescue that followed, government would be a purely passive investor. It would simply take preferred stock, a security that is more like a loan, paying a 5 percent dividend to the government. After some pushback from the banks that didn't really want the money, all of the bankers in the room agreed, taking $125 billion in all.

Paulson's original idea, to use government money not to pump in equity capital but to get toxic assets off the bank's books, was stillborn. Yet the same plan that Paulson rejected was repeatedly revived by his successor, Tim

Geithner, with support from Larry Summers. Geithner unveiled the outlines of his first version of the plan at a press conference on February 10, but he was widely ridiculed for providing no operational details.

The basic concept was that the Treasury would use the remaining $350 billion in TARP funds as backing for more than $1 trillion in other funds from the Federal Reserve and private investors, who would be attracted by guarantees yet to be spelled out. Members of Congress from both parties were withering in their criticism, as was most of Wall Street. Ethan Harris, co-head of US economics research at Barclays Capital, described Geithner's strategy as "shock and uh." The Dow fell by 383 points.

The plan got such a poor public reception that David Axelrod, President Obama's chief political adviser, leaked a story to *The New York Times* pointedly noting that Geithner had won all of the key policy debates inside the administration, and that this stinker of a plan was entirely Geithner's baby. Axelrod was taking pains to distance his president from a Treasury secretary who in a few weeks had gone from hero to goat, in case Obama needed to dump him. A chastened Geithner went back to the drawing board and produced a far more detailed plan on March 23.

This time, the baby had a name. It was called P-PIP, for Public-Private Investment Partnership. P-PIP was a more convoluted variation of the approach that Paulson had rejected as unworkable. Its terms gave private investors most of the gain and taxpayers and the Federal Reserve most of the risk. Specifically, toxic securities held on the balance sheets of banks, delicately renamed "legacy assets," would be offered for sale to investment syndicates, with up to 94 percent of the capital lent by the government and only 6 percent provided by the "investors." Yet the government's private partners were promised 50 percent of the profits. The plan had been drafted mainly by consultants and lobbyists from Goldman Sachs and the giant bond house Pimco, with some help from Warren Buffett.

In *New York Times* writer Andrew Ross Sorkin's account of the genesis of the plan, based on interviews with Buffett and with Pimco executives Bill Gross and Mohamed El-Erian, Pimco "had offered to run the fund pro bono," while Goldman's Lloyd Blankfein "had likewise offered to raise the investor money on a pro bono basis." But of course these were, respectively, America's largest bond fund and its most influential investment bank, not institutions known for eleemosynary gestures. They stood to gain an inside look at the securities and, to the extent that they were doing Treasury a favor, to get an IOU for future use. All had other conflicts of interest, in that they held a lot of depressed securities and stood to gain from creating markets in distressed mortgage-backed bonds that enjoyed new government guarantees. Pro bono, indeed. As 2009 wore on, the government repeatedly withdrew, refined, and reintroduced variations of P-PIP, none of which succeeded in getting much toxic paper out of the banking system. Throughout 2010, the Treasury kept making modifications on the plan, but little of the bad paper moved.

The Bogeyman of Nationalization

Early in the new administration, a debate ensued about whether the government should temporarily take over large insolvent banks. On one side of the debate were Larry Summers, Tim Geithner, and Ben Bernanke. Their preferred policy was to prop up large banks, use incentives and guarantees to enlist speculators to purchase bad assets, and hope that eventual improvements in the real economy would spill back into improved conditions at the banks. Summers's basic argument, laid out to President Obama in a March 31, 2009, memo, was that the government lacked explicit authority to take over large bank holding companies, and if government did so via the back door using negotiated bankruptcies, as in the auto bailout, the exercise might backfire by scaring off private investors. At the time, Summers and Geithner were devising "stress tests" as government seals of approval to lure more private capital back to invest in banks. A receivership for even one big bank, Summers warned, might drive investors away. Of course, a more reliable way to attract private capital to the financial sector was to restore banks to genuine health.

On the other side of the debate were outside economists such as Joseph Stiglitz, Nouriel Roubini, Jeffrey Sachs, Simon Johnson, Paul Volcker, the Congressional Oversight Panel, FDIC chair Sheila Bair, and this writer. As Damon Silvers, deputy chair of the oversight panel, put it, speaking at a conference on the TARP, "The administration makes two assumptions, neither of which are true. First, this is mainly a crisis of confidence. Second, time is on our side." In fact, Silvers added, this was a crisis not of confidence but of *solvency*, and the longer we delayed acknowledging the true conditions of the large banks, the longer the banking system dragged down the rest of the economy. Sheila Bair was emphatically of the view that insolvent Citigroup should be broken up and its good assets sorted out from its bad ones, rather than keeping up the pretense that the bank was solvent.

Administration officials partially sympathetic to the critics' view were chief political adviser David Axelrod, who felt that continuing the Paulson policy of bailing out Wall Street was a political loser, and Christina Romer, chair of the Council of Economic Advisers. She shared the concern that the banks would not resume normal lending until their balance sheets returned to health, and that gradually nursing them back to profitability was a much more circuitous route than a "good bank/bad bank" model, in which the bad assets were removed from an insolvent bank's books. However, Romer, already on thin ice with Summers as overly interventionist, did not press her case with President Obama.

A temporary government takeover of failed banks was repeatedly disparaged by Summers and Geithner as "nationalization." But this was a straw man. Nobody was proposing permanent government ownership of large banks. Rather, the idea was that government should take insolvent banks into temporary receivership, get rid of current management, and do an honest accounting of the holes in their balance sheets. Then government would decide how to make up the loss—how much taxpayer money had to be contributed, and how big a hit the bank's bondholders would take. Once this was done, the bank could either be sold off whole or broken up. Either way, impaired banks would be restored to healthy functioning. With this more direct approach, there would no longer be sick banks, reluctant to extend credit, sandbagging the rest of the economy.

There was a second insidious effect of the strategy of gradually nursing the banks back to health without confronting the underlying disaster of their balance sheets: The Treasury and the Fed had to be extremely protective of bank profits. That meant tightening loan standards at a time when the rest of the economy needed more generous terms. It meant broad toleration of outrageous terms for credit cards and other forms of consumer credit, since these remained profit centers; and it meant defending the trading schemes that generated large bank profits—until the collapse of the next credit bubble. It meant not cracking down on speculative abuses such as credit default swaps that added little to the economy except risks but sometimes made a bundle for banks. And as noted, Treasury refused to get at the root of the foreclosure crisis, since a program of mandatory write-downs and refinancings would also cut into bank profits. By failing to deal honestly with the huge hole in the banks' balance sheets, the Treasury and the Fed condemned the economy to death by a thousand cuts.

Yet another basic flaw was that the Bush-Obama strategy reinforced conflicts of interest. The serial rescues of failing banks amounted, in the words of former IMF chief economist Simon Johnson, to "policy by deal." These deals were hatched in private, over frantic weekends, relying heavily on the advice of a clubby group of Wall Street insiders, all of whom stood to profit by being part of conversations about the government's intentions.

The Treasury had never before been in the position of doling out money directly to failing banks. Unlike the FDIC, whose mandate included taking over and recapitalizing smaller failed banks, the Treasury had neither the staff nor the experience to restructure large banks. Consequently, Paulson had turned heavily to consultants from Wall Street, contracting out both the design and the execution of the TARP program to Wall Street insiders. This practice was continued by Geithner.

Cheap Money, Scarce Credit

The Bernanke-Summers-Geithner strategy created a paradox of cheap money and tight credit. The Fed was keeping short-term interest rates at zero. That policy coupled with the Treasury's guarantee of bank solvency produced a bonanza for the banks and for investors who speculated in their stocks. Indeed, one hedge fund manager, David Tepper, wagered in February 2009 that all the government support would keep banks afloat. He made a big bet on depressed bank stocks. When their stock price recovered later in 2009, he pocketed a cool $2.2 billion for himself and $7 billion for his hedge fund. Several other hedge funds profited handsomely from similar bets. But despite these windfall gains for insiders, the credit wasn't getting to where it was needed.

The commercial lending market offers a vivid example of the problem. When a developer builds an apartment complex, shopping mall, or office building, the normal practice is to get a construction loan from a bank. Then, when the building is completed and the space is leased or sold, a permanent lender pays off the bank and converts the debt to a long-term mortgage. This debt conversion is known in the trade as a "take-out." That permanent lender might be an insurance company, a bank, or an investment banker that turns around and sells the debt as a security to a pension fund, a hedge fund, or some other investor.

In the fevered speculative climate of 2005 and 2006, banks lowered their underwriting standards on commercial construction loans just as subprime lenders did on home mortgages. A similar pattern of overbuilding ensued. By 2008, America was littered with half-empty condo complexes, hotels, office buildings, and shopping malls. This left construction lenders—mostly commercial banks—holding the bag.

An unsold condo complex with a large vacancy rate cannot fetch a permanent lender. In some cases, developers rented out their unsold units and worked out a deal with banks to pay less than the full interest owed on their construction loan. In other cases, banks foreclosed and sold the property to other developer-speculators who could pay the carrying costs, but there were too few of these. By the summer of 2009, the market in conversion of construction loans on condo complexes and apartment buildings had resumed—but mainly in cases where government was guaranteeing the loans. Even with the guarantee, banks would provide the loans only to the extent that condo sales or apartment rentals were at normal levels—which described a minority of the cases. The glut of half-empty dwellings continued to drag down property values across the board and put other mortgages at risk.

The situation, according to one president of a highly reputable national loan packaging firm, was even more dire when it came to shopping malls, hotels, and office buildings. Virtually no creditor wanted to convert construction loans to long-term mortgages, because nobody could forecast vacancy rates. Even construction loans on properties built to order for well-established chains such as Walgreens, where the developer had a signed, long-term lease, were not getting converted to mortgages because investors were simply avoiding the whole sector.

I spoke to a convention of the nation's largest builders of industrial properties in May 2009, and I asked how many had had to forgo deals with willing clients because they could not get bank credit. Nearly every hand in the room went up. Though three months had passed since Geithner unveiled the Treasury's complex, taxpayer-supported bailout programs, the programs' impact on this credit logjam in the huge commercial real estate sector was just about nil.

With these credit markets frozen, weaknesses in the financial economy and in what economists call the "real" economy continued to feed on each other. If banks were holding the bag for construction loans that were not paying returns, their earnings would be depressed and their capital impaired, and they would be more risk-averse about making other loans; even sound industrial projects would wither for lack of credit. If developers were in hock to banks and had difficulty qualifying for new credit, they could not return to their normal business of development. If the landscape was littered with half-empty buildings, nobody in his right mind would build new ones.

By failing to address the problem of depressed bank assets directly, Geithner and the Obama administration prolonged a stalemate that kept the economy mired in stagnation. Trillions of dollars' worth of residential and commercial properties, and the debt instruments on them, were worth less than their book value. As long as this was the case, credit markets would remain risk-averse.

Economists have projected the total shortfall in the balance sheets of banks at about $2 trillion. That sounds like an impossibly large sum. In fact, it is about 15 percent of one year's GDP, or less than one-fifth of the national debt. The costs of *not* fixing the banks will be far more than $2 trillion. Banks normally create credit at a ratio of about 12:1. For every dollar of capital, they can make about twelve dollars of new loans backed by sound collateral. But when their books are clogged with depressed assets, they are reluctant to take new risks and credit remains hard to come by. As Joseph Stiglitz has observed, it would have been far more efficient to take insolvent banks into receivership and use the $700 billion in TARP money to provide capital to clean banks—in turn giving those banks the capacity to extend $8.4 trillion ($700 billion times 12) to the credit-starved economy.

The Japan Trap
The Bush-Obama strategy of nursing insolvent banks back to health, at serious cost to the rest of the economy, repeats an epic mistake made two decades

ago by the Japanese. Like the United States, Japan in the 1980s enjoyed the false prosperity of a financial bubble reinforced by a housing bubble. When the crash came, Japan's Finance Ministry, with its intimate ties to Tokyo's financial elite, could not bring itself to demand an honest accounting. The result was a decade-long period of not quite depression but prolonged stagnation. Even a policy of zero interest rates by the Bank of Japan did not help.

What is all the more remarkable is that Japan suffered its lost decade of growth at a time when the global economy was booming and productive Japan enjoyed an export surplus. This industrial powerhouse of an economy, which had been accustomed to growth rates in excess of 8 percent a year for three decades, went into a period of prolonged stagnation. Between 1991 and 2003, Japan averaged growth of just 1.1 percent per year. Japan's engineers were as inventive as ever, its products just as superb, and its workers just as diligent. This was purely a crisis of Japan's financial system, needlessly prolonged by government's failure to act.

The Japanese financial quagmire was an eerie preview of what the United States would experience a decade later. The causes were the same—too much deregulation and speculation coupled with very low interest rates. And the dynamics of prolongation were the same—a refusal by government to acknowledge balance-sheet realities. Ironically, in the 1990s the US government, along with the IMF, was among those urging the Japanese government to take a far more aggressive stance.

As the Congressional Oversight Panel summarized the experience, "Japanese authorities pinned their hopes on a macroeconomic recovery that would restore the full value of assets and avoid costly write-downs. Regulators permitted lax accounting practices that allowed banks to book the value of their loan assets based on how much they could spare within the capital adequacy ratio. The real financial condition of the borrowers was seldom accurately reflected on the bank balance sheet." Only when a new finance minister cracked down on accounting practices and forced banks to acknowledge losses, in 2003, did the system finally return to health. The panel concluded, "The consensus view among economists who have studied Japan's economy during this period is that Japan simply kept banks in business for far too long with insufficient capital. The unwillingness to acknowledge the harsh reality of the asset bubble burst in the short-term contributed to the very sluggish growth rate of the Japanese economy that lasted for more than a decade." Japan offers a perfect cautionary tale of what not to do—one being repeated chapter and verse by the Obama administration.

How Sweden Did It Right

In the early 1990s, the Swedes, facing a similar financial collapse, modeled their policy closely on the successful experience of the US Resolution Trust Corporation (discussed below). Sweden is often thought of as a social-democratic country, but in the early 1990s it was governed by a center-right coalition. Like Japan and the United States, Sweden had substantially deregulated its banking system in the 1980s. Speculative lending increased, much of it abroad, which is especially risky for a small country vulnerable to exchange rate shifts. And indeed, the financial costs of German reunification in 1989 led the German government unexpectedly to shore up the Deutschmark by raising interest rates. This move in turn put pressure on the Swedish krona.

To defend its currency, the Swedish central bank raised its own interest rates, bursting what had been a bubble in property values. Eventually, the government gave up trying to defend the value of the krona and let the currency float. It quickly lost 15 to 20 percent against stronger currencies, raising the cost of debt service for Swedish banks that had invested in foreign currencies. By 1992, Sweden was in the throes of a full-blown banking crisis.

But unlike the Japanese in the 1990s or the Bush and Obama administrations since 2007, the Swedish government devised a very straightforward restructuring plan. Two large banks were nationalized, and all deposits and creditor claims were guaranteed by the state while the government took adequate time to design a recovery plan. In 1993, a new agency, the Bank Support Authority, thoroughly audited the books of all banks. In a fashion reminiscent of Roosevelt's policy, they were divided into banks that could survive without government help, ones that could make it with capital infusions, and banks that needed to be shut down. Asset management companies, modeled on RTC, were created to find buyers for distressed assets. By 1997, the process was complete, much of the system was re-privatized, and the total cost was about 4 percent of one year's GDP. In American terms, this would be about $600 billion—or slightly less than the cost of the TARP.

Except that Swedish taxpayers got their money's worth, because their outlay quickly restored the financial system and broader economy to health.

History Lessons Ignored

You don't have to go to Sweden to learn how to restore a damaged banking system to health. We've done it twice in our own history—using public solutions. Our first foray into banking remedies was in the 1930s. But a public solution also played out in the late 1980s and early 1990s, after the savings-and-loan industry had succumbed to an orgy of speculative lending permitted by deregulation. The reserves of the agency that at the time guaranteed deposits, the Federal Savings and Loan Insurance Corporation, were wiped out. More than 1,000 S&Ls went bust. Their assets were a mélange of uncollectible loans and messy physical collateral in the form of half-empty condos and unfinished industrial parks. The task was to find someone to buy the assets at a reasonable price and rebuild a devastated thrift sector that was a prime source of home mortgage financing. This was beyond the capacity of private industry.

During the Republican administration of George H. W. Bush, a bipartisan effort in Congress created one of government's great success stories at cleaning up after the excesses of the private sector—the Resolution Trust Corporation. The agency was created in 1989, as part of general reform legislation. Its charter was to sort out solvent from insolvent S&Ls, find buyers for their assets, and rebuild a devastated industry. Ultimately, the RTC resolved 787 failed S&Ls. In a typical process, incumbent management was displaced, equity shareholders lost their investments, bondholders were subjected to a bankruptcy-like proceeding and took partial losses, but depositors were fully protected. Some failed S&Ls were shut down, others were restructured and reopened under new management, and still others were merged into stronger S&Ls.

The RTC proved especially adept at disposing of the bundle of assets, a task for which government is supposedly ill suited. This is a point invariably raised by Larry Summers, who resists the receivership approach on the premise that government can't manage banks. But it could hardly do worse than the current crop of bank executives.

Unlike the Treasury, which has a tiny staff to administer TARP and contracts out its operations, the Resolution Trust Corporation was a government agency lodged at the FDIC. In addition to sorting good loans from bad, it floated new, more transparent securities to raise cash. It devised a sealed-bid auction system to attract buyers for distressed properties that were the collateral for loans. It encouraged bids from bargain hunters. In the end, RTC was widely applauded by most observers as a success story. It relied on Treasury financing that eventually totaled better than $120 billion, which seemed like a huge sum at the time, but it offset the government outlay by recouping value from sold assets.

The difference between RTC and the current TARP program is telling. RTC used taxpayer funds to put a damaged financial industry back on its feet—but it did not bail out incumbent executives and shareholders. On the contrary, the executives that had driven the industry into the ground lost their jobs and the stockholders lost their equity—just as capitalism is supposed to work. A few bottom-feeders who bid for depressed assets made out nicely, but the process of auctioning off these assets was fully transparent. RTC was a public institution accountable to Congress. Unlike the Paulson-Geithner approach, this was not a system of sweetheart deals among cronies conducted behind closed doors. The net benefits of the exercise went mostly to taxpayers. And this exercise in what Summers would disparage as socialism was done largely under a Republican administration!

What Would Roosevelt Do?

There is one other good example from American history: the Reconstruction Finance Corporation. The RFC, which is associated in the public mind with Franklin Roosevelt, was actually created late in the Hoover administration, in 1932. At the time, the banking system was spinning into insolvency, and many large corporations were in bankruptcy.

As established by Congress, the RFC was given direct appropriations of $500 million, with the authority to borrow $1.5 billion more. It was empowered to create a farm credit system; make loans to banks, savings institutions, and insurance companies; refinance railroad bonds; and invest directly in industrial corporations. It was also given the explicit authority to invest in failed banks, so that good assets could be sorted out from bad, and potentially viable banks returned to operation.

When Roosevelt declared his famous bank holiday in March 1933, so that government could perform a triage operation on the banking system, it was the RFC that did the job—closing some banks, allowing others to reopen immediately, and adding public capital to a third category, which would be reopened later. The 17,000 banks that existed in 1932 were shrunken to 12,000. Of the survivors, about half received significant capital infusions from the RFC.

Before it was finally put out of business by a Republican Congress after World War II, the RFC spent just under $50 billion. As chairman of an expanded RFC, Roosevelt named Jesse Jones, a Houston business leader who was also something of a populist. Jones had already been serving as an RFC board member under Hoover and had participated in the RFC's first major bank rescue operation, a $90 million infusion of government capital into the Central Republic Bank of Chicago in June 1932.

At its peak, the RFC held stock in half the nation's banks. Under Jones, the RFC lent or invested capital into not just banks but also industrial corporations, steel mills, railroads, and real estate developers. It underwrote the Rural Electrification Administration, the modern farm credit system, and the Export-Import Bank, as well as municipal bonds for hard-pressed cities and towns blocked from a skittish municipal bond market. Later, it was the government's principal arm for financing the war production buildup.

The RFC was also the source of financing for many of the great public works built during the New Deal, from the San Francisco Bay Bridge to New York's Jones Beach. Jesse Jones prized these projects because they were both useful and "self-liquidating"—the loans were repaid by fees and highway tolls. "Today," Jones proudly wrote in his 1951 memoir, *Fifty Billion Dollars,* "the nation is dotted, from coast to coast and from the Rio Grande to the Great Lakes, with useful monuments to that [RFC] legislation—great bridges, electric power plants and lines, express highways, waterworks, sewer systems, college dormitories, modern low-rent housing, aqueducts, vehicular tunnels, and other facilities."

But there was a radical difference between the current Treasury and Federal Reserve bailouts under the TARP and those supervised by Jesse Jones via the RFC. For one thing, Jones was operating with publicly appropriated money, and he was directly accountable to Congress. For another, the RFC was part of the New Deal and did not have an ideological aversion to putting the public interest first and extracting stringent conditions for the investment of the public money. Jones put directors on company boards and replaced corporate managers. He got authority from Congress to limit the salaries of corporate executives receiving RFC aid, and he used it. Several of the nation's railroads, for example, survived only thanks to RFC loans, and executive salaries were capped at $60,000. Today, the Obama government is having difficulty summoning the political will to cap bankers' salaries at several million dollars. Adjusting for inflation, the RFC found no shortage of entirely competent bankers willing to work for a fraction of that.

Of its $10.5 billion invested in recovery from the Depression, the RFC actually realized a return of about $500 million once prosperity returned. Some $9.3 billion of its later investment in the war mobilization effort was written off as uncollectible, and in effect was a government subsidy to the wartime recapitalization of industry. So in an economic crisis, the question is not whether government "picks winners," but whether it does so competently and transparently.

Although the RFC was one of the most socialistic institutions in the history of the American experience, many conservative experts on financial crises are admirers of the RFC because it kept the Federal Reserve out of the bailout business. The RFC separated the function of recapitalization and resolution of shaky banks and industrial firms from the conduct of monetary policy. The current approach, by contrast, puts the Federal Reserve directly into a function for which it was not designed and which it does not do well—bailing out individual banks without having the capacity or the will to provide hands-on supervision.

Indeed, the policy of the Bush and Obama administrations for the distressed large banks is best described as "forbearance." What does this mean? Waiving accounting standards, weakening regulatory constraints, looking the other way in the face of flagrant conflicts of interest, and not getting involved in bank management decisions despite massive amounts of taxpayer aid. The alternative, as exemplified by the RFC, is a far more hands-on process, with the option of shutting down a failed bank, selling off its assets, or replacing its management.

The only government entity today that behaves roughly like the Reconstruction Finance Corporation is the Federal Deposit Insurance Corporation. However, bank restructuring is only an incidental part of what the FDIC does—and only happens when an insured bank goes broke. Unlike the RFC, recapitalizing and restructuring failed banks is not the FDIC's primary mission. Moreover, the FDIC has authority to liquidate and restructure only banks; it has no authority over bank holding companies, such as Citigroup and Bank of America, which are the largest and most problematic institutions. In the current crisis, the FDIC's process of recapitalization and restructuring of failed smaller banks provided a good model of how to proceed. But FDIC chair Sheila Bair has been the odd woman out in the club of Bernanke, Geithner, and Summers. She was bitterly resented for dissenting from their preferred strategy of propping up and bailing out.

Another path was available. But it was not pursued.

Understimulated

As we have seen, in two of the three key areas of recovery policy—mortgage relief and banking repair—the Obama policy was basically a continuation of Bush's failed policies, with additional subsidies.

In a third key area, economic stimulus, Obama broke some new ground—but not enough. Bush's own stimulus program, enacted in February 2008, spent only about $168 billion, or just over 1 percent of gross domestic product, and most of this was in tax cuts. Though the initial Obama stimulus of February 2009, the American Recovery and Reinvestment Act, spent more money—over $250 billion a year—it was too small to do the job properly given the worsened economy and the offsetting deep cuts in state budgets.

Why the need for a very large government stimulus? When private demand has been undermined by a severe recession, the cascading effects paralyze all the usual sources of recovery in the private sector. Consumers reduce their purchases, workers lose jobs and wages, businesses cut their orders from other businesses, investors are hesitant to commit capital. When recession is intensified by losses in household net worth and a traumatized financial sector, as in the present case, the compounding effects are magnified. In such circumstances, the sole source of purchasing power to revive demand is the government.

Fiscally and politically, the case for a very substantial stimulus was complicated by the fact that in January 2009, the federal government was already facing a large budget shortfall. In fiscal year 2008, under Bush, the deficit had already risen to $459 billion. However, the deficit that President Obama inherited resulted mainly from permanent cuts in the tax code sponsored by President Bush, an expensive war, and revenue losses caused by the recession itself. According to the authoritative Center on Budget and Policy Priorities, domestic government spending was actually a trivial source of increased federal deficits in the years between 2001 and 2008. Bush's tax cuts accounted for 49 percent; the military buildup, another 34 percent; increased entitlements, mainly Bush's Medicare drug benefit (with its gratuitous subsidy to drug companies), 10 percent more. Just 7 percent was the result of all other nonmilitary spending. The Obama stimulus program, at $787 billion, added just 3 percent to the total deficits projected for 2009–19.

It's now clear that Obama's most senior economic aides underestimated the severity of the gathering economic crisis. The most expert members of Obama's team actually had wanted a much larger stimulus but were overruled politically. While Larry Summers was given the job as chief economic policy maker, the more technical post of chair of the Council of Economic Advisers went, as noted, to Berkeley economist Christina Romer. She, like Ben Bernanke, was an expert on the Great Depression. But where Bernanke had focused on its monetary aspects, Romer's interest was on the broader strategies for stimulating recovery via government activism. Read superficially, Romer's work might suggest that she was among those revisionist critics who argued that the New Deal had been a failure because high unemployment persisted right up until World War II. But Romer's point was the opposite. The deficit spending of the Roosevelt years—typically around 4 to 5 percent of GDP—had not been big enough.

Romer knew from her research that in the late 1930s, Congress and the budget hawks in the White House had tried to balance the budget too early in the recovery. The result was the deep recession of 1937, which also cost Roosevelt his working majority of New Dealers in Congress, when Republicans made big gains in the off-year elections of 1938. The proof of the pudding was that when government suspended all the usual rules and incurred a massive deficit of 29 percent of GDP in 1942 for the war effort, unemployment quickly melted to 2 percent.

In early December 2008, as Obama's new team prepared a decision memo for the president-elect, Romer was tasked with assessing the scale of the needed stimulus package. Her technical work convinced her that the cascading effects of losses in consumer wealth, damage to credit markets and bank balance sheets, and worsening unemployment feeding on itself would produce an output gap of around $2 trillion over the next two years. An output gap is the difference between what the economy is capable of producing at or near full employment and what it actually produces. A $2 trillion gap in GDP, Romer calculated, called for a stimulus of some $1.2 trillion over two years, and quite possibly more.

That figure was far larger than what either Summers or Rahm Emanuel considered necessary, prudent, or politically viable. But if anything, even Romer's number proved to be too low. Romer had assumed that unemployment would peak at 8.9 percent. Its actual peak was well over 10 percent and the job losses were far worse than projected. The true two-year output gap for the period Romer measured was closer to $3 trillion. But in presenting a decision memo to the president-elect at a December 16 meeting, Summers offered a range of lower options for stimulus spending, between a low of $550 billion and a high of $890 billion.

At the meeting, there was argument about how fast the government could actually pump the money out, as well as questions raised by Summers about the effect on the bond market if a large deficit caused interest rates to rise. Obama, according to various sources, played a hands-off role and left the final decision to his staff. In the end, Chief of Staff Rahm Emanuel opted for a middle ground and decided that Obama should propose a stimulus in the range of $675 to $775 billion, knowing that Congress still had to act.

The stimulus package was the first big test of Obama's effort to extend an olive branch to Republicans. The eventual bill weighed in at $787 billion. Hundreds of billions in tax cuts were added to attract Republican support. In the final bargaining between the White House and Senate Republicans, crucial aid to state and local government and to public school repair and construction was cut by tens of billions of dollars in order to add more tax breaks. Even so, Obama picked up only three Republican Senate votes.

By ordinary standards, $787 billion is a very large sum of money. But measured against the size of the shrinking economy and the collapse of state and local budgets, it was puny. On paper, the two-year stimulus plan comprised about 2.7 percent of a $14 trillion dollar economy, or about 1.35 percent per year—not much larger than Bush's. But Obama's senior economists underestimated the economy's softness and wanted the money to be spread out over a longer period. So the stimulus was "back-loaded" and actually paid out over three years. By the end of June 2009, only about $100 billion had been spent. Most of the money would not be spent until 2010, and 30 percent of it would not be expended until fiscal year 2011.

States of Distress

The combined shortfall of state and local governments during the same three years totaled about $483 billion. Netting out all levels of government, the overall government stimulus was only around $100 billion a year—a relative drop in the bucket. An additional state and local shortfall of $120 billion is projected for 2012, with Obama calling for a domestic spending freeze.

As the recession deepened, the fall in state and local tax receipts accelerated. Not surprisingly, depressed economic activity reduces revenues from sales, income, and property taxes—the main sources of state and local funds. Because all states but one (Vermont) require balanced budgets, these revenue losses had to be matched dollar for dollar, in the same fiscal year, with cuts in program outlays, layoffs, or increases in state and local taxes. For 2010, the average state revenue shortfall was more than 16 percent—and as high as 35 percent in some states. So about two-thirds of the federal stimulus was undermined by belt-tightening at the state level.

Unlike public works projects that take time to be "shovel-ready," the neutralizing of avoidable state and local budget cuts takes no advance planning whatever. All Washington needs to do is write fifty checks to state treasurers—and layoffs and program cuts are avoided on the spot. A "maintenance of effort" requirement can assure that emergency federal fiscal aid goes to keep existing services and people on the job, and not for state or local tax cuts. As my colleague Larry Mishel of the Economic Policy Institute points out, about half of all spending by state and local governments ends up in the private sector, providing income and jobs to vendors and contractors.

The primary benefits of further stimulus aimed at preventing state and local government from going into free fall are macroeconomic—saving jobs, preventing program cuts, and making sure that states don't worsen consumer purchasing power by regressively raising taxes in a recession. But there is a powerful secondary benefit in preventing a further erosion of trust in government.

When state budgets collapse, states and localities slash services that people need and appreciate. Schools and libraries close, government offices cut hours, class sizes go up, community college budgets take hits. The most creative and valued programs are often the first to go. As public employees are laid off, government's basic capacity to do its job is wrecked. The erosion of confidence of state and local government, due to perverse fiscal policies, spills over into a skepticism about the Obama administration.

According to the Center on Budget and Policy Priorities, by the beginning of 2010 forty-three states had cut services to residents and thirty states had raised taxes. At least twenty-one states had cut low-income health insurance or reduced access to health care; twenty-two states and the District of Columbia were cutting medical, rehabilitative, and home-care services for low-income people who are elderly or disabled. At least twenty-four states were cutting funds for K–12 schooling, early education, and child care, and thirty-two cut support for public colleges and universities.

Students who might stay in college can't afford the higher tuition and join unemployment lines. Despite a provision in the law targeting relief for public education, by October 2009 some 40,000 teachers had lost their jobs. The poor, who have the weakest political voice, typically experience the deepest cuts. *The New York Times* reported that Birmingham, Alabama, cannot afford even to bury the indigent dead. Massachusetts, at this writing, has a new heroin epidemic because it closed drug rehab centers.

The taxes that states raised, typically, were regressive and highly visible taxes such as the sales tax. *Raise taxes and reduce services in a recession?* Republican strategists Grover Norquist and Karl Rove, on their most creative day, could not have imagined a better strategy to crush public confidence in government—and in the incumbent national administration.

Supporters of the administration spent much of 2009 pointing out, correctly, that without the stimulus, things would have been even worse. And that's entirely true. Absent the stimulus, the economy would have declined faster, shed more jobs, and taken longer to recover. But IT COULD HAVE BEEN WORSE makes a lousy reelection bumper sticker.

Polls showed that the public was worried about the deficit. But if you dug a little deeper, the concern was not about rising deficits per se, but of deficit spending going to the wrong people, or high deficits as a symbol of government not doing its job.

The Politics of a Second Stimulus

Late in 2009, the House Democratic leadership, led by Nancy Pelosi, complained directly to President Obama that Democrats would lose control of Congress unless stronger medicine was forthcoming. But the White House remained divided between advisers like Christina Romer, who argued for more stimulus spending, and budget director Peter Orszag, who warned that deficits should not rise. In November, I was invited first to testify to a special meeting of the House Democratic committee chairs on the economic emergency, and then to address the entire Democratic caucus. Beneath the surface harmony with the White House and loyalty to President Obama, there was barely controlled fury that Obama and his team just didn't get it. "He has until 2012 to get this right, but we are going to be hung out to dry next November," said one senior Democratic congressman.

These were elected leaders who took the nation's pulse not through polls or focus groups, but by spending weekends in their districts, listening to the human tragedy of lost jobs, homes, and futures. David Obey, the chair of the House Appropriations Committee, told his colleagues about a visit to a community college in his district where some 400 local workers were in a retraining program. "They were the saddest group of people I've ever seen," Obey said, dismissing the idea that education could be a panacea. "A year ago, they had good jobs, and now they don't have a clue where they're going to end up."

At that meeting, the House Democratic leadership resolved to write their own jobs legislation, as a way to prod the White House. But without strong White House support, the measure faced rough legislative going. In mid-December, by the slimmest of margins, 218–214, the House approved a $154 billion jobs bill, which included emergency aid to the states to prevent layoffs of teachers and first responders, as well as an extension of unemployment benefits. The White House basically sat out the vote. The Republicans were, as usual, united in opposition, and more than two dozen Democrats defected. In early March, Congress passed a paltry $15 billion tax credit for jobs, the stunted fruit of bipartisanship in the Senate.

The White House was whipsawed between concerns about stubbornly high joblessness and pressure to cut the deficit. But this was a false choice. At the White House jobs summit in December, I got a chance to pose the question to Obama directly: How did he reconcile the need for more spending now with the crusade to cut the deficit later? His answer was impressive: "The last thing we would want to do in the midst of a weak recovery," he told me, "is to essentially take more money out of the system either by raising taxes or by drastically slashing spending. And frankly, because state and local governments generally don't have the capacity to engage in deficit spending, some of that obligation falls on the federal government."

This was exactly right. Except that by the time of his State of the Union address, the administration's emphasis was wrong—too little economic stimulus in 2010, too much emphasis on reducing the deficit while the economy was still suffering high rates of unemployment.

Deficit Obsession
Once again, the behind-the-scenes influence of Wall Street was a telling factor. For nearly three decades, Peter G. Peterson, formerly the head of the private equity firm known as the Blackstone Group, has been orchestrating a fearmongering campaign about the future costs of Social Security and Medicare. Peterson was a prime mover behind the Concord Coalition, a leading organization of deficit hawks.

Peterson's story was that future "unfunded liabilities" would crash the economy by draining productive investment, raising interest rates, and frightening foreign creditors. Supposedly, the costs of Social Security were diverting funds needed by younger Americans, though there is no record of Peterson ever advocating more spending on the young. During the late 1990s, when the budget was in balance and endless surpluses were projected, this same story line continued unabated. And during the Bush era, when the prime source of new deficits was the series of Bush tax cuts, the Peterson crowd expended no effort on opposing them. Rather, the real target was social insurance. Should Social Security ever be privatized, it would be a massive source of new profits for financial firms.

Throughout his long career of warning that Social Security and Medicare liabilities would crash the economy, Peterson never called attention to the economic risks that actually did cause the collapse. Nor did he call for more vigilant financial regulation. On the contrary, he made his fortune in one of the least regulated corners of Wall Street, private equity, and cashed in by selling shares in Blackstone to the public right on the eve of the crash. Private equity moguls such as Peterson typically pay a very low rate of tax, taking advantage of Wall Street's "carried interest" loophole, which allows money management fees paid to private equity and hedge funds in the form of carried interest to be taxed at low capital-gains rates rather than ordinary income rates. There is something off when a billionaire lectures ordinary people about the profligacy of their Social Security. Using $1 billion of the money that he took out, in 2008 Peterson created the Peter G. Peterson Foundation to spread the word about the need for budget balance. He hired as his foundation's president David Walker, former head of the General Accounting Office.

You can buy a lot of influence for a billion dollars. Peterson has showered money on a wide variety of institutions, ranging from the *Columbia Journalism Review* to the Brookings Institution and the New America Foundation. He partnered with the Pew Charitable Trusts and *The Washington Post*. Posing as an ideologically neutral source of expertise about the nation's fiscal condition, Peterson even founded an online newspaper, *The Fiscal Times,* and persuaded the *Post* to print its articles in its news pages.

Peterson's contention is that the ordinary legislative process can no longer be relied upon to produce defensible budgets. The Peterson Foundation has been a prime mover behind an extra-legislative budget commission, which would set budget targets that the House and Senate would basically have to vote up or down, with strict limits on the right of debate or amendment.

The economic collapse was a gift to Peterson and kindred budget hawks, because it sent deficits skyward. The Peterson Foundation's propaganda conflates three entirely separate policy challenges—the short-term deficits caused by the recession; the deliberate temporary increase in the deficit produced by necessary economic stimulus; and the long-term (and quite different) fiscal needs of Medicare and Social Security. All these are lumped under the heading "Washington is broken," a line that recurs in nearly all of Walker's extensive public appearances.

In January 2010, Obama's economic advisers seized on the budget commission idea as a way to demonstrate concern for long-term fiscal balance to offset public concerns about short-run deficits. Inside the administration, budget director Peter Orszag was a big promoter of the idea—as was Robert Rubin's Hamilton Project, which Orszag had formerly directed. Congress remained bitterly divided, with a bipartisan group of deficit hawks embracing the Peterson idea, but most of the Democratic leadership opposing it as an extra-constitutional dereliction of Congress's responsibility for taxing and spending. In the end, the measure narrowly failed in the Senate, and Obama then created the commission by executive order.

What is the right way to think about reconciling large short-term deficits with long-run fiscal balance? We surely need bigger deficits for another year or two, to propel a strong recovery. Higher rates of economic growth coupled with progressive taxation can then bring the debt back down to a tolerable scale relative to GDP.

A bipartisan deficit commission is almost guaranteed to emphasize cuts in social outlay rather than a restoration of progressive taxes as the route to fiscal balance. Key Republicans who have endorsed the idea make clear that they want no part of it if tax increases are part of the bargain. On this front, too, the Obama administration has been too quick to pander to Wall Street demands for fiscal restraint, and too slow to lead.

Passing Up Tax Reform

In the administration's budget for 2010, Obama did propose to let the Bush tax cuts expire. But the Obama White House and Treasury explicitly opposed two key reforms that could have netted literally hundreds of billions of dollars a year, relieving the tension between adequate social spending and responsible budget policy. For example, in March 2009, Senator Carl Levin of Michigan and Congressman Lloyd Doggett of Texas introduced legislation, the Tax Haven Abuse Act, to increase the ability of the IRS to collect revenues improperly booked on offshore tax havens. Levin's Permanent Subcommittee on Investigations had conducted extensive hearings on these abuses. In the previous Congress, a similar bill had been co-sponsored by then Senator Barack Obama, who had promised in the campaign to crack down on corporate tax evasion.

The US Treasury estimated that the Levin-Doggett bill would bring in at least $100 billion a year and as much as $130 billion, virtually all of it from tax-evading corporations and very high-income individuals using sophisticated gimmicks to book income offshore in havens with no taxes and no tax treaties with the United States. To put that figure in perspective, it is more than the cost of the Obama health reform. Among other provisions, the measure would treat foreign corporations managed and controlled in the United States as domestic corporations for income tax purposes, and it would close other loopholes that enable various forms of tax evasion using shell companies based offshore. The Government Accountability Office found that 18,857 US companies maintained an office of record in a single building in the Caymans, which in reality has a single occupant, the law firm Maples and Calder. Morgan Stanley has 158 subsidiaries in the Cayman Islands, which are the location of choice for hedge funds.

Corporations and hedge funds mounted a massive campaign to kill the proposal. The administration made no effort to support it. By the time tax legislation emerged from tax writing committees, as the Baucus-Rangel bill, all of its teeth had been stripped in favor of weak reporting requirements. While the Levin-Doggett bill would have raised upward of $100 billion a year, the Baucus-Rangel bill projected raising less than $1 billion. The trade association Cayman Finance, representing that island nation's money-laundering institutions, actually issued a press release congratulating Baucus and Rangel. "The new comprehensive proposal does away with the damaging features of Senator Levin's Stop Tax Haven Abuse Act," said Cayman Finance chairman Anthony Travers, adding that the Baucus-Rangel bill is "entirely consistent with the approach suggested by Cayman Finance in our many meetings with these and other U.S. policymakers."

Even more indefensible was the administration's complicity in a measure that was quietly slipped into 2009 tax legislation extending a Bush-era provision that allows multinational corporations to avoid taxes on dividends. US companies pay tax on worldwide income, but they don't owe tax on income earned through their foreign subsidiaries until it is repatriated. This is called deferral. Obama in the campaign promised to close this loophole when he talked about curbing the tax incentive to shift jobs overseas.

Rules dating to 1962 allowed this kind of indefinite deferral of taxes owed only when a subsidiary is based in a foreign jurisdiction with tax levels comparable to those in the United States. But these rules were weakened by regulation in 1997, and in 2006 the Republicans, in anticipation of the Democratic takeover of Congress, passed a law putting the 1997 loopholes into the tax code. The loophole allows foreign subsidiaries to make payments to one another without triggering US tax. This means that you can pay royalties and interest from France or Germany (high-tax countries) to Ireland (a low-tax country) and escape US taxation entirely. As Reuven Avi-Yonah, professor of tax law at the University of Michigan, explains it, "That is why you can see that a third of US multinational profits overseas are in Ireland, Luxembourg and Bermuda, and why 9 of the top 10 locations have an effective tax rate below 10%."

But in 2009, the Obama administration agreed to legislation making the Bush loophole permanent—costing the Treasury hundreds of billions of dollars and going back on an Obama campaign pledge. This is the kind of insider issue that most voters miss, but that large corporations, banks, and hedge funds appreciate mightily. It tells you that the perception that Obama is closer to Wall Street than Main Street is more than an image problem—it's reality.

The Costs of Complicity

By late 2009, the financial part of the economy was generally booming. It was only the rest of the economy that was sick. The stock market had bounced back more than 50 percent from its March lows. Executive pay was on track to beat even its record year in pre-crash 2007.

A January 2010 tabulation by *The Wall Street Journal* of pay at the thirty-eight top investment banks, hedge funds, asset managers, and stock and commodities exchanges showed an average executive compensation gain of 18 percent—from 2008's $117 billion to about $145 billion. Goldman Sachs set aside a 2009 bonus pool of $16.2 billion, up 47 percent from 2008. This number was slightly lower than expected, to diffuse the political backlash. To further preempt congressional action, Goldman voluntarily paid out its bonuses in deferred stock that would have to be held five years before being cashed in. (A New York steak house favored by investment bankers offered to take stock certificates in lieu of cash.) And CEO Lloyd Blankfein took a relatively modest bonus of just $9 million, as a public relations gesture.

Morgan Stanley recorded the first annual loss in its seventy-four-year history but set aside an astonishing 64 cents out of every dollar of gross revenue for employee compensation—a total of $14.4 for salaries and bonuses. Even Citigroup, which lost $1.6 billion in 2009, managed to set aside about $5 billion in bonuses. In order to get around the TARP's limits on bonuses, Citi during 2009 increased base pay for its top executives by 50 percent. Bank of America, also heavily reliant on taxpayer aid, roughly quintupled its bonus pool for 2009 relative to 2008.

The merger-and-acquisition business was kicking back in. More M&A meant more profits for investment banks, and more confidence that bidding wars for corporate takeovers would prop up the price of stocks. It was one more sign that the bubble part of the economy was recovering smartly, while the real economy lagged far behind.

On all of these fronts—fiscal stimulus, job creation, reviving a collapsed banking system, stemming the epidemic of foreclosures, and insisting that the financial economy serve the real economy instead of being parasitic on it—the Obama program was mostly business as usual. As a result, most economists now believe that we are in for a prolonged period of stagnation—not full-blown depression but slow growth, persistently high unemployment, flat or falling wages, and the possibility of back-to-back recessions as well.

As 2010 dawned, unemployment was rising again. Housing defaults and foreclosures were outpacing the government's meager mortgage modification program. The dangers of a double-dip recession were greater than ever. Health reform had gone from potential big winner to tar baby. And Democrats were increasingly on the wrong side of rising popular backlash.

Jobs, Jobs, Jobs

After a modest gain in November, the economy shed another 85,000 jobs in December 2009, while the measured labor force shrank by 661,000. Had these workers not dropped out, the official rate would have been 10.4 percent. As of December 2009, the economy had lost more than 8.6 million jobs since December 2007. Some 1.5 million workers left the labor force in

2009 alone, and the share of the US population with a job fell to 58.2 percent, a twenty-seven-year low. The share of the population with a job has fallen by 4.5 percentage points since December 2007. As a January report from the Economic Policy Institute observed:

> Given population growth from December 2007 to December 2009, we would have expected the labor force to increase by around 2.8 million over this period. This means that there are now roughly 3.6 million "missing workers," that is, workers who dropped out of (or never entered) the labor force during the downturn. When the recovery begins to take hold and these missing workers start entering or reentering the workforce in search of jobs, it will put strong upward pressure on the unemployment rate.

If we count people who want full-time jobs but are involuntarily working part-time, the unemployment rate is above 17 percent. The typical unemployed worker is now out of work for over twenty weeks. The "long-term unemployed"—those who have been unemployed for six months or more—was 41 percent of the total in January 2010, the highest since the Great Depression. During the entire postwar era, the share of long-term unemployed had not previously risen above 26.0 percent. At this writing, there are 6.3 unemployed workers for every job opening, and that number has been worsening in recent months.

Incomes are falling. Despite rising labor productivity, average weekly earnings grew by only 1.9 percent from December 2008 to December 2009—well below the rate of inflation. As pockets of economic activity have picked up, employers have met the demand mainly by increasing workers' hours or by hiring temps, not by adding permanent jobs. All of this increases insecurity and puts downward pressure on wages, as desperate people are willing to work for less money.

In January 2010, economist Mark Zandi, who has an excellent record of accurate forecasts, projected that the unemployment rate would peak at 10.8 percent in October 2010—on the very eve of the midterm election! That projection, of course, assumes no change in policy. Zandi, who is hardly a radical—for a time he was one of John McCain's advisers—called for an immediate jolt of $125 billion in emergency spending for state and local relief and construction projects plus another roughly $100 billion in tax credits. The Economic Policy Institute, for its part, proposed a $406 billion program of fiscal relief, tax credits, extended unemployment benefits, and direct public service employment to create 4.6 million jobs—which would still be barely half those that the economy needs to get back to pre-recession unemployment rates.

Counting the 8.6 million jobs actually lost since the recession began plus the jobs needed to accommodate normal population growth, there is a jobs gap in 2010 of 11 million. To get back to a pre-recession unemployment rate by 2013, the economy has to create 400,000 jobs every month for the next four years, and at this writing we are still losing jobs.

Small Victories, Big Problems

The pity of it all is that Obama has done many good things for the government and the economy. In the American Reinvestment and Recovery Act of 2009, there were, in embryonic form, a number of initiatives of the sort that American liberals have only dreamed about including almost $100 billion of sundry green initiatives.

Yet if we stay on the current path of government policy, it is hard to see where a durable recovery will come from. The boom years before 2007 turned out to be bubble years, in which consumers felt rich because of inflated housing prices and an overvalued stock market. American households are out about $11 trillion due to losses in housing values and financial investments since the collapse began. During the bubble years they borrowed against rising housing values. Today they are saving rather than borrowing to spend. The existing stimulus spending is already petering out, and the drag will only increase as the government begins trying to reduce the federal deficit. Increased business investment sometimes helps power a recovery, but today business is awash in overbuilt commercial space and corporations are cutting capacity, not adding it.

Despite a cheaper dollar, trade won't save us, either. Though some nations such as China and India never really suffered a financial collapse, American manufacturing is so hollowed out that exports are unlikely to lead a recovery. China continues to discourage imports by keeping its currency undervalued.

Rather than welcoming products made in the USA, Beijing prefers to use subsidies and cheap labor to lure American companies to relocate production in China. In the last quarter of 2009, the trade deficit started increasing again, putting pressure on the dollar. And as the Federal Reserve increasingly plans an "exit strategy" to wean the economy from its heroic and unsustainable use of zero interest rates and defend the dollar, the risk is that higher credit costs will abort a fragile recovery.

Obama's timing, taking office in January 2009, seemed just about perfect for a clean break. There was no doubt that the recession belonged to George W. Bush, no doubt that a drastic change in policy was necessary, and no doubt that Obama had a broad mandate. It is seemingly baffling that a president elected as a change agent opted for so much continuity—until you appreciate that paradox as a reflection of the enduring and bipartisan influence of the financial industry.

CHAPTER THREE

Missing a Rendezvous with Reform

The Obama plan is little more than an attempt to stick some new
regulatory fingers into a very leaky financial dam rather than rebuild
the dam itself.
— JOSEPH NOCERA in *The New York Times*, June 18, 2009

When he took office in January 2009, President Obama had two big economic
challenges—recovery and reform. As we have seen, Obama's temporizing
both delayed economic recovery and squandered leverage for reform.

The administration's long-awaited eighty-eight-page white paper, titled
"Financial Regulatory Reform: A New Foundation," was released June 17,
2009. It was written mainly by Tim Geithner, after months of consultations.
As an indication of continuity with the old order, one of the paper's main
architects was Pat Parkinson, a longtime senior aide and speechwriter to
Alan Greenspan, now a close ally of Geithner.

In his accompanying remarks in the Roosevelt Room, President Obama
described the proposed reforms as "a sweeping overhaul of the financial
regulatory system, a transformation on a scale not seen since the reforms
that followed the Great Depression." But they were nothing of the sort.
Mostly, the reforms were a series of patches that did not challenge the fundamental structure of the system.

At the White House ceremony unveiling the plan, there was a small infor-
mal gathering prior to the president's speech. As an invited guest, I chatted
with Larry Summers. He was feeling vindicated, even defiant. "The critics
who were attacking us back in February for not nationalizing banks have
been proven wrong by events," he pointedly said. "Credit conditions have
improved and growth will turn positive next quarter." Dan Tarullo, who had

been appointed to be the Fed's man on financial regulation, was in a buoyant mood. "Remember that Cooper Union speech?" he asked me. "Well, we delivered on it."

Except they didn't. The plan was more notable for what it left out than for what it included. It left largely intact the doctrine of "too big to fail." There was no serious effort to discourage huge financial institutions, whose scale added nothing to efficiency, from growing even bigger. The hope was that government would develop better tools to keep these giants from going off the rails, including higher capital requirements.

There were no meaningful measures to reform the corruption of credit rating agencies, whose complicity with the issuers of deceptive securities such as subprime bonds had been so central in the collapse. There was no engagement with the fundamental conflict of interest that had enabled big conglomerates to help take down the system—by mixing commercial banking with speculative proprietary trading and the creation of exotic securities. The advice of Paul Volcker to restore something like the Glass-Steagall wall between commercial banking and more speculative activities was ignored. Obama would accept it only a year later. The white paper was somewhat better on regulation of derivatives. It proposed reforms to make trading of standard (but not custom) derivatives more transparent and less prone to fraud and manipulation, though this was later watered down.

As weak as the reform plan posed by the June document was, it was even further weakened in the legislation that the same Treasury Department sent Congress in August, and then weakened again in Congress with the complicity of Geithner's Treasury.

The initial plan did not challenge compensation schemes that rewarded executives for pumping up company stock prices. It called for international guidelines on compensation standards, monitoring of pay levels by the Fed, and for temporarily imposing some pay limits on banks that took TARP money, but once banks paid back the money, they would be no longer subject to pay constraints.

The crisis of mortgage foreclosures, worsening by the day, was not addressed. The plan proposed only the most minimal changes in the whole system of "securitization"—the conversion of loans into bonds and derivatives. The one robust feature of the plan, a proposed consumer protection agency, became an instant object of industry attack and scant administration defense.

At the most fundamental level, the Obama blueprint left largely intact the broader business model that had enabled the financial industry to take down the economy. There was no serious effort to shrink the financial sector back down to a scale that would leave it as servant of the rest of the economy rather than master, or to promote a comprehensive simplification of the system or a reining in of the exotic abstractions that produced such profit for the financial sector and such risk for the larger economy. Nothing would interfere with the long-term trend in which bankers and investment bankers all tended to behave more like hedge funds—engines of speculation for their own enrichment rather than sources of credit for productive investment. The private, government-blessed institutions of self-regulation, such as the Financial Industry Regulatory Authority, which had failed utterly, were left intact. The Federal Reserve, as a banker-oriented and quasi-private agency with immense public functions, was left unreformed—and given even more powers as super-regulator. It was a reform effort worthy of a McCain administration.

The contrast with the early Roosevelt administration could not have been more dramatic. In FDR's first year, Congress enacted the Glass-Steagall Act, radically limiting the business model of combined commercial banking and securities trading that had promoted dangerous levels of speculation. The government acted to sort out weak banks from strong ones and added deposit insurance—and after 1933, weaknesses in the banking system ceased to be a drag on the recovery. In 1933 and 1934, the Roosevelt administration acted to push through Congress a new Securities and Exchange Commission to bring investment bankers, broker-dealers, and stock exchanges under much tighter public scrutiny and to limit conflicts of interest. And in 1935, Roosevelt persuaded Congress to enact the Public Utilities Holding Company Act, curbing another of the worse abuses of the 1920s, the pyramiding of layers of holding companies and the watering down of stock, using vast amounts of undetected leverage against a very thin capital base. It was the credit default swap scandal of its day. And through the creation of the Home Owners Loan Corporation and the original, public Federal National Mortgage Association (Fannie Mae), the New Deal built a whole new system of reliable mortgage finance. The Roosevelt reforms didn't just limit potential for individual abuses. They remade the entire financial system.

And although the June white paper included some fine rhetorical generalities about policy objectives, the fine print gave most of the details away. The banking industry pronounced itself mostly satisfied with the plan. And worse was yet to come as the industry began exerting its influence on Congress.

Too Big Not to Bail

At the heart of the corrupted financial system was the problem known as "too big to fail." As Lehman Brothers and AIG showed, some institutions had been allowed to grow so big, so opaque, and so interconnected that just letting them collapse was not an acceptable option. What, then, to do about very large institutions to prevent them from putting the entire system at risk?

There were basically two preventive remedies, only one of which was partially embraced by the Obama administration. One was to restore the Glass-Steagall wall. The abuses that led to the collapse demonstrated the importance of reviving the principle that if you're a bank operating with government-insured deposits and access to Federal Reserve advances, you must be limited to relatively safe and prudent sets of activities. Alternatively, if you are a trader or an investment bank with no special government seal, operating with your own capital and that of investors pursuing risk and reward, good luck to you—but don't expect to be bailed out if you make bad bets. The mischief of the past decade was that institutions with no special government monitoring and no claim on government help put the system in such jeopardy that government had to bail them out anyway. So in order to make Glass-Steagall work, there also had to be limits on permissible activities and interconnections, coupled with regulation of currently unregulated shadow banks such as hedge funds. However, the administration initially rejected both Glass-Steagall and regulation of shadow banks.

A second possible approach was to discourage bigness per se, either by stricter limits on the total share of bank deposits that any one institution could hold, or by anti-trust enforcement, or by increasing capital requirements in direct proportion to a bank's sheer size. A rather weak, discretionary version of the capital requirement was included in the white paper, which proposed that the regulatory standards for very large firms "including capital, liquidity, and risk-management standards should be stricter and more conservative than those applicable to other financial firms," but left the details to the regulators.

Rather, the administration's main remedy for the too-big-to-fail problem was to punt it to the Federal Reserve, which could gain new powers as a "systemic risk regulator." That sounded plausible, but in the run-up to the collapse the Fed had totally bungled its existing regulatory responsibilities. This was partly due to the fact that recent incumbent chairmen, Ben Bernanke and Alan Greenspan, were congenitally opposed to regulation, but it also reflected the franchise and structure of the Fed, as an agency largely beyond democratic accountability and one whose regional operating arms were owned by member banks.

Regulation delegated to the Fed, in practice, is done not by its board of governors, who are presidential appointees, but by the examination and supervision departments of the regional reserve banks, which are private institutions owned by the banking industry and which report to a local board appointed by bankers. The Federal Reserve Bank of New York regulates most large bank holding companies. The Fed, absent fundamental reforms in its structure, was simply too cozy with the banks to entrust it with this new mission—which would require it to crack down on the most lucrative activities of the very banks that owned it.

In our system, the Fed has three fairly separate jobs that are best left distinct: monetary policy, regulatory policy, and lender-of-last-resort. Under Bernanke and Geithner, it added a fourth—chief bailout agency. From the era of Greenspan on, it performed none of these jobs well. But the Obama plan proposed to give the clubby and unaccountable Fed additional powers as a super-regulator of "systemic risk."

In conducting monetary policy, the Fed mainly manipulates short-term interest rates and the supply of money in order to balance the goals of high growth and full employment against the goal of low inflation. As countless speeches of Bernanke and Greenspan revealed, both men deceived themselves into thinking that the past decade was a serene period when the US economy could enjoy the holy grail of relatively high growth and low inflation. Their premise was that the world was "awash in liquidity," thanks to the high savings rates of Asia, which financed America's need for investment at low interest rates, and that trade with countries that produced cheap consumer products was keeping inflation low. Greenspan and Bernanke simply missed the financial bubble developing right under their noses, which was one of the main sources of the ostensible cheap and plentiful credit. Worse than missing it, they enabled it. As soon as the bubble burst, the credit disappeared. Then, under the guise of promoting recovery, they acted to enable the next bubble.

With the repeal of the Glass-Steagall Act in 1999, the Fed was given the responsibility of supervising the consolidated company at the holding company level. But the Fed was substantially asleep at the switch as big banks and their holding companies got more deeply into speculative trading. It not only missed subprime as a retail abuse, but it missed the abuses of off-balance-sheet entities and the immense risks that financial conglomerates were creating for the system as the main wholesale financiers of retail subprime companies.

The Fed's role as lender-of-last-resort in a crisis—it is empowered to flood the system with money when liquidity dries up and to take other actions such as lending against sound collateral—got hopelessly conflated with the bailouts of individual institutions. The Fed, working with the Treasury, got deeply into the business of "bank resolution," an activity even further beyond its core franchise. The Fed was not just extending emergency credits to provide general liquidity when markets were drying up, but working with the Treasury to devise survival plans for particular banks, many of them insolvent. This latter function went beyond both the Fed's charter and its institutional competence.

Logically, the central bank does not also need to be the bank regulator. Those functions are divided in Britain, which has a Financial Services Authority as regulator and the Bank of England as central bank. They are also divided on the European continent, which has a European Central Bank as monetary agent but leaves bank regulation at the national level.

Paul Volcker eloquently summarized the problems with the Treasury's conception of too-big-to-fail in testimony before Congress:

> The approach proposed by the Treasury is to designate in advance financial institutions "whose size, leverage, and interconnection

could pose a threat to financial stability if it failed". Those institutions, bank or non-bank, connected to a commercial firm or not, would be subject to particularly strict and conservative prudential supervision and regulation. The Federal Reserve would be designated as consolidated supervisor. The precise criteria for designation as "systemically important" have not, so far as I know, been set out. However, the clear implication of such designation whether officially acknowledged or not will be that such institutions, in whole or in part, will be sheltered by access to a Federal safety net in time of crisis; they will be broadly understood to be "too big to fail".

Think of the practical difficulties of such designation. Can we really anticipate which institutions will be systemically significant amid the uncertainties in future crises and the complex interrelationships of markets? Was Long Term Capital Management, a hedge fund, systemically significant in 1998? Was Bear Stearns, but not Lehman? How about General Electric's huge financial affiliate, or the large affiliates of other substantial commercial firms? What about foreign institutions operating in the United States?

All hard questions. In practice the "border problem" seems intractable. In fair financial weather, the important institutions will feel competitively hobbled by stricter standards. In times of potential crisis, it would be the institution left out of the "too big to fail" club that will fear disadvantage.

Only when Obama's back was to the wall did he begin paying attention to Volcker, in December 2009. Meanwhile, the idea of giving the Fed even more power ran into headwinds in Congress. The Republican right, as much as the Democratic left, resented the central bank as a clubby affair controlled by big-city bankers.

Throwing Consumers a Bone

In the one dramatic departure from business as usual, the Treasury plan proposed to create a Consumer Financial Protection Agency (CFPA). This plan, the brainchild of Harvard law professor Elizabeth Warren, would take enforcement of consumer protection away from existing agencies including the Fed, none of which did it very well. For most banking agencies, consumer protection was a low priority, and it ran counter to their self-conceived missions as agencies whose main purpose was to serve the needs of their clients, the banking industry. In the crisis, there was also a plain conflict of interest between the goal of the Treasury and the Fed of rebuilding bank profits and the need to protect consumers from excessive bank charges.

In 2008 and 2009, when regulators were supposedly cracking down on banking abuses, bankers just kept inventing new ones. Hidden overdraft charges and disguised fees on prepaid debit cards went through the roof. A report by the Center for Responsible Lending calculated that banks raked in nearly $24 billion in overdraft charges in 2008, and were profiting at a higher rate in 2009. Once a small fee to cover interest and processing costs, overdraft charges have increased to an average of $34 per incident, and have become a profit center. Banks, devastated by the balance sheet casualties of their speculative trading activity, were trying to recoup by gouging consumers.

The argument of Warren and other supporters of the idea was that traditional bank regulatory agencies had just dropped the ball on consumer protection. During the era of excess, when speculative financial innovations set the stage for a crash, regulatory agencies hadn't just neglected the systemic risks in inventions such as credit default swaps, collateralized debt obligations, and excessive leverage. They had also ignored abuses on the retail side of banking, such as usurious credit card practices, hidden overdraft fees, and racial targeting for more costly forms of credit, as well as financial products that were inherently deceptive. These abuses were not necessarily systemic risks—sometimes they were just consumer rip-offs. But the two kinds of regulatory default came together in the subprime crisis, where a product that was fraudulently created and marketed was also a time bomb for the entire financial system—and both aspects were just waved through by regulators. As Warren put it, "There are two reasons to have stronger consumer protection of financial products. First, to protect the American middle class. Second, to protect the American financial system."

Throughout this period, the Fed had plenty of authority to head off abuses but refused to use it. Warren argued for the commission as a counterweight;

if there had been such a commission charged with reviewing consumer financial products, it would have instantly spotted both the retail abuse and the systemic risk in subprime lending. Ideally, such a commission would function almost like the Food and Drug Administration, vetting proposed new financial products for safety and effectiveness before they were turned loose on the financial system and the gullible public, or the Consumer Product Safety Commission, requiring recalls of defective financial products, and insisting that along with complex and hard-to-fathom products banks should also offer "plain vanilla" ones like traditional thirty-year fixed-rate mortgages.

To the delight of Warren and other supporters, the administration white paper contained a vigorous version of the proposed agency. The CFPA would gain new consumer protection powers over currently unregulated retailers of credit, such as nonbank mortgage companies, check-cashing companies, payday lenders, wire-transfer companies, tax preparers, and other operators with a history of predatory price gouging. Studies showed that their clients, mostly the working poor, often faced interest charges well in excess of 100 percent. It would also have authority over debt collectors, debt counselors, companies proposing to help consumers get mortgage modifications, and other nonfinancial companies that extended credit to consumers. And it would have authority over nonbank businesses that provided retail credit, such as auto dealers, many of whom had a long history of gouging the unwary. The idea was to have a single consumer financial agency, with a single set of standards, regulate both banks and nonbanks when it came to consumer credit.

The language of this section of the white paper was markedly different from the rest. It read as if it had been written by someone genuinely committed to radical reform. Much of the rest of the report read as if it had been written by lawyers for banks.

In addition to Elizabeth Warren, who as chair of the Congressional Oversight Panel was not a member of the administration, a big supporter of the consumer agency was Assistant Treasury Secretary Michael Barr, who had served in the Clinton Treasury under Rubin and Summers and had then taken a position at the University of Michigan Law School. Barr was well respected at the Geithner Treasury, though he was not a member of the Wall Street club. Yet the proposal probably would have gone nowhere but for the support of an unlikely ally, Barack Obama. According to my reporting, this provision was the sole element of the reform package to which Obama paid close personal attention. (As the bill worked its way through Congress, though, his attention was elsewhere.)

Why did Obama weigh in on this provision? Just weeks before he released his white paper, the president had been in a very good mood at a May 22 White House ceremony celebrating his signing of a small but significant first piece of financial reform legislation initiated by Democrats in Congress, the Credit Card Act. That act limited overcharges and required greater disclosure. The measure played well in the media and in the polls. Given the widespread and largely accurate perception that the administration was too close to the big banks, Obama liked the idea of another counterweight. His chief political adviser, David Axelrod, concurred, and the White House intervened to direct Treasury to include the consumer protection agency. This passed the initiative to Barr, who was a genuine enthusiast. In this section of the white paper, presumably drafted by Barr, the Treasury did not mince words.

> The spread of unsustainable subprime mortgages and abusive credit card contracts highlighted a serious shortcoming of our present regulatory infrastructure. It too easily allows consumer protection values to be overwhelmed by other imperatives—whether short-term gain, innovation for its own sake, or keeping up with the competition. To instill a genuine culture of consumer protection and not merely of legal compliance in our financial institutions, we need first to instill that culture in the federal regulatory structure.

Treasury proposed to put the new agency in charge of all consumer financial protection, giving it sweeping powers to subpoena information and issue regulations. On the crucial issue of preemption of stronger state laws, the white paper declared that "the CFPA's strong rules would serve as a floor, not a ceiling." It proposed new tools, such as the authority to ban clauses requiring mandatory arbitration (invariably on terms favorable to the creditor) in cases of dispute. And the paper added one new idea, strongly supported by advocates of simplification and transparency.

We propose that the regulator be authorized to define standards for "plain vanilla" products that are simpler and have straightforward pricing. The CFPA should be authorized to require all providers and intermediaries to offer these products prominently, alongside whatever other lawful products they choose to offer. Even if disclosures are fully tested and all communications are properly balanced, product complexity itself can lead consumers to make costly errors. A careful regulatory approach can tilt the scales in favor of simpler, less risky products while preserving choice and innovation.

The paper added, "We propose that the government do more to promote 'plain vanilla' products. The CFPA should be authorized to define standards for such products and require firms to offer them alongside whatever other lawful products a firm chooses to offer."

Simpler, more transparent financial products are usually less costly to consumers and less lucrative to bankers. They don't lend themselves quite so readily to complex and opaque securitization. This provision was a breath of fresh air, not just because it clearly put the government on the side of consumers who were often bewildered or deceived by overly complex products, but because it was the one section of the white paper that acknowledged a more fundamental public policy challenge—the need to drastically simplify the entire financial system. Not surprisingly, the banking industry went all-out to kill or cripple the proposal, and substantially succeeded.

The Empire Strikes Back

The American Bankers Association contacted members of the House Financial Services Committee with a simple message. Those who voted to weaken the proposed consumer agency would be rewarded with campaign contributions, while those who supported it could expect money to go to their opponents. The ABA particularly targeted the fifteen committee members who were also members of the pro-business New Democrat Coalition, many of whom were in swing districts and facing close elections in 2010. These centrist Democrats in turn appealed to Chairman Barney Frank not to put them in the position of having to cast a vote that might offend the bankers.

The ABA's immediate legislative goal was to get rid of the bill's teeth, such as the "plain vanilla" provision, as well as its preemption language allowing states to enact stronger consumer protections. The ABA also wanted the bill weakened so that most authority would be left with the traditional tame regulatory agencies that had failed to head off the abuses responsible for the crisis. That would leave a much narrowed new consumer agency regulating only the banks' competitors, such as freestanding check-cashing offices and mortgage companies.

In early September 2009, the US Chamber of Commerce launched a $2 million ad campaign targeting the provisions in the plan that authorized the proposed agency to regulate nonbanks. The initial ad featured a friendly neighborhood butcher. "The economy has made it tough on this local butcher's customers," declares the announcer, "but now Washington wants to make it tougher on everyone." The ad went on to warn, preposterously, that the proposed protections would end up increasing the cost of credit.

By late September, before the bill was even out of committee, House Financial Services chairman Barney Frank had gotten the message. On September 22, he sent a letter to all the members of the committee, announcing that his draft of the bill would exclude from coverage retailers such as the butcher who extended credit to his customers, who was of course a stalking horse for bigger players; Frank obligingly agreed to exempt all "nonfinancial" businesses that extended credit to consumers, such as auto dealers. In addition, several major financial industries were exempted, including accountants, tax preparers, and credit reporting agencies. The marketing of IRAs, Keoghs, and 401(k) accounts was also exempted. So a whole area of potential consumer credit abuses was simply removed from the agency's jurisdiction.

The white paper had aptly observed that "the Federal Trade Commission has a clear mission to protect consumers but generally lacks jurisdiction over the banking sector and has limited tools and resources to promote robust compliance of nonbank institutions. Mortgage companies not owned by banks fall into a regulatory 'no man's land' where no regulator exercises leadership and state attorneys general are left to try to fill the gap." However, Representative Frank proposed to leave some of the jurisdiction with the FTC, and he explicitly moved enforcement of the important Community

Reinvestment Act back to the same banking agencies that had failed to use its provisions to head off the subprime disaster.

Responding to the industry's lobbying, Frank proposed to explicitly ban the agency from requiring banks to offer simple products as well as hard-to-fathom ones. In his letter to committee colleagues, he wrote

> **No "Plain Vanilla" Requirements.** Financial institutions will **not** be required to offer plain vanilla products and services, and CFPA will not have authority to approve or change business plans. [emphasis in the original]

In short, the CFPA, the one portion of the administration reform plan with some real teeth, was undermined by the leading liberal House Democratic banking legislator. And he had some help downtown. In carefully choreographed testimony before Frank's committee on September 23, Treasury Secretary Geithner said, "In general, we are very supportive of the changes as proposed by the Chairman," adding that there had been "a lot of concern" that the plain vanilla language would put the government in the position of overriding the business judgment of bankers. But of course, that was the whole point. The "business judgment" of bankers had taken down the whole system.

In October, as the bill was going through the committee markup, the auto industry mobilized its Republican and New Democrat allies to explicitly strip out the provision giving the new commission authority to regulate terms of consumer credit extended by car dealers. Often, the terms of credit are opaque to the borrower and are a bigger source of profit to the dealer than the markup on the car. An amendment to the (already weakened) draft bill offered by Republican John Campbell of California excluded auto dealers from the commission's purview. The amendment was approved, 47–21, with the committee's New Democrats voting with the Republicans.

Industry executives and New Democrats were thrilled. Once again, financial industry lobbyists proved stronger than reformers. Once again, the Wall Street–oriented people inside the administration such as Geithner had outplayed the relative interventionists—including in this case the president himself. Preoccupied as Obama was with Afghanistan and health reform, this level of detail passed beneath the presidential radar.

Here was a classic case where a president might have cast some shame on the industry figures opposing pro-consumer reform and put some salutary pressure on pro-industry Democrats. But throughout 2009, this president simply did not operate that way, and Chief of Staff Rahm Emanuel has repeatedly warned consumer and labor groups not to criticize centrist Democrats. What is depressing is that the Democrats capitulated to industry and to Republicans without a fight. How much better it would have been, win or lose on this provision, to have kept the teeth in the bill, and then smoked out Republicans for casting an anti-consumer vote.

With the administration largely disengaged, the provision was on track to be even further weakened in the Senate. Senator Dodd advised the measure's champion, Elizabeth Warren, that the consumer agency would have to be gutted or dumped entirely. Only in January 2009, the day after the surprise loss of Ted Kennedy's former Massachusetts Senate seat, did Obama belatedly weigh in, as part of his new populist persona, to try to salvage the measure. Obama's aides let the press know that he had summoned Dodd to the White House to tell the Senate Banking Committee that inclusion of a strong consumer agency was "non-negotiable." At this writing, Dodd has made a deal with the Republicans to put the consumer agency under the Fed.

Derivatives: The Great Cave-In

A similar fate awaited the administration's commitment to tough regulation of derivatives. This was the great black hole of the financial system. Credit default swaps that were built upon layers of leverage had been at the center of the collapse. Despite the unwinding of contracts that occurred in the aftermath of the collapse, the notional value of derivatives contracts still ran well into the hundreds of trillions—more than ten times world GDP—and bankers and traders still relied on derivatives for outsize profits (and risks).

Derivatives, let's recall, operate at one or more layers of abstraction from real economic transactions. A mortgage loan, for example, is a real transaction. A bond backed by a subprime mortgage loan is a real security, as is a package of such securities. But financial engineers created synthetic packages of bonds backed by mortgage loans, as derivatives. And a credit default swap, which is an insurance policy against such packages of bonds going bad, is even further removed from financial reality. So-called naked credit default swaps were "insurance" for a security that the insuring party did not own. They were pure gambling. At each stage of abstraction, derivatives invite pyramids of leverage and huge speculative profits for insiders—as long as the bubble keeps inflating. AIG wrote hundreds of billions of dollars' worth of swaps backed by none of its own capital; it was *all* leverage. When the bubble bursts, the losses can be as infinite as the capital is infinitesimal.

In both the Clinton and Obama administrations, chairmen of the Commodity Futures Trading Commission had warned against the catastrophic potential of derivatives, and both had been isolated by other, more pro–Wall Street officials. In 1998, then CFTC chair Brooksley Born had defied the entire senior ranks of the Treasury and the White House National Economic Council by putting out a draft proposal for tighter monitoring and regulation of derivatives. After applying relentless pressure on Born to back down, and ultimately driving her out of the government, the administration (led by Robert Rubin and Larry Summers) supported a bill drafted by Wall Street and Enron and sponsored by Republican senator Phil Gramm of Texas explicitly prohibiting the kind of regulation that Born and her deputy Michael Greenberger had in mind. The bill had the Orwellian name of the Commodity Futures Modernization Act. It prohibited the federal government from regulating financial swaps either as insurance or as securities, and for good measure prohibited regulation of energy derivatives. All too knowingly, the law even barred state regulators from regulating derivatives as a form of gambling.

In the battle over derivatives reform, the details are a little technical but worth grasping, because they epitomize the power of Wall Street to block reform and the penchant of both the administration and senior congressional Democrats for backing away from transformational reform.

The core issues were these:

- Would the 2000 act, prohibiting the CFTC from regulating all kinds of derivatives including credit default swaps, be reversed, and would the SEC be given adequate powers to regulate all kinds of securities-based derivative transactions?

- Would all derivatives contracts be required to be traded on regulated exchanges?
- Would they would be subject to anti-fraud and anti-manipulation requirements, transparency, effective self-policing, and limits on leverage?
- Would the CFTC have the power to review and limit the trading positions of major players, so that it could spot and head off either deliberate market manipulation or herd instincts that created risks to the system?
- Would there be loopholes for customized (over-the-counter) derivatives? If there were, this would only invite more and more creative use of such loopholes. Most supposedly "customized" derivatives are actually standard products, but they generate extra profits for the banks that create them, since there is no basis for comparative pricing.
- Would there be any other loopholes that would permit bankers and traders to evade regulation and supervision?

The industry position was clear. Bankers and traders wanted as little regulation as possible. The financial industry was promoting the idea that standard derivatives should be traded through private, industry-created and industry-supervised "clearinghouses." This was the old ploy of self-regulation to head off real regulation. If the financial industry had its way, customized derivatives, a huge source of profit, would remain private contracts between two parties, not subject to exchange trading, or limits on speculation.

In written commitments to skeptical senators in May 2009, senior Treasury officials committed the administration to tough reforms. But there was some slippage between what Treasury had promised and the principles laid down in the administration's white paper. There was a further weakening between the June white paper and the draft legislation that Treasury sent Congress on August 12. That proposed legislation did increase the power of regulators to require much greater disclosures, and to impose aggregate limits on the positions held by any trader. It required that standardized derivatives—though not customized ones—be traded on regulated exchanges. But the draft bill created new loopholes added at the instigation of industry lobbyists.

For example, a huge exclusion was introduced for swaps and similar derivatives related to foreign currencies. Speculation in the movement of foreign currencies had been central to the collapse of the Long-Term Capital Management hedge fund in 1998, the first of the advance tremors signaling that something was seriously amiss.

A second loophole excluded transactions between regulated swaps dealers and customers that were nonbanks. This was an invitation to creative evasion. The administration draft also failed to require that dealers maintain collateral in segregated accounts, so that counterparties could be paid in the event of a panic. And the actual legislation was further weakened by a highly effective industry lobbying campaign.

Business's Class Solidarity

The banking industry seized on the ploy of having customers play the public face of the opposition to tough derivatives regulation. This maneuver was orchestrated by the National Association of Manufacturers and the Securities Industry and Financial Markets Association, working closely with the bankers. On October 2, key legislators working on derivatives received a letter that began,

> The undersigned companies and trade associations—representing diverse segments of American industry and serving virtually all U.S. consumers—support efforts by Congress to improve transparency, accountability and stability in the nation's financial markets. As you develop a regulatory framework, we strongly urge policymakers to preserve the ability of companies to manage their individual risk exposures by ensuring access to reasonably priced and customized over-the-counter (OTC) derivative products.
>
> Business end-users rely on OTC derivatives to manage risks including fluctuating currency exchange, interest rates, and commodity prices. By insulating companies from risk, customized OTC derivatives provide businesses with access to lower cost capital—enabling them to grow, make new investments and retain and create new jobs.
>
> In contrast, some reform proposals would place an extraordinary

burden on end-users of derivatives in every sector of the economy—including manufacturers, energy companies, utilities, health-care companies and commercial real estate owners and developers. Specifically, proposals that would require all OTC derivatives used by business end-users to be centrally cleared, executed on exchanges or cash collateralized or subject end-users to capital charges, would inhibit companies from using these important risk management tools in the course of everyday business operations. These proposals, which would increase business risk and raise costs, are at cross purposes with the goals of lowering systemic risk and promoting economic recovery.

The letter came from a hastily contrived letterhead group, the Coalition for Derivatives End-Users, and signed by every major industry trade association, as well as individual corporations including Apple, Coca-Cola, Intel 3M, Procter & Gamble, Johnson & Johnson, and so on, more than 100 in all. The coalition was the handiwork of a Washington lobbying firm, The Raben Group, headed by Robert Raben, a former senior aide to . . . Barney Frank. So it goes.

Raben's career and modus operandi are worth a brief digression, because they epitomize how Wall Street dominates Washington. After serving for seven years as Frank's counsel on the House Judiciary Committee, Raben moved to the Clinton administration, where he served as assistant attorney general for legislative affairs. He then set up a lobbying firm in 2001, hiring about three dozen former congressional and administration officials from both parties. He developed a reputation as a lobbyist with especially good access to Democrats that industry needed. As a liberal on social issues, Raben did a lot of work with the Hispanic community on immigration issues; he worked with the civil rights community, and also the gay and lesbian community. However, when it came to serving Wall Street clients, Raben's liberalism largely evaporated. He was offering access.

The assertions in the coalition letter were complete nonsense. The reforms would not impede the access of ordinary businesses to legitimate hedging of, for example, prices of oil or wheat, interest rates, or yen—the long-standing, economically defensible uses of options and futures. Businesses remained

free to trade on regulated futures markets. The proposed reforms for stan-
dardization, exchange trading, and transparency, however, would damp
down the kind of extreme speculation in complex derivatives that crashed
the economy, in which there is no underlying commercial transaction being
hedged—merely pure financial gambling. Far from raising costs to end users,
greater transparency and tough controls on market manipulation would
reduce costs because they would increase price competition. However, they
would reduce excessive profits going to bankers and traders. The willingness
of industry associations representing bank customers to carry water for the
bankers was a revealing illustration of both the power of banks and the soli-
darity of the business class as a whole.

But there was worse to come. Barney Frank circulated his own draft
derivatives bill on October 2—and it was far weaker than what Treasury
had proposed. According to well-placed sources, major sections were literally drafted by lawyers for the banking industry. The 187-page bill was
a Christmas present of gifts for traders and investment bankers. Far from
embracing needed reforms of the very sector that had crashed the economy,
Frank's bill weakened existing law.

Corporate Democrats in Command

The details of the battle over derivatives regulation, and the roles played
by different factions in the administration, pro–Wall Street Democrats, and
Barney Frank, could literally consume a whole book. The story reveals, in
cameo, just how Wall Street still dominates Washington despite inchoate
popular resentment against the forces that caused the crash. The industry has assumed that the whole derivatives issue is so complex to the lay
public and such a game of inside baseball with few forces on the other side
that it could easily prevail. But the emblematic details of the capitulation
are not hard to grasp, and they convey the larger story. Here's one vivid
illustration.

In 2008, the price of crude oil was going berserk, for no good reason other
than the activities of Wall Street speculators. It rose from about $60 a barrel
in June 2007 to a peak of $147 in the summer of 2008, then returned to $70
by summer 2009. The sudden price rise was suspect, given that the economy
was in a deepening recession. Congress was feeling the wrath of voters, who

were furious at $4-per-gallon gas. As congressional hearings and investigations subsequently revealed, the price swings were purely the result of excessive speculation by Wall Street, not supply and demand.

In late summer 2008, as gas prices and tempers soared, Congress was on the verge of passing a Democratic leadership bill limiting speculation on energy futures. The bill got fifty-three votes in the Senate, though it never made it into law. But the speculators and traders saw regulation coming, reversed their strategy, and made a bundle by shorting oil, and the price plummeted, dropping to as low as $33 a barrel. The volatility was huge, with no fundamental change in supply and demand. This was pure speculation at work.

When he became chairman of the CFTC in 2009, Gary Gensler, a former trader at Goldman turned reformer, was determined to crack down on excessive Wall Street speculation in energy derivatives. He was appalled to find that a regulation that existed on paper was being sabotaged in practice by the CFTC staff. In principle, only end users with a legitimate reason to hedge commodity prices, such as oil refiners, grain companies, airlines, or truckers, are permitted to take unlimited positions in derivatives, since they have a legitimate business purpose other than speculation. Gensler discovered that the CFTC staff had been extending this exemption to purely *financial* players on the theory that they had a legitimate commercial purpose—to hedge their own speculative financial exposures, the way a gambler lays off bets.

The most prominent of these was his old employer, Goldman Sachs. Goldman's game was to persuade investors to expect increases in the price of, say, oil, and then enlist them to make financial bets on rising prices, using derivatives created by Goldman. Goldman would then go into the futures markets and cover its own risks, using regulated futures products. Since Goldman was closer to the market than its customers, in its own proprietary trading it could go long or short, depending on what the pattern of swap purchases suggested about which way the market was going. During the up cycle, these financial maneuvers created the appearance of a spike in real-world demand for oil, reinforcing the perception that demand for oil was outstripping supply and raising prices still further—creating even more profit opportunities for Goldman, both as middleman and as speculator. At this writing, oil has rebounded to $75 a barrel, and Goldman's research department is helpfully predicting that it is headed for $200, which stimulates more demand for more speculation in rising prices, and more business for Goldman's swaps desk, and more outsize profits.

In three days of CFTC hearings on energy position limits in July and early August 2009, Gensler called the financial executives on the carpet and announced his plan to deny purely financial middlemen the right to hold unlimited positions in swaps and kindred derivatives. At the hearing, Blythe Masters of JPMorgan Chase and Don Casturo of Goldman Sachs rather lamely argued that it was not fair to impose position limits on the financial houses, that the demand was coming from investors. "I don't see a Goldman swaps desk as a passive mechanic, and the billions of dollars of transactions that you do as a passive mechanic," Gensler shot back.

Frank backed Gensler on position limits but caved in to industry on several other key issues. Frank's draft bill even contained a provision resolving pending litigation in New York in favor of the banks. The case involves a glass manufacturer being sued by major banks for failing to make payments on misleading derivatives. The Frank bill provided, astonishingly, that even if a bank creates a deceptive derivative in violation of the 2000 act, it cannot be sued for damages. This was part of a bill being touted as reform.

The Frank bill also provided a giant loophole that makes it possible for banks to avoid the requirement that derivatives be traded on regulated exchanges, where there are requirements for collateral, position limits, and anti-fraud and anti-manipulation protections. The administration bill had a narrower loophole that allowed "customized" derivatives to be unregulated contracts between just two parties.

When Frank's draft bill was released the evening of October 2, Americans for Financial Reform (AFR), the coalition of consumer groups serving as the one counterweight to the bankers, went into shock. "This bill is literally worse than nothing because it eliminates what few regulatory protections exist," Professor Greenberger told me. "It would be better to kill it." The groups, which had been treating Frank with kid gloves, asked for a meeting. A senior staffer, citing a busy schedule, grudgingly found time for a short meeting on Monday, October 5. He tried to reassure the consumer groups that they were reading too much into the bill, but it soon became clear that they had a better understanding of what was really in it and who had really drafted it than Barney Frank or his staff.

After the meeting, the consumer groups learned that there would be a hearing in just two days, that the witnesses had already been invited, and that the witness list was closed. The groups were even more appalled when they learned that all of the witnesses were from either Wall Street, allied industry groups fronting for the banks, or academics sympathetic to the industry view. The list included witnesses from Goldman; Cargill, the giant grain trader; Morgan Stanley; the Managed Funds Association; Deere & Company; and the Wholesale Markets Brokers' Association—all supporting a weak bill. There was not a consumer representative or other critic on the list. In their testimony, all congratulated Frank for his weaker draft, or proposed further weakening. This was a pure gift to the committee's New Democrats—led by Representative Melissa Bean of Illinois—and the financial engineers whose interests they fronted for.

Succumbing to a chorus of indignation, Frank eventually permitted a single critic at the witness table. He explicitly vetoed Michael Greenberger, the most technically expert of the available witnesses, on the grounds that Greenberger had a "known history" (as if Goldman Sachs didn't). Robert Johnson, a former chief economist of the Senate Banking Committee and onetime associate of George Soros, was allowed to appear on behalf of Americans for Financial Reform. Johnson is a well-informed critic of financial deregulation, but not as expert on derivatives as Greenberger. Frank did not deign to sit as chairman while Johnson testified. He turned the gavel over to Representative Bean. Having fawned over the industry witnesses, she cut off Johnson.

Another figure who went into shock upon seeing Frank's "discussion draft" was CFTC chairman Gary Gensler. He had already gone out on a limb, in a point-by-point letter sent Congress on August 17 criticizing Geithner's proposed derivatives bill as far too weak. Now Frank's bill was even weaker. During that first week in October, Gensler spent several hours on the phone with Frank and his staff, trying to persuade them of how destructive their bill was. But the bankers were succeeding in isolating or at least constraining Gensler. He was branded as an uncooperative outlier within the administration. Frank told colleagues that Gensler was somewhat "utopian." Gensler, the former Goldman Sachs trader, like the former Federal Reserve chairman Paul Volcker, was the unwelcome radical in the room.

Gensler was very polite but firm in his public testimony to Frank. He urged the committee to report a bill at least as strong as the one drafted by the Treasury, and he demolished the weakness of Chairman Frank's discussion draft, paragraph by paragraph.

By contrast, when the industry-written discussion draft was circulated, Frank won the lavish praise of the more conservative, pro-banker Democrats on his committee. In a series of closely orchestrated statements, the New Dems stroked their chairman. Bean said, "This bill moves us in the right direction by reducing risk to the economy with robust and dynamic oversight of major market participants, while preserving appropriate risk-management tools for end users."

"The New Democrat Coalition applauds the work of Chairman Barney Frank and the members of the Financial Services Committee for crafting a proposal to provide greater regulation and transparency to the over-the-counter derivatives market," said Congressman Joseph Crowley (D-NY), chair of the New Democrat Coalition. "I congratulate my fellow New Dem Members, 15 of whom serve on the Financial Services Committee, for their work with Chairman Frank to reform our financial system to provide greater protections for American consumers and businesses while ensuring continued access to valuable tools to manage risk. New Dems are dedicated to continuing our work with Chairman Frank to reform the derivatives market and our financial system as a whole."

"I want to thank Chairman Frank for accepting suggestions from the New Democrat Financial Services Task Force in crafting new rules for derivatives trading," said Gary Peters of Michigan. "These changes will provide additional clarity for industry while still maintaining tough standards that will prevent abuse."

Another New Democrat, New York's Michael E. McMahon, added, "For all those who believe we need comprehensive, thoughtful regulatory reform, Chairman Frank is exactly the leader you want to have in the fight. Chairman Frank's draft provides a solid start to discussions about reforming the derivatives market. A year ago, many critics of derivatives were ready to eliminate the entire over-the-counter market. This reaction was unreasonable and not in the best interest of our economy. The Frank proposal addresses the systemic risk issues by mandating exchange clearing and trading for the majority of products while preserving the over the counter market for specialized contracts."

Frank's capitulation to the industry was a wake-up call to the AFR consumer coalition. Until the events of the first week in October, this large and unwieldy coalition had tiptoed very gingerly around the volcanic Frank. There was no criticism of the chairman, only the most politely worded pushback against selective provisions that the coalition didn't like, such as Frank's decision to exempt auto dealers from the proposed Consumer Financial Protection Agency, or to remove its jurisdiction over the Community Reinvestment Act. But the groups had gained nothing by being polite.

A charitable reading of Frank's actions would suggest that he was simply bowing to political reality; without the support of the fifteen pro–Wall Street Democrats on the committee, there would be no bill. Every Republican on the committee was totally aligned with the banking industry. Since 2006, the membership of the Financial Services Committee has swollen from under forty to a ridiculously large seventy-one members (over Frank's objection), because it is a popular destination for members looking for industry campaign contributions. According to the Center for Responsive Politics, the eleven first-term members on the committee, mostly from swing districts, raised an average of $1.09 million each from the financial industry for the 2010 campaigns. This is a bargain with the devil. If the Democrats are not seen as delivering help for regular people, because members like these take dives on key votes in order to raise industry donations, no amount of campaign money will save them.

However, a principled chairman is not without a fair amount of power to cajole and horse-trade in order to get good legislation. In June 2009, Chairman Henry Waxman, dealing with a similarly fractious Energy and Commerce Committee, managed to outmaneuver the pro-industry Democrats as well as the Republicans and pass a decent energy bill.

A less kind reading is that Frank simply bought in to the Geithner-Summers view of reality, one very close to the self-interest of the big banks, and that Frank was not interested in compromising his alliance with the administration. An even less charitable view would point to Frank's own financial contributions from the banking industry, over $1 million in 2009, money that he didn't need given his ultra-safe seat.

But it's also worth recalling where the fifteen pro–Wall Street members of the New Democratic Coalition came from. Most, as we saw in chapter 1, were the legacy of Rahm Emanuel, from his days as chair of the Democratic Congressional Campaign Committee. When Emanuel gave up his House seat to become Obama's chief of staff, his recommendation was to continue this strategy of putting corporate Democrats on the Financial Services Committee. The House leadership obliged.

The corruption of the House Financial Services Committee is emblematic of the neutering of the Democrats as a progressive party. And the corruption extends to the committee staff. According to a superb investigative piece by Ryan Grim and Arthur Delaney published by The Huffington Post, of the 253 current and former committee staffers who left between January 2000 and December 2009, 31 Democratic staffers and 53 Republican staffers have been registered lobbyists, nearly all with the financial industry, and none with public interest groups. A staffer looking to a future career as a lobbyist is not going to urge a chairman to embrace tough consumer legislation.

Obama AWOL

As the committee worked its will on the crucial derivatives issue, Tim Geithner, the author of the administration positions of June and August, distanced himself from the tougher provisions that remained in the draft legislation. When the New Democrats on Frank's committee forced the committee to report a badly weakened bill, Geithner actively supported Frank's bill. Frank, for his part, expressed the hope that the bill might be strengthened by the Agriculture Committee, which shares jurisdiction over derivatives legislation. This was improbable, since the Ag Committee is chaired by Congressman Collin Peterson of Minnesota, a Democrat so conservative that the Democratic Caucus nearly stripped him of his chairmanship for regularly voting with the Republicans.

Frank and Peterson at last took HR 4173, the Wall Street Reform and Consumer Protection Act, to the floor of the House on December 9. In the last-minute jockeying before the floor action, pro-banker New Democrats led by Representative Bean threatened to oppose the entire bill unless their demands for further weakening were satisfied and included in the final "managers' bill" offered by the two chairmen.

One such provision, accepted by Frank, limited the ability of states to go beyond the federal consumer protection floor. It gave the power to decide when federal law preempted state law to the bank-friendly Office of the Comptroller of the Currency rather than the new Consumer Finance Protection Agency. Another very contentious provision would have killed the CFPA entirely. In a compromise, a weakened version of the new agency remained in the draft bill, but opponents were promised a floor vote on the amendment to kill it.

In this case, the administration favored keeping the watered-down consumer protection agency in the bill but did no lobbying on its behalf. Lengthy negotiations with conservative Democrats led by Bean were held in Speaker Pelosi's office, and included two senior Treasury officials, Deputy Secretary Neal Wolin and Assistant Secretary for Financial Institutions Michael Barr, with House Majority Leader Steny Hoyer working out the compromise.

On the floor, the amendment by Democrat Walt Minnich of Idaho to strip the consumer agency from the bill narrowly failed, 223–208, but with 33 Democrats voting with Republicans to kill the agency. The measure stayed in the final House-passed bill, but the banking lobby vowed to kill the provision in the Senate.

This was the very week that President Obama went public with a rare criticism of the banks on the CBS show *60 Minutes,* and even called leading bankers to the White House to urge them to do more on mortgage relief and small-business lending. But this uncharacteristic pressure from Obama was widely understood as a kabuki ritual purely for public consumption. No warnings were issued to bankers receiving emergency aid to stop trying to gut the consumer protection bill.

On the crucial issue of derivatives, the provision that ultimately emerged from the bargaining between Frank and Ag Committee chairman Collin Peterson was exceedingly weak, though slightly better than the bill that had emerged from Frank's House Financial Services Committee after the lobbyists got through with it. The bill did require major participants in the swaps market to report their trading activities to their regulator, either the CFTC or the SEC depending on jurisdiction. It did include a provision empowering regulators to act against outright fraud and manipulation. Major swaps dealers were required to have adequate capital. And the CFTC was authorized to set limits on positions in cases of speculation in physical commodities, such as oil or wheat futures.

However, huge loopholes remained for "over-the-counter" derivatives. Trades for standardized derivatives were required to be done on clearinghouses, but not on more tightly regulated exchanges. States continued to be barred from regulating speculation in derivatives as gambling, and they were now also barred from regulating credit default swaps as insurance. The massive loophole for foreign exchange speculation remained. On this set of issues, the Treasury aligned itself with the industry, arguing against attempts to close these loopholes.

The legislation was also weakened in several subtle ways. For example, the original draft bill that went into the final House markup session authorized the CFTC and the SEC to ban "abusive" swaps. By the time the final draft was sent to the House floor, that had been weakened merely to empower the regulators to report such abuses to Congress.

During the floor debate, three senior members of the House Democratic leadership proposed an amendment to close the major loopholes in the derivatives section. The amendment was co-sponsored by Representative John Larson; chair of the House Democratic Caucus Chris van Hollen, who succeeded Rahm Emanuel as head of the Democratic Congressional Campaign Committee; Rosa DeLauro, co-chair of the Steering and Policy Committee; and a back-bench Democrat, Bart Stupak of Michigan, who is a social conservative but an economic populist. "Under this amendment, the CFTC and the SEC will be granted authority to prohibit swap transactions that pose a risk to the financial marketplace," Stupak told the House. "Certain swaps, such as naked credit default swaps, are pure speculative bets that a company will fail and should be banned." Stupak added that the amendment "also narrows the definition of determining which companies are and are not bona fide hedging end users," so that pure speculators would not be treated as legitimate hedgers. Finally, Stupak explained, the amendment provided that illegal swap transactions would not be enforceable in a court of law.

Representative Stupak, acting as lead co-sponsor, thanked the two key committee chairmen, Frank and Peterson, for their help. But when Collin Peterson's turn to speak came, he spoke in opposition. "We believe that if we ban these products," Peterson said, "they will simply move overseas and outside of our ability to regulate them." The amendment went down.

On the crucial issue of whether to give bankruptcy judges the authority to modify the terms of mortgages, the House had already approved an identical measure as a stand-alone bill, known as the Helping Families Save Their Homes Act of 2009, passed in March 2009. But when the measure, which had been killed by the Senate, was proposed as a floor amendment to the Frank financial reform bill, forty-five members changed their vote from aye to nay, and the amendment failed. According to the Center for Responsive Politics, the forty-five faithless members who switched their votes received a total of $3.4 million from financial industries over the past election cycle. Several represented districts hard hit by the foreclosure crisis, including California Democrat Jim Costa, whose San Joaquin Valley district has the nineteenth worst foreclosure record in the country; Republican Mario Diaz-Balart of Greater Miami (twenty-third worst); and Democrat David Scott of suburban Atlanta (twenty-seventh worst.)

The seriously weakened bill passed the House, 223–202, along a mostly party-line vote. All Republicans opposed it, as did some twenty-four conservative Democrats. Among the Democrats who would not bring themselves to vote aye were progressives Marcy Kaptur and Dennis Kucinich of Ohio, and Bart Stupak of Michigan.

Where in all of this was Barack Obama? Nowhere. The president was preoccupied by health reform, Afghanistan, Guantanamo, and other issues. To the extent that Obama was willing to occasionally work the phones and lobby key legislators, the health legislation sucked out all the oxygen in the room. With Obama not personally engaged, the key decisions were made by Geithner and Summers, whose own impulses were even more pro–Wall Street than the president's. Nobody was alerting the president to the further watering down of his own white paper. "Doing financial reform in 2009 without the personal involvement of Barack Obama," said Michael Greenberger, "was like trying to pass the Securities Act of 1933 without Roosevelt."

Thus the poisonous mix that undermined serious financial reform: the temporizing of the Obama administration; the relentless power of financial and business elites to suborn key Democrats; the nexus of lobbying, campaign contributions, and the revolving door between Congress and

K Street; the arcane character of many of the issues coupled with the gross disparity of resources between self-interested financial elites and the outgunned consumer and labor groups; and a chief executive who was largely AWOL.

The Senate is not expected to act until late spring 2010. If the Senate, with its disabling filibuster rule, does not strengthen the House-passed bill, the doctrine of too-big-to-fail will survive. Some, perhaps most, derivatives will be allowed to be traded off exchanges where they will not be subject to price competition or regulatory oversight. Hedge funds and private equity companies will still have only the most minimal oversight. There will be only token democratization of the Federal Reserve. The resolution system for dealing with zombie banks will formalize the seat-of-the-pants process invented by Hank Paulson and Tim Geithner: Taxpayer money and Federal Reserve advances and loan guarantees will be used rather than having bondholders take the loss.

This set of slender reforms is far too weak to fundamentally alter the behavior of the financial system that caused the crash. Mainly, it creates additional risk for taxpayers, increases costs for ordinary borrowers, and expands the role of the Federal Reserve far beyond normal monetary policy, upping the risk of inflation later on.

In January 2010, a new element entered the equation: the personal involvement of Barack Obama. The president called for three major reforms—a surtax on bank profits, enactment of a new Glass-Steagall Act, and passage of a strong consumer protection agency. It remains to be seen whether Obama will put real political weight behind these hopeful pronouncements. Chris Dodd was plainly annoyed that the administration had sprung the Glass-Steagall idea on him with no notice or consultation and viewed it more as a grandstand ploy than a serious commitment. At a February 3 hearing of the Senate Banking Committee, with Paul Volcker and Deputy Treasury Secretary Neal Wolin in the witness chairs, Dodd acidly observed that the White House's abrupt embrace of a new Glass-Steagall Act "seemed to many to be transparently political." At this writing, Dodd is working with Banking Committee Republicans to craft a bill that is far weaker than the House bill. None of the president's stated priorities is likely to survive.

Obama has to decide whether he is serious about legislating—and on what side. For now, the banking industry is calling the shots on Capitol Hill, enabled by Obama's own economic team. Unless the full power of the presidency is brought to bear against the immense undertow of Wall Street influence, America will continue to miss its rendezvous with reform.

CHAPTER FOUR

Crony Capitalism

> Barack Obama ran for president to restore America's role in the world, reform our healthcare system, achieve energy independence and prepare our children for a 21st century economy. He did not run for president to manage banks, insurance companies or car manufacturers.
>
> —LAWRENCE SUMMERS, June 2009

Despite the financial industry's central role in creating the crisis, Wall Street continues to occupy a privileged place in the American political economy. The strategy begun by Hank Paulson in September 2008 and continued by the Obama team throughout 2009 is best understood as a series of deals for favored insiders and firms rather than as a strategy of broad economic recovery. Crony capitalism got us into this mess, and crony capitalism accurately describes the strategy of both the Bush and Obama administrations to contain the damage at the expense of more fundamental reform.

Conservatives are fond of declaring that it's not government's job to "pick winners and losers." Markets do that. But the system of backroom rescues created on the fly initially by Paulson, Bernanke, and Geithner, and later continued by the overlapping team of Bernanke, Geithner, and Summers, was structured to allocate taxpayer capital to favored institutions. The winners won big and the losers lost everything.

It is hardly surprising that the first institution forced into a shotgun merger on highly unfavorable terms was Bear Stearns, a financial house regarded as vulgar, arriviste, and not a member of the club. Bear's profits were in high-stakes trading, not in genteel investment banking (though in the bubble years after 2003, even the most white-shoe firms were aspiring gamblers, too). Bear, however, remained an outlier. When the Fed in 1998 asked the entire Wall Street fraternity to fund a pool of money to keep the collapse of the hedge fund Long-Term Capital Management from crashing the system, Bear's famously profane chairman, Jimmy Cayne, was the one banker to refuse to ante up.

Right after they forced Bear into a fire sale to Morgan, Treasury and the Fed changed the rules so that Bear might have been saved. When an embittered Cayne gave an extended series of interviews to financial writer William Cohan, he defended himself, on the record, in language that used to be unprintable. "The audacity of that prick in front of the American people announcing he was deciding whether or not a firm of this stature . . . [Bear Stearns] was good to get a loan . . . like he was the determining factor," Cayne said, referring to Tim Geithner. "This guy thinks he's got a big dick. He's got nothing, except maybe a boyfriend."

The other outlier firm not even given the courtesy of a shotgun merger, but just allowed to collapse entirely, was Lehman Brothers, an investment banking house with few of the intimate ties to the Treasury and the Fed enjoyed by the two ultimate insiders, Citigroup and Goldman Sachs. Not incidentally, Lehman was an archrival of Goldman. Had it been Goldman that found itself with a run on the bank in mid-September 2008, it is inconceivable that Paulson would have just let it go.

Citi and Goldman had by far the most incestuous relationship with the government, and with each other. Hank Paulson and Robert Rubin had both been at the pinnacle of Goldman Sachs, as had the chairman of George Bush's National Economic Council, Steve Friedman. After leaving government, Friedman became chair of the Federal Reserve Bank of New York. Rubin had gone from the Clinton White House to become chairman of the executive committee of Citi. Not surprisingly, Citi and Goldman both played an outsized role in devising the government's response to the crisis and in using the crisis to feather their own nests.

The Privileged Role of Citigroup

When Robert Rubin became chairman of Citi's executive committee in 1999, he soon became a relentless force prodding the bank to pursue ever greater risks. In the speculative credit boom that took off in 2002 and 2003, Rubin saw other banks making huge returns and felt that Citi was missing out. He personally recruited some of the fanciest traders from places like Goldman and Morgan Stanley. The CEO who had brought in Rubin as chair of Citi's executive committee was Sandy Weill, who had assembled Citi as the ultimate financial conglomerate, with help from Rubin's efforts to repeal the Glass-Steagall Act. Yet Weill, who retired in 2002, was a less aggressive and more prudent banker than his successor, Chuck Prince.

Prince, previously the bank's legal counsel, was far less knowledgeable about exotic securities than Weill and relied increasingly on Rubin for strategic advice. Rubin's counsel was to invest more heavily on riskier bets, especially collateralized debt obligations (CDOs) backed by mortgages or other loans, to be packaged by Citi, sold to investors, and sometimes held in Citi's own off-balance-sheet affiliates. A former senior Citi executive told *The New York Times*, "Chuck was totally new to the job. He didn't know a CDO from a grocery list, so he looked for someone for advice and support. That person was Rubin. And Rubin had always been an advocate of being more aggressive in the capital markets arena. He would say, 'You have to take more risk if you want to earn more.'"

The Securities and Exchange Commission, investigating Citi's exposure after the Bear Stearns collapse in March 2008, was told by Citi executives that Citi considered problems with its portfolio of mortgage securities so remote that it excluded that possibility from its risk analysis. Citi judged the risk of default at less than .01 percent, a figure apparently pulled out of thin air. It also had appallingly lax internal controls. Citi's chief of risk analysis, David Bushnell, who was supposed to be supervising the risks taken by senior traders like Tom Maheras, was a social friend and fishing partner of Maheras, and he was treated as more the junior executive than the supervisor.

Citi was a bit late to the speculative party, but the bank made up for its tardiness with dizzyingly risky plays. The firm was especially vulnerable because it was an archipelago of separate business empires built by Weill, now linked by a CEO who was more of a manager than a strategist. Unlike its nimbler rivals, JPMorgan Chase and Goldman Sachs, which dumped mortgage securities early on, Citi was very late to see the collapse coming. In September 2007, when CEO Chuck Prince learned for the first time that Citi's exposure to mortgage-backed securities totaled a staggering $43 billion, Maheras, a Rubin favorite, assured Prince that these securities were just fine. So when the crash came, Citi took a real beating.

Propping Up a Corpse

When Paulson called in the chiefs of the nine largest banks and arranged for a direct infusion of government funds on favorable terms, Citi desperately needed the money, taking $25 billion and on very favorable terms. At the time, Citi's bonds were so heavily discounted in money markets that it was costing Citi about 22 percent interest to borrow money in the marketplace. The government was charging only 5 percent.

Even though Citi's market capitalization was now less than the value of the money that Treasury was investing, making the government effectively the majority owner, Treasury constructed the bailout so that the government would get no meaningful rights of ownership. Instead, the deal was structured so that the cash would be in preferred rather than common stock, with the government also getting warrants (the right to purchase stock) that were unlikely to be exercised. Treasury declined to replace management or seek seats on Citi's board.

The lending program under which Citi and the other eight banks got the TARP money was known as the Capital Purchase Program, or CPP. As outlined by the Treasury on October 14, it had quite specific terms. To qualify, the banks had to be *solvent*. The program was described not as bailing out failed banks but as shoring up the capital footings of those that were shaky but viable. This was a reasonable premise, but it turned out to be a convenient fiction.

Soon afterward, Treasury unveiled a second program, known as aid to Systemically Significant Financial Institutions (SSFI). This emergency pipeline was created with AIG in mind, and the terms were very different. AIG had already gotten $85 billion of emergency cash through an ad hoc bailout cobbled together by Treasury and the Fed with funding from the Fed under emergency powers dating to the Depression, even before Congress enacted TARP. Now, with Congress having approved $700 billion for a broad range of rescues, Treasury created the SSFI spigot for failing institutions with the potential to wreak havoc on the entire financial system. But the money came with serious strings. In the case of AIG, the government had already gotten 79.9 percent of the company's equity, though it behaved as a relatively passive investor.

Thus the basic architecture of TARP, as hastily concocted by Paulson:

Solvent but shaky institutions get cheap loans from the Treasury under the Capital Purchase Program, and keep their independence. Failed institutions that pose big risks to the system can get even more money, but get taken over.

But no sooner had the Treasury completed its second round of aid for AIG than Citi came knocking on its door again. As things turned out, Citi's $25 billion under the CPP was not nearly enough. Citi had belatedly tabulated its losses, and they were more like $65 billion. Its stock had plummeted, from a peak of more than $55 dollars per share in 2007 to $27 in January 2008. (Bob Rubin in 2006 managed to cash in $12.1 million of options before the collapse.) Now, in November 2008, Citi was trading at under $4. It would eventually bottom out at less than a dollar. Its executives had lost more than 90 percent of their stock holdings. Citi's market capitalization was now down to about $20 billion, or less than the money Treasury had just advanced it. By any normal measure, the bank was insolvent.

So the week before Thanksgiving, while President-elect Obama was building his economic team, Rubin personally contacted his old Goldman partner Hank Paulson to ask for more money. In addition, Rubin wanted the government to guarantee a large pile of securities that were deeply underwater. After a few days of dickering, the Treasury came across with a remarkably generous deal. Citi would get another $20 billion, plus the guarantee of $306 billion of depressed securities, later modified to $301 billion.

The additional $20 billion in cash was not provided under the Capital Purchase Program, which required that participating banks be basically solvent, which Citi clearly wasn't. Nor was it provided under the SSFI program, which required that a failed institution be taken over, which Citi was not. As Damon Silvers, the deputy chairman of the Congressional Oversight Panel, later put it, "Citi got the money under no program whatever, it was just money." After the fact, the Treasury made up a program name. The special deal for Citi was called the Targeted Investment Program, or TIP. It was well targeted, and a generous tip indeed. "That was the moment it became a true sweetheart deal," Silvers added. Later, TIP was used to infuse additional funds into Bank of America, after it became clear that the Treasury and the Fed had strong-armed B of A into acquiring Merrill Lynch, which turned out to be much sicker than either the government or the acquiring bank appreciated.

The details of Treasury's guarantee of $301 billion of Citi's junk securities holdings were even curiouser. The particular securities to be guaranteed were not even identified. And it was not made clear whether the $301 billion referred to book value, market value, or something in between. But the government was suddenly on the hook for $301 billion of Citi's losses, of which Citi agreed to eat the first 10 percent, as a kind of insurance premium. In the meantime, Citi could continue to carry these assets on its books as if they had real value.

Only in late January 2009 did Citi's new CEO Vikram Pandit—who had taken the reins in December—publicly identify, in general terms, what was in the pool, as part of a presentation to investors and securities analysts. The government-guaranteed toxic stew included $154.1 billion of mortgages, $16.2 billion of auto loans, $21.3 billion of "other consumer loans," $12.4 billion of commercial real estate loans, and $13.4 billion of corporate loans, as well as $31.9 billion of distressed securities and $51.5 billion of off-balance-sheet lending commitments. As of late 2009, the Congressional Oversight Panel had not been able to get either Treasury or Citi to divulge how much the assets had been marked down to get to the $301 billion valuation, or whether this was book value. In August 2009, Neil Barofsky, TARP's special inspector general, begin a full audit of the November 2008 Citi deal, at the request of US Representative Alan Grayson, one of Treasury's critics on the House Banking Committee.

Friends in High Places

At the time of the bailout, Michael Froman was simultaneously serving as a senior executive at Citigroup and as head of the economic unit of the Obama transition team in charge of recommending people for the top economic jobs. Froman actually continued working at Citi right into early January, when he joined the White House senior staff (and collected a payment from Citi of $2.25 million). Tim Geithner, then still the president of the New York Federal Reserve, was auditioning with Froman for the post of Obama's Treasury secretary at the same moment that he and Paulson were considering Citi's request for $25 billion under a program that had to be invented after the fact. Literally hours after Citi's request was approved, on November 22, Geithner was named secretary. The decision to hire Geithner, of course, was made well above Froman's pay grade; it was made personally by Barack

Obama. But such was the clubbiness between Citi and both administrations that nobody even worried about the appearance of a conflict.

During the marathon round of phone calls about the Citi rescue the weekend before Thanksgiving, Geithner was closely involved in the negotiations. He recused himself from direct dealings with Citi only after his name was leaked as Obama's likely Treasury secretary, but he continued taking Rubin's calls. With the official handoff at Treasury from Paulson to Geithner, Citi's privileged access was uninterrupted.

At the time of the bailout, Citi was much farther underwater than either Bear Stearns or Lehman Brothers had been, with $1.23 trillion in off-balance-sheet exposures to high-risk securities. Paulson and Geithner testified to Congress that they had let Lehman Brothers go bankrupt because they didn't have the authority to save it. But they somehow managed to save Citi (and its incumbent executives and shareholders) literally by making programs up as they went along. Nowhere in the TARP legislation, Treasury's rules for the TARP program, or anywhere else was there authorization for the sweetheart deal that Citi got as a Thanksgiving present.

It is hard to imagine any other institution in America being treated with this kind of favoritism, except perhaps Goldman. "Sandy Weill paid Bob Rubin more than a hundred million dollars over nearly a decade," said Robert Johnson, a former investment banker and onetime chief economist of the US Senate Banking Committee. "In that one deal, Weill and Citi were repaid a thousand times over."

As a financial strategist, Robert Rubin had proven worse than useless. The trading risks that he had promoted to Citi's CEO Chuck Prince cost the bank hundreds of billions in losses. But as a political fixer, Rubin was still pure gold. The deal was a huge windfall to Citi in more ways than one. Prior to the government guarantee, Citi's stock had been sinking like a stone. Markets knew that the bank was insolvent. Short sellers were piling on, driving the share price down to less than a dollar. When the deal was announced, signaling that the government would do whatever it took to keep Citi afloat and that the company would not be forced to undergo the kind of restructuring typical of FDIC-led liquidations where shareholders lose all, Citi stock rebounded, by 58 percent in one day, and eventually by more than 400 percent.

Within the ranks of senior government officials, the only serious voice speaking out against this blatant favoritism came from Sheila Bair, the hold-over Republican chair of the FDIC. Bair was appalled. She was accustomed to a transparent process at the FDIC whereby insolvent institutions were seized, their shareholders wiped out, and their management replaced, so that the bank could be reorganized and put back in service. Citi was not just a bank but a holding company, so its reorganization was beyond the FDIC's jurisdiction. But, Bair reasoned, if the Treasury could follow this approach with the world's largest insurance conglomerate, sprawling AIG, Treasury could surely do it with Citi. Treasury's contention that it had no authority to "resolve" Citi, she felt, was nonsense. If the practical choice was between bankruptcy and cutting a deal on Treasury's terms, Citi would surely come around, as AIG, Merrill Lynch, and Bear Stearns had all done. Citi, in Bair's view, was insolvent and should be broken up.

But Bair's opposition cut no ice. On the contrary, she was painted by the Paulson-Geithner camp as rigid, unrealistic, and self-serving. And Citi's special treatment did not end there.

Citi's Government Contracts

Citi also benefits from lucrative government contracts for its little-known unit called Global Transaction Services, or GTS. While the rest of Citi has been struggling, the government has made sure that GTS is an expanding profit center. GTS transfers money—more than $3 trillion daily—for several government agencies, including the Federal Reserve. It has the government contract to transfer funds to pay military contractors in Iraq, to operate the Cash for Clunkers program, and to supply financial aid to auto suppliers; it even handles all US passport applications. Some of these contracts were negotiated on an arm's-length basis with competing bidders; others were sole-source deals.

With this subsidized head start from government business, Citi's GTS unit has positioned itself to be the lead global player in the business of money transfer for other corporations, governments, and international entities such as the World Bank. The profits of this government-subsidized unit allowed Citi to survive the bad years. In 2005 and 2006, the unit accounted for well under 10 percent of its profits, according to *The Wall Street Journal*. In 2007, when Citi was barely in the black, that jumped to 60 percent. In 2008, when

Citi lost money, the unit helped offset other losses with some $3 billion in net income, while in 2009 it again accounted for nearly half of Citi's net profits.

Seemingly, this unique franchise is another rationale for not breaking up Citi. In November 2008, when Citi's survival was on the line, CEO Vikram Pandit cited the GTS global entanglements and responsibilities as one more reason why Citi could not be allowed to fail. *The Wall Street Journal* quoted one Citi executive: "100 governments around the world would be trying to figure out how to pay their employees." But this is another straw man, for simply letting Citi unravel was never under discussion. The issue was whether government should take Citi into a receivership.

Losing Money, Rewarding Executives

In July 2009, New York attorney general Andrew Cuomo revealed that even as Citi was writing off $65 billion in losses and taking $45 billion in taxpayer money, the firm continued to pay outlandish executive bonuses. Cuomo reported that Citigroup and Merrill Lynch suffered losses of more than $27.7 and $27.6 billion, respectively. Yet Citigroup paid out $5.33 billion in bonuses in 2008; Merrill, $3.6 billion. Cuomo wrote, "Together, they lost $54 billion, paid out nearly $9 billion in bonuses, and then received bailouts totaling $55 billion."

At Citi, the top four executives shared bonus compensation totaling $43.66 million, while the next four got $37.47 million—after Citi survived only thanks to massive taxpayer bailout.

Cuomo further reported:

> For three other firms—Goldman Sachs, Morgan Stanley, and JP. Morgan Chase—2008 bonus payments were substantially greater than the banks' net income. Goldman earned $2.3 billion, paid out $4.8 billion in bonuses, and received $10 billion in TARP funding. Morgan Stanley earned $1.7 billion, paid $4.475 billion in bonuses, and received $10 billion in TARP funding. JPMorgan Chase earned $5.6 billion, paid $8.69 billion in bonuses, and received $25 billion in TARP funding. Combined, these three firms earned $9.6 billion, paid bonuses of nearly $18 billion, and received TARP taxpayer funds worth $45 billion.

Compensation soared at the big banks during the boom years. But then when the bust came, and the banks lost huge sums and had to be rescued by taxpayers and the Fed, the bonanza for executives just continued. Amazingly, pay and bonus levels did not fall. As Cuomo's investigation further revealed:

> At Bank of America, compensation and benefit payments increased from more than $10 billion to more than $18 billion in between 2003 and 2006. Yet, in 2008, when Bank of America's net income fell from $14 billion to $4 billion, Bank of America's compensation payments remained at the $18 billion level. Bank of America paid $18 billion in compensation and benefit payments again in 2008, even though 2008 performance was dismal when compared to the 2003–2006 bull market. Similar patterns are clear at Citigroup, where bull-market compensation payments increased from $20 billion to $30 billion. When the recession hit in 2007, Citigroup's compensation payouts remained at bull-market levels—well over $30 billion, even though the firm faced a significant financial crisis.

Perhaps the most shocking comparison is between Citi's net earnings (or losses) and its total employee compensation. In 2006, its last boom year, Citi reaped a net income of $21.538 billion and paid compensation of $30.277 billion. Two years later, it lost $27.684 billion. Yet despite having laid off about 20 percent of its workforce, its compensation tab actually increased to $32.440 billion, of which more than $5 billion was in bonuses. How could a firm that lost tens of billions and required $45 billion of taxpayer money to stay in business have the nerve to pay bonuses at all? Only because it had very good friends in very high places.

In June 2009, the ever unrepentant Citi created a plan to raise base salaries of key employees by up to 50 percent, because its huge losses and flat stock left less room to pay the large customary bonuses using stock gimmicks for the year 2009. At that point, the government's nominal stake in the company was 34 percent, even though a fair accounting would have given the government majority control, since the $45 billion of direct cash pumped into Citi was almost double the value of Citi's common stock. But the Treasury had deliberately lowballed the value of its taxpayer contributions to the humbled banking giant.

Treasury's terms were more like a gift than an investment. The government, which had all the bargaining power, offered taxpayers a far worse deal than comparable deals being negotiated during the same period at arm's length in the free market. The most generous taxpayer subsidy went to the sickest bank—Citigroup. This might have been defensible had government been given controlling interest in the bank and exercised that interest as a majority shareholder to replace incompetent management, alter the bank's business model, and reform the outrageous compensation structure. But this course was exactly what Summers and Geithner, just like Paulson before them, did *not* want to do.

Business, as Usual

You might imagine that the new Obama team would be less inclined to give Citi and other mega-banks the kind of sweetheart deals offered in 2008 by the Bush team. But nothing was more revealing of the continuity and favored treatment than the terms by which the three weakest banks were permitted to exit the TARP program in late 2009. The whole premise of TARP was to shore up bank balance sheets so that banks could attract private equity capital and have more capacity to resume lending. But this strategy was breached by the Obama administration when banks wanted out of TARP in order to avoid its ceilings on executive pay.

In fall 2009, Bank of America, Wells Fargo, and Citigroup, representing almost one-third of the country's bank assets, kept pressing the Treasury to be permitted to exit TARP. Their main motive was to escape the pay ceilings. Despite Geithner's sympathies, he at first argued that they were still too weak. Before they could exit, he insisted, they needed to raise more capital—so that the money provided under TARP would be replaced by real equity and not by accounting tricks. By year end, however, Geithner bent his own rules and gave in, placing the banks in an even weaker lending position. There was no reason for this capitulation other than the banks' desire to evade the executive pay limits.

Citi was permitted to cobble together a deal that included a $17 billion sale of stock and a contribution of cash, lubricated by a well-timed decision by the IRS to waive a tax rule. That waiver allowed Citi to claim a $38 billion tax break against losses despite an ownership change as it paid back the government, something not normally permitted. The IRS is a quasi-independent agency housed at the Treasury. Ordinarily, its rulings are insulated from politics. The last time that political neutrality was breached was under Richard Nixon, and the misuse of the IRS played a role in Nixon's impeachment. But in the case of Citigroup, there is little doubt that the IRS accommodated the political appointees at the Treasury in timing the ruling to facilitate Citi's exit from TARP. However, though the tax break would cost the Treasury $38 billion over time, it was useful only to offset *future* Citi tax liabilities. It did nothing for Citi's true balance sheet at the time of its exit strategy. Basically, Citi's exit terms swapped common stock for preferred, leaving its real capital footings unchanged.

And when the government tried to dispose of its own preferred shares as part of the Citi exit deal, it found that markets had seen through Citi's brave talk about its improved condition. In an embarrassing setback to the escape plan, Treasury had to delay its own sale because there were too few buyers and Citi's stock price dropped under $4 a share—less than what the government had paid. Bank of America, meanwhile, sold $19.3 billion in stock to satisfy Treasury's demand that it strengthen its balance sheet. But these sales actually diluted the value of the shares of existing stockholders and left the bank worse off.

A senior regulatory official told me, "If you replace TARP capital with cash, your capital structure is weaker. Cash is gone on the asset side, a hunk of capital is gone, and debt-to-equity ratio is worse." The question even came up in President Obama's December 13 interview on CBS's *60 Minutes,* when correspondent Steve Kroft asked the president point-blank whether the banks were fleeing from TARP to escape its pay ceilings. Obama replied, "I think in some cases that was a motivation." The president went on to offer some rare, hot rhetoric about the bankers. "You guys are drawing down $10, $20 million bonuses after America went through the worst economic year that it's gone through in decades, and you guys caused the problem. And we've got 10 percent unemployment. Why do you think people might be a little frustrated?"

But at the very moment that Obama was trying to sound like a populist, his appointees were working hand-in-glove with the banks to expedite their exit. In an effort to duck responsibility for the decision to let the big banks exit TARP, Treasury officials even blamed it on the Federal Reserve. According to officials I spoke with, this claim is nonsense, since TARP is the Treasury's program and the day-to-day negotiations about exiting TARP were with senior Treasury officials. The truth is that Treasury got the Fed to agree to accept responsibility because the Fed is not required under the TARP program to account to Congress for its actions. In a hearing of the House Oversight Subcommittee, Chairman Dennis Kucinich of Ohio had this exchange with Herb Allison, the assistant Treasury secretary in charge of TARP:

> **Allison:** We don't make the determination of when Citi can repay the Treasury for our investment in the company. That decision is made by the regulator . . . the Federal Reserve in this case.
>
> **Kucinich:** Well, they're the regulator, but we're the shareholder. When do we find out? When do you find out? Do you find out when you read about it in the newspaper?
>
> **Allison:** When the regulator informs us.
>
> **Kucinich:** The Fed doesn't ask you if you have any position on this, they just tell you they're doing it. Is that what you're saying?
>
> **Allison:** We don't exercise regulatory oversight over the banks. That's a matter for the regulatory agencies.
>
> **Kucinich:** But we are holding all these billions in shares. Shouldn't the government have any ability to decide when the banks would exit from TARP?

Allison's alibi was, to put it mildly, less than truthful—but emblematic of the way the Treasury under Tim Geithner favored the big banks over the public interest. The facts are these: Treasury conducted the day-to-day negotiations with the big banks over their exit from TARP. The Federal Reserve was technically required to sign off on the exit plans but was not actively involved in the details. My sources say that the Fed was requested to let the banks off the hook early by Obama's chief of staff, Rahm Emanuel.

Every Day Is Payday

At the heart of the financial collapse was a misalignment of incentives between the way executives and traders are compensated and the risks they take. In the hedge fund world, there is a revealing little phrase—IBGYBG. It stands for "I'll be gone, you'll be gone"—as in "Let's do this deal, cash in, and leave some other sucker holding the bag." Critics of this entire way of life have long argued that if you want to reform Wall Street, you need to reform executive compensation.

But executive compensation actually presents two very different challenges. One is taking the profit out of trading strategies that benefit only insiders and pass along systemic risks. A hedge fund executive can make more than $1 billion a year adding no value to the real economy. Banks that increasingly behave like hedge funds contend that they need to pay traders in proportion to the profits that they make for the bank—or lose this talent to competitors. No executive compensation scheme is going to limit trading profits. The best remedy for this aspect of the problem is to use taxes and regulation to discourage the entire business model of highly leveraged trading, often on inside information, as parasitic to the real economy.

Ordinary executive compensation is another story. In the past three decades, the compensation of chief executives has increased from something like 24 times that of the average worker to around 300 times. There is no evidence whatsoever that the talent of chief executives increased by anything like this multiple. As countless books and articles have documented, skyrocketing executive pay is simply the result of a power grab, facilitated by crony boards of directors and a system in which compensation consultants are rewarded for recommending higher pay packages.

There are a couple of separate problems with out-of-control executive pay. One is simple fairness—why should the boss be paid 300 times the earnings of the average worker? The other has to do with misaligned incentives. If a senior executive is compensated by stock options or other bonuses based on this year's profits, the executive will have an incentive to take big risks to manipulate quarterly earnings and the short-term share price, rather than pursing corporate strategies that add long-term value. Innumerable studies document that executive pay diverges from the true performance of the company. In the recent financial collapse, executives who pursued strategies that were ultimately disastrous for their companies and for the larger economy nonetheless cashed in big.

Critics have proposed a variety of remedies, including "say on pay" rules, in which shareholders get the right to approve pay packages; more power for outside directors on corporate boards to set executive compensation; and most importantly, regulations that require bonus compensation to be deferred, so that it more closely tracks the true long-term success of the company. Such proposals have come before the Securities and Exchange Commission from time to time, and they have always been beaten back by industry pressure. No general measures on executive pay were included in the Obama administration's program of financial reform. Indeed, when the exorbitant bonuses for 2009 became public information, Christina Romer, the administration's chief economist, was dispatched to appear on CNN. "This big bonus season," she said, "is going to offend the American people. It offends me . . . You would certainly think that the financial institutions that are now doing a little bit better would have some sense." Romer spoke almost as if she and her boss were pure bystanders—as if the administration, which had bailed out the entire banking system, had no power to reform compensation practices.

As noted, TARP did include a provision authorizing the government to limit compensation in the case of companies that received "exceptional assistance" from the bailout program. This turned out to be seven of America's largest financial corporations. The Obama administration appointed a special master for executive compensation, popularly known as the Pay Czar. The job went to a lawyer named Kenneth Feinberg, who had won wide respect for his service administering a fund providing a different kind of compensation—for the families of the more than 3,000 victims of the 9/11 attacks. He allocated some $7 billion in awards and persuaded 98 percent of the recipients to accept his formula rather than challenging it in court.

Negotiating with seven of America's largest companies to accept limits on pay turned out to be a somewhat tougher challenge. Feinberg has confirmed that he was under relentless pressure from Tim Geithner's Treasury not to go too hard on the bankers—on the premise that they needed to retain competitive talent. However, these banks *survived* thanks only to the taxpayer bailouts, and it seemed unconscionable for taxpayers to reward executives of failed enterprises.

Feinberg devised what might be a template for broad reform of executive compensation. Negotiating pay packages for 136 top executives, he traded somewhat larger salaries and bonuses than he thought justified (upward of $6 million) for provisions that most of the compensation would be deferred in the form of long-term stock. The pay would be excessive, but at least the executives would get incentives to pursue long-term value rather than short-run speculation. This took strenuous bargaining. AIG executives pressed hard for all-cash compensation, telling Feinberg that company stock then trading at around $40 a share was basically worthless—quite an admission. According to Steven Brill, writing in *The New York Times*, top Treasury officials pressed Feinberg not to be so tough on AIG.

In the end, however, Feinberg's astute tightrope act was largely for naught, because Geithner simply allowed the banks to exit TARP early. Once they were out from under the Treasury's jurisdiction, the banks were free to pay their executives whatever they liked. The Obama administration might have used Feinberg's work as a model for broader reform of executive compensation based on securities law rather than on the emergency assistance of TARP. But no such proposal was forthcoming. Instead several of the large banks, led by Goldman Sachs, as a "voluntary," preemptive move, shifted more of the bonus compensation to stock awards that had to be held for at least five years. But recent history shows that these moves, unless mandatory, are easily gamed. For examples, when stock option awards did not pay off because the stock had fallen, several large companies "reloaded" and issued new options, to guarantee that their executives would be rewarded no matter what the firm's actual performance.

Goldman Rules

To appreciate the unique power of Goldman Sachs, the alma mater of both Robert Rubin and Henry Paulson, there is no better moment to begin than the critical month of September 2008. This was the month when the financial dominoes were falling, and when Hank Paulson finally decided that he was out of ad hoc tricks and needed Congress to appropriate close to a trillion dollars in bailout funds. As Paulson, Geithner, and Bernanke scrambled to devise a rescue, they relied heavily on two private citizens, bankers Bob Rubin and Goldman Sachs CEO Lloyd Blankfein. Neither was in the role of financial statesman, but rather of self-interested special pleader.

Goldman was one of two private companies heavily involved in the design of the several rescue operations of the Treasury and the Fed—the other was Pimco, the nation's largest bond house. In the fateful meetings that consigned Lehman, Goldman's archrival, to oblivion, Blankfein was the one competing banking executive who was in on the crucial conversations. Paulson was on the phone to Blankfein several times daily. Sometimes Blankfein was in the role of adviser; other times he was a potential merger partner; still other times, a prospective investor of securities the government hoped to unload. Often his multiple roles were blurred. According to *New York Times* reporter Andrew Sorkin's account, it fell to Warren Buffett to warn Paulson that the whole show was becoming too incestuous.

And just two days after Lehman collapsed, on September 15, when the Treasury reversed course and decided that it had to rescue AIG, with Federal Reserve loans initially totaling $85 billion and jerry-built aid from Treasury, the Fed, and the FDIC ultimately swelling to a total of $185 billion, Blankfein was also intimately involved in these conversations. The intrepid Gretchen Morgenson of *The New York Times* obtained phone records, through a Freedom of Information request, revealing that Paulson talked to Blankfein twenty-four times between September 16 and September 21 at the height of the crisis, far more than he spoke to any other executive. During this period, Paulson spoke only four times to the hapless CEO of Lehman, Richard Fuld.

The Incestuous Case of AIG and Goldman

The decision to use government funds to make sure that AIG not just be left to go bankrupt was defensible in principle. AIG truly did pose systemic risks. After the decision to let Lehman go, the stock market was in free fall and other credit markets were nearly frozen. With the insurance conglomerate as the largest writer of credit default swaps—insurance on bonds—a collapse of AIG would have domino effects across the financial economy, triggering cascading losses and turning crisis into catastrophe. But the fishy part of the deal was allowing the government aid to be used as a pass-through to other firms *that had not yet suffered losses* on securities guaranteed by AIG.

Goldman Sachs, for one, was on the hook for $12.9 billion in securities insured by AIG. But these securities had not defaulted. Yet when he negotiated the deal for AIG to get $85 billion from the government, Paulson's assumption was that $12.9 billion of the taxpayer money would be passed through directly as a windfall to Goldman. Indeed, that was part of his motivation. In July, when Goldman exited the TARP program early and bought back its warrants for $1.1 billion (after initially offering $650,000), the stated rationale was that Goldman didn't need the government's money. Skeptics asked why Goldman had taken the $12.9 billion of government-funded AIG money, and why Paulson and Geithner had not just permitted that transaction but facilitated it.

When Special Inspector General Barofsky finally assembled enough of the facts to issue a comprehensive report in late November 2009, his findings were devastating. The Fed, in this case represented by Tim Geithner, then president of the Reserve Bank of New York, simply refused to use its leverage to negotiate with Goldman to take less than 100 cents on the dollar for positions that would have been worth a fraction of that if AIG had failed. Barofsky also nailed the dishonesty in Goldman's claim that it had other ways of covering its losses and didn't really need the taxpayer money. Goldman and other banks got a total of $62 billion thanks to the AIG rescue. The New York Fed gave the banks $27 billion in cash and permitted them to keep $35 billion more in collateral already put up by AIG. "By providing A.I.G. with the capital to make these payments," Barofsky's report stated, "Federal Reserve officials provided A.I.G.'s counterparties with tens of billions of dollars they likely would have not otherwise received had A.I.G. gone into bankruptcy." The $13 billion in taxpayer funds conveniently covered most of the $17 billion that Goldman paid out in bonuses.

In negotiating this sweetheart deal, Paulson also violated the terms of his own appointment as secretary of the Treasury, which explicitly required him to recuse himself from any decision involving his former employer Goldman Sachs, unless he received an ethics waiver from government lawyers. Throughout the weekend of September 13–14, however, Paulson was intimately involved in discussions at the New York Fed, which then resulted in the AIG and Goldman deals. It must have dawned on him that he was committing a conflict of interest in violation of his written ethics commitment, because he subsequently sought a waiver, which was granted after the fact, on September 17.

Meanwhile, the New York Federal Reserve Bank, then headed by Tim Geithner, directed AIG to withhold from its annual filings with the SEC the details about its payments to Goldman and other banks during the crisis. This fact came out only in January 2010, when Darrell Issa, the ranking Republican on the House Oversight and Government Reform Committee, released five months' worth of e-mails between AIG and the New York Fed, beginning in November 2008. Geithner insisted that he had not been involved personally—that this guidance had come from the Fed's lawyers. But Issa and others contended that the New York Fed has pressured AIG into violating securities laws requiring full disclosures to investors.

The fact that a senior Republican is leading the attack bodes well for a liberal–conservative coalition eventually getting to the bottom of the sweetheart Goldman-AIG-Paulson-Geithner deals. Critics led by former officials Bill Black and Eliot Spitzer have called on the three government trustees, who represent the government's 79.9 percent share in AIG, to voluntarily release additional e-mails.

It is now well established that in the fall of 2007, Goldman was aggressively marketing to its customers collateralized debt obligations backed by subprime loans and other shaky collateral—at the very same time that the firm was betting against them using short selling. On its face, this seems like a gross violation of securities laws. At this writing, investigators at the SEC are determining whether to proceed. The SEC has determined that as early as January 2008, Goldman, which was betting heavily against the mortgage market, was pressuring AIG to advance Goldman increasing amounts of cash as the value of mortgage-backed securities declined. The more this market collapsed, the more profit Goldman gained, both because it was shorting these securities in the marketplace and because it had insured them with AIG against declines in their value. AIG accused Goldman of lowballing the value of its mortgage securities and refusing to allow independent third parties to provide valuations, so that it could squeeze AIG for more cash. As the market spiraled downward and AIG bled cash, there was one other nice touch. Goldman's equity research department, in an August 2008 report, advised investors to avoid AIG's stock. Goldman got paid off on supposedly worthless securities at the trough of the collapse, at 100 cents on the dollar, via the government bailout of AIG. The value of many of these securities has since recovered.

In January, one other tantalizing detail came out. Hank Greenberg, the man who built AIG into a massive conglomerate, alleged in an interview with *The Wall Street Journal* that machinations by Goldman Sachs contributed to AIG's abrupt collapse in yet another respect. According to Greenberg, prior to 2006 the swaps created by AIG—insurance contracts against a security defaulting—were paid off only at maturity in the event of a default. But in 2005, the International Swaps and Derivatives Association (ISDA), a group in which Goldman is a major player, drafted new standards that shifted much more of the risk off customers such as Goldman and onto insurers like AIG. With the new standards, AIG would have to part with cash—collateral—as the market value of the securities was declining. These allegations do need to be taken with a grain of salt, since Greenberg is a self-interested player with a stake in repairing a badly damaged reputation and making AIG's failure somebody else's fault. Yet the ISDA did in fact modify its standards in 2005—and these contentions add one more piece to the puzzle still to be sorted out by the oversight panel, the Financial Crisis Inquiry Commission, congressional investigations, and the SEC. At the very least, they suggest that self-regulatory standard-setting bodies such as the ISDA have far too much power, and that regulators are still too hands-off. They also add one more element to the picture of a Goldman Sachs far too cozy with the Treasury and the Federal Reserve at the expense of the public interest.

Revolving Doors
During the same period, Goldman converted from an investment bank to a bank holding company. This gave it access both to the Fed's discount window and to TARP money. Under the Fed's emergency powers, Goldman had enjoyed access to Fed advances since the summer of 2008, but this made it official.

One by-product was a nice personal windfall for yet another insider, Steve Friedman, former CEO of Goldman, former chief economic adviser to President Bush, and at the time also the chairman of the board of the Federal Reserve Bank of New York. With Goldman's new status as a bank holding company, the reserve bank that Friedman chaired was now Goldman's primary regulator.

Friedman was a member of Goldman's board and held a large block of Goldman stock. His participation in the Fed's decision to change Goldman's status violated the conflict-of-interest rules of the Fed. At Friedman's request, officials of the New York Fed asked for a waiver of the rules. While the request was pending, Friedman, who had inside knowledge of how the Fed was treating Goldman and could anticipate that markets would react favorably, purchased 37,300 Goldman shares. By the summer of 2009, he had reaped close to $3 million in profit. After more than two months, the general counsel of the Federal Reserve, Scott Alvarez, granted the waiver (after Friedman had purchased the stock) on the inventive grounds that Friedman had inadvertently found himself in violation of the Fed's conflict-of-interest rules because of events beyond his control—namely the New York Fed's decision (in which Friedman was involved) to expedite Goldman's conversion to a bank holding company. A more disinterested ruling by either the general counsel of the New York Fed or the Board of Governors' counsel would have immediately required Friedman to recuse himself from any decision benefiting Goldman, or to not purchase additional shares, or both. It is a measure of the clubbiness of the whole affair that Friedman told the press he didn't see anything wrong with his conflicted roles or his financial transaction.

At the time, Friedman was also heading the search committee for a new president of the New York Fed to replace Tim Geithner. The job went to yet another Goldman executive, William C. Dudley. The general counsel of the New York Fed, Tom Baxter, who is supposed to be the guardian of the ethical standards of the institution and the public interest, told *The Wall Street Journal* that it made sense to allow Friedman to remain as chairman and as head of the search committee, because he is "the kind of person we needed to head the search"—as if only Friedman were capable of doing the job. On May 7, 2007, after the *Journal* printed details of the conflict, Friedman, stung by the bad publicity, stepped down as chairman of the New York Fed, insisting that he had done nothing wrong. The ever helpful general counsel, Tom Baxter, put out a statement that Friedman's purchases of Goldman Sachs stock in December 2008 and January 2009 "did not violate any Federal Reserve statute, rule or policy." By then, Friedman was almost $3 million richer, Goldman was $23 billion richer thanks to the two infusions of taxpayer cash, and the New York Fed presidency was safely in the hands of a Goldman man.

Astonishingly, in late January 2010, Goldman executives began discussing with regulators the idea of *giving back* their bank holding company status, and reverting to a pure investment bank, to escape the tighter supervision for which Obama had begun campaigning. The most galling premise is that the regulators would just allow Goldman to assume whatever guise its executives found most expedient at any particular time.

A perfectly charming illustration of the way Goldman invests in public officials is the case of Gene Sperling, who was the last head of Clinton's National Economic Council. When Bush took over, many of the Clinton alums headed to Wall Street. But not Sperling, who was known as a centrist policy wonk. He impressed even his critics by taking positions at think tanks—the Center for American Progress and the Council on Foreign Relations. By 2006, it was increasingly likely that the next administration would be Democratic, and that Sperling would likely have a senior position in it. According to some fine investigative reporting by Bloomberg News, Goldman Sachs helpfully created a position for Sperling as adviser to its foundation, paying him $887,727 in 2008—chump change for Goldman, but a small fortune for a policy wonk (whose day job at the Council on Foreign Relations paid $116,653). Now Sperling is a senior economic official in the Obama administration. If you were he, would you cross Goldman?

Goldman alums are ubiquitous in the financial system and in government's revolving door. Besides Rubin and Paulson, Neel Kashkari, the first head of TARP, came from Goldman. Likewise Josh Bolten, George W. Bush's chief of staff at the time of the serial bailouts. When Paulson, reflecting the government's nominal ownership of AIG, needed an executive to represent the government's interest, he selected yet another former Goldman colleague, Ed Liddy, a member of Goldman's board. During the week from hell in mid-September, Paulson relied heavily on both Kashkari and another former Goldman partner and Paulson crony now serving as a senior Treasury official, Steve Shafran. With the shift to Obama, the Goldman alums include Gary Gensler, head of CFTC, and Mark Patterson, Geithner's chief of staff. The general counsel to TARP, Tim Massad, was a lawyer with Cravath, Swaine and Moore, one of Goldman's outside law firms. For good measure, the World Bank, the New York Stock Exchange, and the Federal Reserve Bank of New York are also headed by Goldman men. In Republican and Democratic times alike, Goldman's influence is unmatched.

At the time of the key bailout decisions, the heads of several of the banks that benefited were also Goldman alums, including Robert Steel of Wachovia and John Thain of Merrill Lynch. Thain's Goldman connection is of more than passing interest, since the Fed and the Treasury bent the rules and quite possibly broke the law in order to pressure Bank of America to consummate its rescue of a collapsing Merrill Lynch, so that Bank of America's shareholders ended up taking a far bigger hit than Merrill Lynch's, despite the fact that Merrill was the institution about to go under. The additional $20 billion that B of A received under the TIP program in January, plus the Treasury's guarantee of another $118 billion in toxic assets (mostly from Merrill Lynch), constituted a kind of restitution from Treasury for the bank's coerced agreement to take on far greater losses than it had bargained for back in September.

In this episode, too, Goldman people were ubiquitous. Ken Wilson, a recently retired Goldman vice president, was advising Paulson on the deal. And Bank of America's top outside adviser, J. Christopher Flowers, who vetted Merrill's books for B of A CEO Ken Lewis and pronounced them more than sound enough to go forward with the deal, was also a former Goldman investment banker.

With this level of interlocks, it would be astonishing if Goldman and its allies did *not* get sweetheart deals. If you compare the degree of insolvency of Bear Stearns and Lehman Brothers with that of the banks that got saved, you might be forgiven for concluding that the most serious mistake that Bear CEO Jimmy Cayne and Lehman CEO Richard Fuld made was not being Goldman men.

As the Goldman dynasty continued into the Obama era, Mark Patterson, who had headed Goldman's Washington office, got an ethics waiver from one of the most ethics-conscious administrations in history. The double standard of kid-glove treatment for Wall Street executives joining the Treasury was in sharp contrast to the rather rigid rules applied to many other officials. Peg Seminario, one of the most admired experts on worker health and safety, has served as the AFL-CIO's expert on the Occupational Safety and Health Administration. She was one of the finalists to be appointed head of that long-neglected agency. But Seminario was registered as an AFL-CIO lobbyist. No special waiver was granted to her, and the job went to someone else.

Tom Malinowsky, the DC director of Human Rights Watch, had dutifully registered as a lobbyist so that he could lobby Congress and the Bush White House against torture. The Obama administration considered him for a top human rights job but told him that he was disqualified because he had been a lobbyist! Meanwhile, Tom Donilon, who had lobbied extensively on behalf of Fannie Mae and orchestrated damage control for Fannie at the time when the mortgage giant was the subject of extensive investigations, managed to get himself a waiver. He served first as head of the Obama transition team's unit on the State Department—and then transitioned himself into a job as deputy national security adviser.

Good Day at BlackRock

Yet another highly dubious aspect of the entire Treasury strategy has been the heavy reliance on private firms both as strategic advisers to the government and as inside-track investors. BlackRock, for example, manages $1.3 trillion in assets for an array of clients. The firm, whose CEO Larry Fink enjoys excellent contacts with Henry Paulson and his successors in the Obama administration, has won myriad contracts to manage various pools of private money that is temporarily under the stewardship of one or another government agency.

BlackRock now has contracts to help manage the aftermath of the Bear Stearns takeover, as well as assets from AIG and Citigroup. When the government ended up with some $30 billion in toxic assets from the JPMorgan Chase takeover of Bear, it hired BlackRock to manage them. The firm is advising the Federal Reserve on its strategy to stimulate the housing market, as well as Fannie Mae and Freddie Mac (Federal Home Loan Mortgage Corporation), the now-nationalized mortgage companies. Fink has bragged to the press and to his clients about his insider status. "It gives comfort to our clients that we are being involved in some of the solutions of our economy, and it allows us to show our clients that we are being asked in these difficult situations to provide advice," he told a gathering of Wall Street analysts in December 2008, a time when he was advising both the outgoing Bush team and officials of the incoming Obama administration. "I mean it is a great seal of approval," he added. "I'm running out of here to go meet with Treasury to talk about plans later this afternoon." Officials of both administrations confirm that they talked with Fink daily, sometimes several times in a single day.

One Fed policy directly influenced by Fink was the Fed's decision to extend the government safety net to money market mutual funds. These funds are lightly regulated and have enjoyed no special government guarantee (or regulation). Americans have used them as checking accounts or demand savings accounts, taking advantage of the slightly higher interest rates. The presumed safety of the funds is in their very short-term investments, which are rolled over daily. Investors are able to withdraw their funds at will. Until 2008, no major money market fund had ever traded at less than par—100 cents on the invested dollar. But in the great freeze-up of September 2008, one of the funds that was heavily invested in Lehman Brothers announced that it was now worth only about 97 cents on the dollar. This created a stampede out of money market funds into Treasury securities, including a withdrawal of $38 billion from BlackRock's funds. After Bernanke's unprecedented guarantee, the money came right back.

The contracts from the Treasury to manage various pools of toxic assets that government took over gives BlackRock privileged insights into the thinking of key government officials such as Summers and Geithner and increases the risks of "front running," or trading ahead of other investors based on insider knowledge (an action that is illegal but widely practiced). The potential for conflicts has been criticized by leaders of both parties but has not led to changes in government policy.

"They have access to information when the Federal Reserve will try to sell securities, and what price they will accept. And they have intricate financial relations with people across the globe," complained Senator Chuck Grassley of Iowa, the ranking Republican on the Senate Finance Committee. "The potential for a conflict of interest is great and it is just very difficult to police."

Without singling out BlackRock, Neil Barofsky warned of the conflict of interest that occurs when a private firm such as BlackRock is managing assets both privately and for the government. It could use federal subsidies to overpay, thus raising the market value of comparable securities in its own portfolio. "In other words, the conflict results in an enormous profit for the fund manager at the expense of the taxpayer," Barofsky wrote in his April 2009 report. According to the Congressional Oversight Panel, the Treasury has at least thirty-seven employees of private investment firms serving as consultants.

Double Standards

The flip side of these sweetheart deals is a series of double standards—very gentle and generous treatment for Wall Street, especially for favored firms on Wall Street—and free-market, devil-take-the-hindmost treatment for everyone else. Following the decisions to throw Bear Stearns and then Lehman Brothers to the wolves, Bernanke and company changed the ground rules immediately afterward. Had they done so a week earlier, both firms would have survived. In the case of Bear, the Fed agreed to make available to damaged financial institutions $200 billion in Treasury securities in the form of loans backed by distressed collateral that nobody else wanted, starting March 27—when it was too late for Bear. In the case of Lehman, the Fed and the Treasury declined to advance Lehman government funds, as they did for AIG literally the same week, under the emergency clause giving the Fed authority to provide funds to virtually any firm, given "urgent and exigent" circumstances. That clause has been on the books since 1933.

Geithner, defending the decision to let Lehman go down, later told financial writer William Cohan, "[C]entral banks do liquidity, they don't do insolvency. No central bank I'm aware of has the authority to put capital into financial institutions. That's what governments exist to do." In light of actual events that followed, that assertion was a breathtaking misrepresentation, to put it kindly.

In the months after the Treasury and Fed decided to let Lehman go bankrupt, the Federal Reserve again and again went beyond its usual role of "doing liquidity" precisely to "do insolvency." The law authorizes the Federal Reserve to lend only against sound collateral, but it repeatedly lent against junk. This was particularly the case in its extraordinary loans to Citi, Bank of America, Merrill, and AIG. Indeed, in the case of the support to Citi, the whole point was to lend against junk. And in the various permutations of schemes to pump money into sick banks, the typical formula was that the Treasury would put up money appropriated by Congress, and the Fed would then lend some multiple of it. Without these loans, several institutions would have been revealed as insolvent. Historians will long debate the economic impact of these different standards for different distressed banks.

A Shotgun Merger for Merrill

The Fed's double standard in its treatment of Bank of America and of Merrill Lynch is also telling. There was only one precedent for this coerced merger—the forced takeover of Bear Stearns by JPMorgan Chase in March 2008. After the fact, it certainly appeared that the government brokered a deal that was overly sweet for Morgan. But six months later, Bernanke, Geithner, and Paulson had a lot more experience, making the differential treatment of Merrill Lynch and Bank of America even less excusable.

In the immediate aftermath of the decision to let Lehman go bankrupt, Paulson and company resolved not to repeat the error with the even larger Merrill Lynch. But the terms turned out to be a windfall for Merrill's shareholders and executives, and a huge tax on B of A, the nation's largest institution and one that was in relatively sound shape compared with the Wall Street banks that had caused the meltdown. In the deal put together that September week, Bank of America offered to purchase Merrill for an astonishing $50 billion, a price of $29 a share, or a 70 percent premium over the stock's closing price the previous week before rumors of the deal started percolating. B of A's Ken Lewis had coveted Merrill, and clearly overpaid for it, but the deal was urged on by Paulson.

Thanks to the diligence of New York State attorney general Cuomo, who unearthed unsavory details of government strong-arming, we now know that after Lewis got a better look at Merrill's rapidly deteriorating balance sheet, he wanted out of the deal—and was prevented from walking away or even renegotiating terms by alarming brass-knuckle tactics on the part of Bernanke and Paulson. As a consequence, B of A's shareholders, who had invested in what was hitherto a quite solvent bank, took a huge and probably illegal beating. Between September and February, the stock lost about 90 percent of its value. The only comparable losses were in the share prices of outfits such as Citi, which unlike B of A were true insolvent zombies. The precarious shape of B of A was primarily the result of a deal that the bank had a perfectly legal right to exit, because of a material deterioration in Merrill's condition.

Cuomo's investigation began with a probe of why Merrill went ahead and paid $3.6 billion in executive bonuses during the period when the deal was still pending, despite its massive and mounting losses and the plain fact that it was insolvent but for the government-backed rescue by Bank of America. Turning over this rock, Cuomo unearthed a much more consequential scandal.

As sworn depositions to Cuomo's investigators by Paulson, Bernanke, Lewis, and others confirmed, and subpoenaed e-mails only embellished, Lewis realized as the fall wore on that Merrill was in worsening shape. Under the terms negotiated in September, the deal was due to close January 1. First, however, it had to be approved by B of A's shareholders at a meeting on December 5. Under the securities laws, Lewis had not just a right but a legal obligation to inform his shareholders of the significant deterioration in Merrill's condition. At the time of the preliminary takeover in September, it appeared that Merrill's losses for the year would be modest. By late November, they looked to be more than $9 billion. Lewis had a clear right to walk away from the deal by invoking the "material adverse change" (MAC) clause, which is standard in takeovers.

But when Lewis and his team advised the government of what they had learned about Merrill's dire condition, they received mainly threats. If Lewis tried to back out of the deal, or even to renegotiate its terms, the Treasury and the Fed would get him fired, and B of A would never get a penny more in government aid. Basically, the government coerced Lewis to violate the securities laws. When his shareholders considered and approved the deal on December 5, Lewis, under pressure from the government, told them nothing of what he knew about Merrill's worsened condition, which was certain to crash the price of B of A stock once the information became public when Merrill's year-end numbers were released. This seemed a prima facie violation of the SEC's Rule 10b5 prohibiting any material omission or misrepresentation in the purchase or sale of a security.

In August 2009, the SEC sued Bank of America for failing to disclose to its shareholders Merrill's true deteriorating condition prior to the shareholder vote on the deal in December 2008. The SEC calculated that the losses added up to more than one-third of the deal's value, representing a fundamental change to the deal. "Nevertheless," said the SEC, "despite its representation that it would update shareholders, BOA kept them in the dark as they were asked to vote on the proposed merger." The bank sought to settle the case with the SEC, which was under some political pressure not to further weaken the damaged firm. But the presiding judge, Jed Rakoff, rejected the proposed settlement. The SEC and B of A then negotiated a much stiffer fine of $150 million; at this writing, Judge Rakoff is weighing whether to accept the new settlement.

Meanwhile, Bank of America is also being sued by the California Public Employees' Retirement System (CalPERS) and the California State Teachers' Retirement System (CalSTRS), the two huge California state pension funds, which together owned $38.5 million in B of A shares and suffered a loss in excess of $200 million. The suit contends that B of A management had a plain duty to disclose to shareholders what had been learned about Merrill's diminished condition prior to the December 5 vote.

As Cuomo's probe, congressional hearings, and further investigation by the Congressional Oversight Panel revealed, Lewis raised with Paulson and Bernanke the possibility of backing out of the deal at several meetings in December. Paulson threatened to fire him and his whole board. Bernanke wrote his colleagues in an e-mail that he viewed Lewis's threat to invoke the MAC clause as "a bargaining chip, and we do not view this as credible at all." In the end, a shaken Lewis went ahead with the deal, causing B of A stock to bottom out at under $4 a share. It has since recovered to about $15, courtesy of serial taxpayer bailouts.

What's curious is not just the threats. Bernanke and Paulson were right to worry that if the deal blew up, it would be massively destabilizing for the still very fragile financial system. What's odd is that they also flatly closed the door on a renegotiation of the deal's terms. After all, the JPMorgan Chase/ Bear Stearns deal had to be renegotiated back in March 2008, after a drafting error was discovered in the legal documents. This gave Bear some belated leverage, but by then both the government and JPMorgan Chase realized that the initial $2-a-share fire-sale price was unjustifiably cheap, and the deal was quickly quintupled to $10 a share. The broader effect on money markets was exactly nothing.

By the same token, it was obvious by December 2009 that charging Bank of America $50 billion for a mortally wounded Merrill Lynch was highway robbery. But Bernanke and Paulson had Lewis right where they wanted him, were disdainful of the damage to the larger acquiring institution and its shareholders, and slammed the door on any kind of renegotiation. It's hard to avoid the conclusion that Merrill Lynch was just a more intimate member of the Wall Street club than Bank of America, an outsider institution founded by an immigrant that had grown into America's largest bank. B of A, whose headquarters had been in San Francisco, moved to Charlotte, North Carolina, after a big merger with Nations Bank, formerly North Carolina National Bank. But compared with outfits like Goldman, Morgan, and Citi, it was a Wall Street outsider. To be sure, many of the errors and blunders were those of Ken Lewis. But once again, the odor of double standard hung over the behavior of the Fed and the Treasury. In effect, one arm of the government, the Treasury and the Fed, coerced a private firm to commit what had all the elements of an illegal act—and then another arm of the government, the SEC, proposed to penalize the firm for complying. Shades of Kafka!

As Elizabeth Warren, chair of the Congressional Oversight Panel, aptly wrote to Treasury Secretary Geithner,

> [T]his interaction among Treasury, the Board, and B of A is a warning of the dangers that can arise when the government acts simultaneously as regulator, lender of last resort, and shareholder. [Treasury had purchased $15 billion in convertible preferred stock and warrants of B of A on October 28, 2008; as indicated above, it purchased an additional $20 billion of B of A preferred stock and warrants on January 16, 2009.] The TARP by its very nature creates conflicts of interest for Treasury and the Board. The conflicts can arise not only when the nation's senior financial officials are faced with decisions by a private institution that they believe would adversely affect the stability plan, but also when they are asked to make regulatory decisions that affect the institutions in which the government holds shares.

Wall Street versus Main Street

An even more fundamental double standard was in the way big, money-center banks were treated compared with the treatment of smaller community banks that typically serve smaller businesses. Commercial banks with holding company affiliates, such as Citi, got into trouble by creating, trading, and investing in exotic securities. Though their more clever brothers such as Goldman created junk only to sell it off (and even short it), Citi's own portfolios were disproportionately clogged with these bad bets. The same was true of the feckless investment banks such as Bear Stearns, Merrill Lynch, Lehman Brothers, and Morgan Stanley. The first three went out of business as independent firms. Morgan Stanley survived only with substantial government aid, on terms almost as generous as those granted to Citi.

But smaller commercial banks, for the most part, did not go in for this brand of gambling. Despite their theoretical right, after the 1999 repeal of the Glass-Steagall Act, to underwrite securities if they so chose, they were either not large enough or just not inclined to enter that risky business. Rather, their portfolios were mostly in traditional commercial and residential loans.

Thousands of small and medium-size community banks were the unsung heroes of this whole sorry affair, because they stuck to their knitting and did not lower their standards. But independent commercial banks that had behaved more prudently suffered nonetheless because of the general spillover of the havoc wrought by Wall Street. Many ordinary businesses and consumers, hit hard by the recession, fell behind in their loan repayments; loan portfolios that looked just fine in 2006 did not look so good in 2009. A survey of 773 smaller banks by the Aite Group, conducted for the Independent Community Bankers of America (ICBA) in early 2009, found that 73 percent reported an increase in delinquencies and defaults since the crisis began.

But because these institutions did not pose any systemic risk, few received any TARP money. Instead, they often received the third degree from business-as-usual bank examiners, who required smaller banks to raise additional capital or increase their loan-loss reserves. In 2008, regulators increased required bank capital ratios from 8 percent of loans to 10 percent, and they increased them again in 2009 to 12 percent in cases where banks had a large volume of real estate loans. To add insult to injury, community banks found themselves with an increase in the premiums paid to the dwindling FDIC insurance fund.

A new emergency premium, to be assessed on the 8,305 federally insured institutions on June 30, 2009, was 20 cents for every $100 of their insured deposits. That compares with an average premium of 6.3 cents paid by banks and thrifts in 2008. And then in October 2009, facing near insolvency of the FDIC's funds after 106 bank failures, the FDIC required the banks to pay three years' premiums in advance. This was small change for the big houses like Goldman and Morgan Stanley, which did not go in for retail deposits, but a large hit for smaller banks.

In addition, an analysis by Dean Baker of the Center for Economic and Policy Research found that the spread in the cost of funds between small banks and big ones widened significantly after the Treasury and Fed first got into the bailout business with the Bear Stearns rescue. Using public-record data from the FDIC, Baker calculated that between 2000 and the first quarter of 2007, the cost of funds for small banks was only about a quarter point (0.29 percent) more than for large ones, defined as banks with over $100 billion in assets. But from late 2008 through 2009, when investors took for granted that large banks would be bailed out, that spread widened to more than three-quarters of a point (0.78 percent), a significant competitive disadvantage. Baker calculated that this taxpayer subsidy to the eighteen largest banks during that period totaled $34.1 billion a year.

The August 2009 report of the Congressional Oversight Panel, criticizing the double standard in favor of large Wall Street banks, observed, "Small banks' troubled assets are generally whole loans, but Treasury's main program for removing troubled assets from banks' balance sheets, the PPIP [Geithner's program to encourage speculation in depressed securities] will at present address only troubled mortgage securities and not whole loans."

Members of the Independent Community Bankers of America, representing all but the very largest banks, complained bitterly about this double standard, and so did several of the presidents of regional Federal Reserve Banks outside New York. Jack Hopkins, president of CorTrust, a $550 million South Dakota commercial bank, told a Senate Banking Committee hearing, "Community banks played no part in causing the financial crisis and have watched as taxpayer dollars have been used to bail out Wall Street investment firms and our nation's largest banks considered 'too big to fail.' During this same time period, dozens of community banks have been allowed to fail while the largest and most interconnected banks have been spared the same fate due to government intervention."

Hopkins, testifying on behalf of the ICBA, described "a very harsh examination environment from field examiners" and a "disconnect between the public statements from policymakers [promoting expansion of credit] in Washington and the treatment of local banks during examinations." He told of one banker who "called the regulator to inquire about receiving TARP funds [and] he was questioned as to why he needed the money. When he explained he wanted to supplement his capital position and also make more loans, the regulator told him the agency didn't want banks making more loans in this environment. This attitude has led many community banks to conclude there is reluctance to extending TARP money to community banks and that the program was primarily designed to assist large, troubled banks. Community banks in danger of failing would not be eligible for TARP funds."

Thomas Hoenig, the president of the Federal Reserve Bank of Kansas City and the longest serving of the regional Fed bank presidents, repeatedly argued against the favoritism shown money-center banks at the expense of non–Wall Street banks. "The banks that behaved well are getting little if any help," he told me, "while the ones that caused the crisis are getting taxpayer bailouts."

In short, you could only get TARP money if you didn't really need it— unless you were a big Wall Street bank. In that case, the Fed and the Treasury would keep making up program categories to find one that justified a massive bailout.

Stressing Credulity

From the perspective of smaller traditional bankers, the "stress tests" for the nineteen largest financial institutions, created by the Treasury and the Federal Reserve in the spring of 2009, rubbed their noses in the double standard. The very term *stress test* is financial industry jargon for a modeling exercise that is supposed to determine how a class of investment will perform under adverse circumstances. The stress tests are typically devised by the bank's own staff, and their accuracy depends entirely on their assumptions. In the great collapse of 2007–09, not only did investments and institutions fail but so did the banks' stress tests.

The Bernanke-Geithner stress tests of April 2009 were a cynical device to build public confidence in busted financial institutions, and not incidentally to restore faith in their pummeled share prices. In effect, they were reverse-engineered. The conclusion came first—they were literally designed so that no institution would fail.

When he announced the results on May 7, Fed chairman Bernanke declared that "more than 150 examiners, supervisors, and economists" had conducted several weeks of examinations of the banks. But if you do the arithmetic, that is about seven examiners per bank, and all of the stress-tested nineteen banks were $100-billion-and-up outfits! When an ordinary commercial bank, say a $10 billion institution, undergoes a far less complex routine examination of its commercial loan portfolio, it involves dozens of examiners. The stress tests were not true audits of just what was on the banks' balance sheet; they were modeling exercises, relying on the banks' own accounting, rigged so that all would pass.

To nobody's great surprise, the stress tests happily revealed that no major bank was insolvent, and the nineteen largest banks collectively needed to raise only about $75 billion in additional capital, although their losses might total as much as $599 billion. Citigroup, queen of the zombie banks, remarkably enough, was said to need only $5.5 billion in additional private capital. You could make up that paltry sum with a fraction of Citi's executive bonuses.

In early 2009, there was one other huge regulatory favor to large money-center banks. The normal accounting standards, which are set by an independent nonprofit body, the Financial Accounting Standards Board, require banks' balance sheets to mark down depressed assets to their current market value. Otherwise, investors and regulators have no way of telling what a bank is really worth. But the industry campaigned for a suspension of the markdown requirement, and both the Treasury and key congressional leaders applied extreme pressure to the FASB until it buckled.

The suspension of mark-to-market accounting, undertaken very reluctantly in April 2009 by a split vote of the FASB, was made retroactive to

January 1, 2009, and enabled even banks as deeply wounded as Citi and Bank of America to report first-quarter profits thanks to creative bookkeeping. These misleading results, in turn, served the goal of Treasury and the Fed to use the rosy "stress tests" results to restore confidence. For example, Bank of New York Mellon was able to book a onetime increase in first-quarter 2009 earnings of $676 million (on net income of $322 million) after retroactively implementing FASB's more lax standard on valuing toxic assets. Banks took advantage of the new rule through simple accounting manipulations. As the Congressional Oversight Panel's investigation found, banks "moved securities from their trading account to available-for-sale and held-to-maturity accounts to take them out of an automatic mark-to-market classification and into classifications that fall under the new rule." The panel further warned, "[T]he new rule reduces investor transparency as institutions are not required to use observable market inputs if the bank managers consider the market to be 'distressed.' As such, investors have difficulty valuing assets that fall under the new rule."

But while the large Wall Street banks could use the FASB suspension of mark-to-market accounting to make their balance sheets and reported earnings look a lot better than they really were, this form of inventive accounting was not available to the smaller banks whose assets were mainly in the form of whole loans and not exotic securities. The FASB suspension of mark-to-market accounting did not apply to traditional loans. Either the loan was performing (being paid on time), or it wasn't. If the borrower was late in paying interest or principal, the bank had to come up with more capital. Once again, small banks and their real-economy clients were paying for the sins of large ones.

The clients, in many cases, were small businesses. And though the stock market rebounded smartly in the second half of 2009, the small-business sector of the economy, which generates most of the jobs, was dead in the water. Smaller banks, under the gun to strengthen their balance sheets, were reducing lines of credit—even though their own cost of money was close to zero. With one hand, the administration was making credit as loose as possible. With the other, it was discouraging banks from extending it to retail customers.

When I put this question to Tim Geithner in December 2009, he acknowledged that the problem was dire. "Small businesses are harmed four different ways," he said thoughtfully. "The community banks, which are small businesses' main source of credit, are reducing their balance sheets. These banks have taken a huge hit from commercial real estate. Small businesses also rely on credit card borrowing and home equity loans for working capital, and these sources of credit are also less available." Good points—but Geithner had no effective policy for addressing the problems. Only in February 2010 did the administration, under pressure from Congress, belatedly propose $30 billion in TARP funds for small-business lending.

According to FDIC officials, hundreds more community banks, the prime source of small-business lending, are expected to go broke in 2010, further restricting bank credit. What to do? Goldman to the rescue! One member of the administration economic team pointed to a small program at Goldman Sachs, which doesn't do much retail lending, in which Goldman offered to take small-business loans off the books of community banks at a substantial discount. This official thought that hedge funds might be induced to lend money to small businesses—at 14 percent interest. "If you are shut out of credit markets entirely," he told me, "14 percent isn't so bad"—this at a time when the Fed's short-term lending rate to Wall Street banks was zero.

When Government Got Tough: The Auto Rescue

Another stunning case of double standard was the difference between the Obama administration's treatment of the faltering auto industry and its coddling of Wall Street's biggest banks. Domestic manufacturing has been the stepchild of public policy for at least three decades. Except where national defense is concerned, administrations of both parties have disdained the idea of industrial policies, and government has increasingly taken the view that it doesn't matter where production is located. US trade policy has turned a blind eye to the mercantilist maneuvers of other nations in practice, as long as they genuflected to "free trade" in theory. Wall Street's goal of opening up the world's financial markets has taken precedence over a level playing field for US manufacturers.

Business-oriented US administrations and their corporate allies reasoned that it didn't really matter where production was located as long as the parent company made a profit. There were, however, two huge hidden costs to this policy. One was our chronic and widening trade deficit. The less we made, the more we had to import. The other cost was a cumulative loss of basic manufacturing capacity.

Of course, government policy alone was not the entire cause of this erosion. Some large companies, such as General Motors, simply failed to make competitive products. Though unions have been blamed for the declining fortunes of basic industries like autos and steel, the fact is that Germany has stronger unions and better-paid workers, but it has a national commitment to industrial excellence. Even Japan pays its factory workers wages comparable to those earned by Americans. Neither nation has a system where individual corporations are stuck with costly health and pension benefits, and both have governments that care where production is located.

As Detroit lost market share, it also lost political influence. The declining clout of the automakers, compared with the permanent influence of Wall Street, is perfectly captured in this tale of two bailouts. The auto restructuring also provides a blueprint of what the banking policy might have been, if the administration had shown the same backbone in its dealings with Wall Street that it did with Detroit.

At the time the Obama administration took over, GM was hemorrhaging money. The Bush administration, in its waning days, had reluctantly advanced the automakers money from the TARP program. Though supposedly a free-market conservative, Bush did not want the auto industry to collapse on his watch. But his administration had no systematic plan for restructuring the automakers. So, unlike the Geithner policy for the banks, which in many ways was a holdover from the Bush administration, the Obama auto policy began with a clean slate.

The auto executives badly bungled their initial plea to Congress, having flown to Washington on private jets. In December, Josh Bolten, Bush's chief of staff, attempted to work with Nancy Pelosi on a temporary fix, but Congress's attitude was hardening. Finally, after a round of concessions by the United Auto Workers and key bondholders, who agreed in principle to swap their debt for equity, the Bush administration agreed to provide a loan of $17.4 billion from TARP funds to GM and Chrysler (Ford decided it could survive without government funds). This was just enough money to hand the problem to the new administration.

Between the election and the inauguration, there were leaks indicating that Obama intended to appoint a "Car Czar" to work out the terms of a rescue and restructuring of the auto industry. Weeks went by with no announcement. Behind the scenes, the administration was trying to clear the way to name yet another influential Wall Street investment banker, Steven Rattner. But Rattner's private equity fund, the Quadrangle Group, was the subject of a criminal investigation for alleged payoffs to intermediaries to win contracts with the New York State pension fund. Summers and Geithner wanted Rattner, but the White House political operatives could not decide whether he was an acceptable risk.

On February 12, the White House astonished Washington, Detroit, and Wall Street by hiring Ron Bloom, a trade unionist and political radical, as chief of an auto industry task force reporting to Treasury Secretary Geithner. A week later, Rattner was added to the task force and in effect became Bloom's co-director, a lower-profile solution that the White House hoped would be consistent with Rattner's legal complications. For several months, the two worked together on the auto deal, but as Quadrangle's problems mounted, Rattner resigned in July.

Bloom is literally a category of one. He had begun his union career as an organizer for the Service Employees International Union. He soon came to appreciate that labor and capital were no match, and he became intrigued with what a small number of trade unionists, beginning in the 1970s, called "capital strategies." Bloom got himself admitted to the Harvard Business School, earned his MBA, and went to work on Wall Street for firms that provided expert advice to unions in restructuring deals where workers were asked to trade wage and benefit cuts for a share of company ownership. But Bloom went far beyond simply helping unions make sure workers' interests were fairly represented, and he became an architect of innovative restructuring deals. He apprenticed at Lazard Frères under famed investment banker Felix Rohatyn, then became a partner in a small firm devoted entirely to helping unions do financial deals. Bloom later returned to the labor movement as a special adviser to the president of the United Steelworkers. Bloom is widely credited with helping to reinvent a leaner and more competitive domestic steel industry that still makes room for unionized workers.

Having worked on Wall Street as an innovative analyst and architect of restructurings, Bloom won the respect of Obama's economic team. He was also valued as a man who was trusted by the unions and could persuade them to support a bargain that entailed painful cuts in wages and benefits. Having been a key strategist in labor negotiations for more than two decades, Bloom also could be tough as nails with industry.

The deals that Bloom and Rattner eventually worked out for General Motors were light-years away from the deals that Bernanke and Geithner had struck for the big Wall Street banks. Concessions, and direct government engagement, that were supposedly impossible in the case of the money-center banks suddenly became possible for GM and Chrysler.

In the deal that the government struck with GM, an expedited bankruptcy proceeding got a reorganized GM back in business in an almost inconceivable forty days. The government put in $65 billion of TARP money, becoming a majority shareholder. And the government's role was far more hands-on than in its light-touch treatment of favored Wall Street banks.

Hardball in the Public Interest

On February 17, GM and Chrysler submitted their restructuring plans to the Treasury task force. Bloom and Rattner, acting in the role of investment bankers on behalf of the government, rejected the plans as unrealistic and worked with the executives on more plausible ones. In late March, Rattner delivered the message to GM's CEO Rick Wagoner that he had to go. He was replaced by a new chief executive who was a GM veteran, Fritz Henderson, who was acceptable to the government. Henderson would soon be fired by the new board as hopelessly steeped in the old GM culture.

The Treasury's expedited bankruptcy was designed to allow a leaner GM to emerge, stripped of cost centers that were dragging it down, with a fighting chance for survival. Key to the deal was making both the UAW and GM's senior bondholders make major sacrifices. The union took steep wage cuts, and its pension fund traded preexisting guarantees of retiree and health payouts for the far shakier proposition of ownership of a large block of company stock. This was structured through a Voluntary Employee Benefit

Plan, a variation on a union health and pension fund. After some dickering, the union got $6.5 billion in GM stock, a 17.5 percent stake, plus warrants that could raise ownership share to 20 percent. Actual health and pension benefits were no longer guaranteed. They would depend on the health of the company, its dividend and share price.

Analysts had scoffed at the possibility of getting buy-in from the other major stakeholders—the owners of the automakers' debt. But the Treasury team, in this case, was willing to play real hardball. In the Chrysler negotiations, Bloom, Rattner, and the Treasury team offered a swap of equity for debt, compensating bondholders at just 29 cents on the dollar. Some big hedge funds balked, believing that if the debt holders bargained hard and hung together, they could get a better deal. But the government had an ace up its sleeve. About 70 percent of Chrysler's debt was held by four large banks that were recipients of TARP money: Citigroup, JPMorgan Chase, Goldman Sachs, and Morgan Stanley. These banks were advised that they were expected to take the deal. When the big banks agreed to settle at 29 cents on the dollar, the hedge funds, after some arm-twisting, followed.

President Obama had made it clear that Detroit had to be given one last chance. On March 30, he declared, "We cannot and must not, and we will not let our auto industry simply vanish," he said. "This industry is like no other—it's an emblem of the American spirit, a once and future symbol of America's success." Once the detailed negotiations began, he stayed fairly aloof. But in April, when the deal was hanging in the balance, the president took the uncharacteristic stance of publicly shaming the hedge funds that had been holding out for a better bargain. Announcing the Chrysler bankruptcy and restructuring on April 30, he declared, "[A] group of investment firms and hedge funds decided to hold out for the prospect of an unjustified taxpayer-funded bailout. They were hoping that everybody else would make sacrifices. Some demanded twice the return that other lenders were getting. I don't stand with them. I stand with Chrysler's employees and their families and communities."

Tom Lauria, a lawyer who represented Perella Weinberg, owner of a major hedge fund, told an interviewer that Rattner had threatened to destroy the firm's reputation if they tried to block the deal. The White House denied this, but Perella quickly caved. Somehow, the firm got the message. In the end, Chrysler's restructuring took just thirty-six days and GM's only forty. By August, stimulated by the government's Cash for Clunkers program, the automakers were scrambling to hire new workers.

This was the kind of White House that was absent in the public debates about the executive bonuses, the sweetheart deals, and the need for much tougher regulation of Wall Street. By fall, the very banks that had survived thanks to taxpayer bailouts were strenuously lobbying to kill any legislative or regulatory constraints on their toxic business models—and the administration was entirely quiet.

Consider all that happened in the auto deal that was supposedly impossible in the case of, say, Citigroup. Critics of the banking bailout, including this writer, have argued that the banking policy failed to do three things. It failed to radically restructure zombie banks as a condition of government aid. It did not demand of the banks a revised and plausible business plan. And the government did not require equitable burden sharing among all the "stakeholders," including employees and creditors. The leading economic officials of two administrations, Bush and Obama, argued that this course was not a good idea—government did not know enough about banking to second-guess bankers, government lacked the authority, and government should restore confidence, not rock the boat.

The auto restructuring gave the lie to these contentions and achieved all three goals—a radical restructuring; fair burden sharing among employees, executives, and bondholders; and close government oversight. Whether GM can ultimately build a car that consumers want to buy, of course, will be up to the ingenuity of GM.

But the GM and Chrysler deals showed that government had the leverage and the negotiating skills to bargain hard. The auto deals demonstrated that, with the right experts in charge, government could improve upon the myopic assumptions of industry executives. Several of the Wall Street deals—Bank of America's purchase of Merrill Lynch and Morgan's of Bear Stearns—also showed that the Treasury and the Fed could drive a hard bargain—but on behalf of a powerful set of insiders, not taxpayers.

A Corporate State

The remarks of Lawrence Summers, which serve as an epigraph to this chapter, come from a major policy address that Summers delivered to the Council on Foreign Relations on the eve of the June 2009 release of the administration's financial reform program. Summers was repeating an argument he had made repeatedly inside the administration: The government, in his view, is no good at managing companies, even companies bailed out at taxpayer expense. Obama evidently agreed, for he took Summers's advice that his recovery program should be based on propping up and bailing out failed private financial institutions, not transforming them—or the financial system.

In fact, Summers's comment reflected an ignorance of American history. Twice before—in the 1930s with the Reconstruction Finance Corporation, and again in the 1990s through the Resolution Trust Corporation that cleaned up the private sector's savings-and-loan disaster—government in fact had proven far better than Wall Street at recapitalizing failed banks and managing them in the public interest until their assets could be sorted out and the banks returned to health.

The habits of crony capitalism are odious not just for the conflicts of interest and the grotesque rewards to insiders—but because they stand between Obama and a robust economic recovery.

Simon Johnson analogizes the US financial morass to familiar crises that he dealt with as chief economist of the International Monetary Fund. The common element, he argues, is simple corruption—top government officials using public funds to protect or revive busted cronies in the financial elite, thus prolonging the crisis. In a startling piece published in *The Atlantic* in May 2009, Johnson compared the US to other corrupt cases that the IMF had dealt with over the years. "The challenges the United States faces are familiar territory to the people at the IMF," Johnson wrote. "If you hid the name of the country and just showed them the numbers, there is no doubt what old IMF hands would say: nationalize troubled banks and break them up as necessary." Johnson's article was a bombshell. It marked his break with the global financial elite. The insight was less remarkable for what it said than for who was saying it.

By early 2010, after nearly three years of financial crisis, the outlines of a new economic order in America were becoming distressingly clear. As in the 1930s, the government had amassed increased power over the private market economy. Interventions that had been unthinkable before early 2007 became commonplace. Government was deeply and reluctantly involved in industries from banking to autos. Yet despite Obama's rhetoric of deep change, the understood purpose of these interventions was not to reshape the balance of power in the larger political economy, but *to shore up the status quo*. The Treasury and the Federal Reserve, the latter institution largely shielded from public or congressional accountability, were making decisions, often on the fly without stated criteria, about which of America's largest banks and corporations shall live and which ones shall die; which ones shall enjoy massive government subsidies and loans from the Federal Reserve, and which shall be left to the brutal verdicts of what was left of free markets.

The 1930s also saw a very substantial increase in government's power. But there was one huge difference. In the '30s, that power was wielded on behalf of a drastically reformed economy. Government policy put in place constraints on economic concentration and on the financial liberties taken by Wall Street, direct public sponsorship of projects to benefit the common man and woman, and legal and political support for trade unions and mutual institutions as counterweights to private financial power. By contrast, in the era after the Crash of 2007, the increased state power, if anything, reinforced the financial elite, now with the additional weight of government intervention.

In the years after Roosevelt, the state, a more engaged citizenry, a strengthened trade union movement, and a mostly progressive Democratic Party roughly offset the concentrated economic and political power of organized finance. Even under the Republican Eisenhower administration, a well-regulated economy was aptly characterized by economist John Kenneth Galbraith's concept of "countervailing power." Government was the flywheel. In that era, it sounded ridiculous when archaic Marxists characterized the state as "the executive committee of the ruling class." But in the Bush and Obama eras, the Fed and the Treasury often behaved precisely as the Washington branch of Wall Street. For this collusion, Obama was attacked as a socialist!

The disgrace of the reign of finance created an opportunity to build a radically different economy and to energize a resurgence of progressive politics. Instead, it brought us closer to a corporate state.

CHAPTER FIVE

Obama's Loyal Opposition

Too big to fail has failed.

—THOMAS HOENIG, president,
Federal Reserve Bank of Kansas City

One of the hallmarks of failed national policy is presidential reliance on insiders who live in a bubble where dissenting voices are excluded and the conventional wisdom becomes an echo chamber of reinforcement. Supposedly, the insiders—the best and brightest—simply know more than the critics. Lyndon Johnson's Vietnam fiasco was one classic case of this pathology. Herbert Hoover's reliance on Wall Street advisers was another, George W. Bush's certitude that Iraq was behind the 9/11 attacks was a third.

For Obama's senior economic aides and their Wall Street allies, there was only one path to recovery, and it required first and foremost the restoration of profits in the financial industry. However, there were plenty of other available experts, inside and outside the administration, equally or more knowledgeable, recommending an entirely different and more effective approach. For the most part, they were marginalized or ignored.

One such group included some of the members of Obama's own core economic team, such as economic advisers Jared Bernstein, Christina Romer, and Austan Goolsbee. But because of the dominance of Summers and Geithner, reinforced by Rahm Emanuel, the mild dissenters within the administration had to watch their backs. Summers and Geithner were fanatic on the subject of loyalty. "Not a team player" was one of Geithner's most damning expressions and a label to be avoided.

The most important voices pressing for an entirely different approach to recovery and reform have been outside the administration. They included

House Speaker Nancy Pelosi, some congressional committee chairs, individual back-bench senators and representatives, and government agencies beyond direct White House control, as well as dissenting economists such as Joseph Stiglitz and Paul Krugman. Taken together, their work shows the better path that might have been—and could still be.

New COP on the Beat

Of the administration's loyal opposition inside Washington, the two shrewdest and best-informed agencies were the Congressional Oversight Panel (COP) and the FDIC, both headed by tough, knowledgeable, and principled women, Elizabeth Warren and Sheila Bair, respectively—and both beyond the immediate control of the White House and Treasury. The panel was legislated as part of the Emergency Economic Stabilization Act passed in October 2008 creating Hank Paulson's $700 billion TARP bailout program. COP was given the broad authority to hold hearings, issue monthly reports, and request documents from the Treasury. The same legislation also created a companion investigative body headed by a special inspector general for TARP, who worked closely with the panel. Taken together, the several thousand pages of hearings and reports of the panel and the inspector general provide the most comprehensive and coherent available critique of administration policy on the bailout of Wall Street.

The legislation authorized the Democratic House Speaker and Senate majority leader to appoint three of the panel's five members, with the other two being named by their Republican counterparts. For his pick, Senate majority leader Harry Reid tapped Warren, a Harvard law professor specializing in bankruptcy law. Warren's knowledge of bankruptcy took her into the issue of why households were going broke at record rates, even before the 2007 bust. She wrote a popular book with her daughter, Amelia Warren Tyagi, *The Two-Income Trap,* on the economic squeeze facing middle-class families. Part of this story reflected predatory financial abuses, and Warren was the leading proponent of a financial product safety commission. She was the kind of regulatory progressive that Obama had avoided appointing to key economic positions in his administration. Though Warren did not begin her term as a full-spectrum expert on the entire banking system, she was a very quick learner, and she sensed the vacuum of informed progressive criticism of the administration approach.

Warren was born in Oklahoma in 1949 and vividly remembers her parents' and grandparents' recollections of the Great Depression and Roosevelt. "People like my grandparents knew two things about Roosevelt," she says. "He made it safe for you to put your money in banks, and he put the government on the side of helping ordinary folks." Warren was taken completely by surprise when Senator Reid, whom she had never met, phoned to ask her to serve on the panel. When her phone rang, she did not even recognize the name, and mistook him for a state senator. Senate sources say Ted Kennedy suggested her to the majority leader.

The two other Democratic members of the panel, Damon Silvers of the AFL-CIO and Richard Nieman, the New York State superintendent of banks, agreed that Warren should serve as chair, and the COP began work in December 2008. It would spend the next year in a series of skirmishes with Geithner's Treasury that reveal the larger fault lines of financial reform.

As one of the nation's leading experts on bankruptcy, Warren has strong views on how a capitalist system should deal with failed companies, and her views are quite at odds with the Paulson-Geithner-Summers position. As Warren explains, bankruptcy is our system's method of dealing with capitalism's inevitable casualties. Bankruptcy, she says, "is where you take your failures." Bankruptcy treads a nice line between averting unnecessary wider damage on the one hand, and not creating incentives for risky behavior on the other. For the most part, the bankruptcy remedy works well. When a company finds itself effectively insolvent, it can use a bankruptcy proceeding to wipe out its debts and reorganize itself with a relatively clean slate. But the company can't just stiff its creditors willy-nilly. The process is all carried out under the supervision of a federal judge and requires a comprehensive and accurate accounting of assets and liabilities.

Typically, in a Chapter 11 proceeding, shareholders are wiped out, and bondholders get in line with other creditors for a piece of the remains. Once an accounting of assets and liabilities is performed (by an independent outside party who reports to the judge), the creditors can then be paid at so many cents on the dollar as part of a court-supervised reorganization plan that also considers what resources are needed for a viable successor company to continue operating. For instance, the plan would not permit auctioning off plant and equipment of a viable enterprise to satisfy creditors.

During this whole process, a court appointee, not incumbent management, is in charge. Sometimes, the judge concludes that management was not culpable for the firm's failure (which might have been caused by wider business conditions) and allows managers to keep their jobs. In other cases, where management is seen as weak, incompetent, or at fault, top managers are replaced as part of the reorganization. Sometimes, when it is too far gone, the company simply shuts its doors, under a different chapter of the bankruptcy code, and the remains go to creditors. The differences between this process for dealing with failed enterprises and the Paulson-Geithner-Summers-Bernanke approach to propping up zombie banks could not be more stark.

With the bankruptcy system (and its counterpart for failed banks, known as resolution or receivership), investors and executives have fair warning that if an enterprise goes bust, they will lose their stake. Entrepreneurs know that if they take excessive risks, they are likely to lose their jobs as well as the value of their stock. By allowing a reorganization under court supervision, we permit the viable assets, including plant, equipment, goodwill, and workers' jobs, to have an afterlife. And by refusing to bail out the casualties, government allows capitalism to work as advertised. Government avoids creating what economists call the "moral hazard" of inviting excessive risks by just mopping up the losses and making failed executives and their shareholders whole. The American system of bankruptcy works much better than the European counterpart, in which the penalties for failure are so draconian that it is seldom used, and very large companies that fail are typically taken over by the state or given subsidies to continue operating.

"For years," Warren says, "large companies tried to argue that they were indispensable and tried to get government aid. But for the most part, government held the line. The Chrysler bailout of 1979 was a breach, but it was not repeated. The bailout of Continental Illinois Bank was done under the bankruptcy laws, and shareholders were wiped out.

"In the 1990s, Enron went crazy looking for a bailout. They dominated futures markets in electricity. They argued that if we go down, the lights will go out all over America. But government said no. Then along came Bear Stearns, which got direct government help. We pinned five dollars to the dog's collar and hoped that somebody would take him."

At the time, Bear Stearns seemed to be another one-off, like the government-engineered emergency rescues of Chrysler in the late 1970s and of Long-Term Capital Management in the late 1990s—just three such bailouts in four decades. But as Warren observes, the whole world changed with the October 2008 passage of the TARP program and the way Paulson, Geithner, and Summers went about implementing it. Suddenly, in broad swaths of American capitalism, *there was no penalty for failure.* Government was guaranteeing the whole financial system, or at least those parts of it deemed large enough to pose wider risks to the system. "The banking system had to be saved," Warren says, "but the idea that American taxpayers should put our money behind equity [shareholders] of particular banks was something brand new and dangerous."

In September 2008, as Fannie Mae, Lehman, AIG, Merrill Lynch, Washington Mutual, and others were collapsing or being rescued, Warren was starting the fall semester of her bankruptcy course. "I taught Lehman on Monday, and AIG on Tuesday," she says. "I asked my students to think about what AIG meant. You could see the wheels turning. After a while I called on a student, who more or less spoke for the whole class. AIG meant, the student said, that if you make yourself big enough and interconnected enough to everyone else, the government bails you out. And that's exactly what it meant. For the first time, government was standing behind equity."

Warren felt passionately that this was the wrong way to proceed. So when she became chair of the Congressional Oversight Panel just a few months later, she became a relentless force for questioning why the government did not use something more akin to the bankruptcy process for failed banks. In an early conversation with Neel Kashkari, the young investment banker from Goldman whom Paulson had named to head the TARP program, Warren pressed Kashkari on why Citigroup's shareholders should be bailed out. Why should Citi be propped up rather than broken up? Kashari's answer: We don't want government owning banks, and we want private money coming back in. Warren found that rationale, which continued under Summers and Geithner, completely unconvincing and perverse. "The way you get new money to come in," she says, "is to wipe out the old debts, in a bankruptcy proceeding. And the way you get government off the hook is to use a resolution process similar to a bankruptcy so that the bank can be returned to new private ownership with a clean balance sheet."

Ordinarily, the vice chairman or deputy chairman of this sort of oversight body represents the minority party. But through a fluke in the hastily written TARP legislation, this was not required. So a second Democratic appointee of the oversight panel, Damon Silvers, was designated by Warren to serve as vice chairman. Silvers had been appointed jointly by Majority Leader Reid and House Speaker Pelosi. His day job is associate policy director and special counsel to the president of the AFL-CIO, in charge of issues involving capital markets. But that title understates his expertise. The labor movement gets involved with issues of financial market regulation and corporate governance through its defense of members' pensions, its occasional use of proxy fights in labor disputes, and its general interest in how capitalism is regulated. Silvers is universally regarded as the labor movement's best-informed expert on all of these issues, and one of Washington's most effective left-of-center players on financial regulatory policy.

And if labor was to be represented on the panel, it was logical that capital should get a seat—except that the banking industry was well represented all too well by the panel's two Republicans, former New Hampshire senator John Sununu and Texas representative Jeb Hensarling. However, the third Democrat on the panel, Richard Nieman, is a former longtime bank executive who spent much of his career at Citigroup.

Nieman could charitably be described as a Wall Street Democrat. Before being named to the post of state banking commissioner, he spent ten years at Citigroup rising to the position of general counsel of the Global Equities Group, and then he became director of regulatory affairs—chief lobbyist—for the accounting giant PricewaterhouseCoopers. Nieman often wrangled with the other two Democrats on the panel. The fact that one of the three Democrats on the COP needed to be a Wall Street ally is a telling indicator of the quiet influence exercised by financial elites, day in and day out, even in a financial crisis of the industry's own making.

The panel's reports walked a tightrope between open opposition and nuanced critiques of elements of the administration program, but they added up to a devastating and well-documented indictment. Professor Warren herself became something of a public figure and more effectively staked out a coherent dissenting analysis than either of the congressional banking committee chairmen. The panel left little doubt that they would have preferred a "resolution" approach to the problem of zombie banks rather than the Treasury strategy of propping them up.

As the oversight panel kept reporting, you could cherry-pick indicators of financial health, such as narrowing spreads between ultra-safe Treasury securities and ordinary forms of credit, and make it seem as if market conditions were improving. But the fact remained that in practice, credit was hard to come by for a great many borrowers. Geithner blamed this on the depressed conditions in the rest of the economy—creditworthy customers were just not borrowing. For Warren and Silvers, it was an indication of a continuing negative feedback loop in which weak banks, weakened lending, and weak consumer demand were dragging one another down.

The panel and the special inspector general regularly called attention to the multiple conflicts of interest in Geithner's bailout schemes. Testifying before the House Committee on Oversight and Government Reform on July 22, Inspector General Barofsky bluntly declared, "TARP has become a program in which taxpayers (i) are not being told what most of the TARP recipients are doing with their money, (ii) have still not been told how much their substantial investments are worth, and (iii) will not be told the full details of how their money is being invested."

The inspector general was particularly aggrieved that Treasury had refused to impose adequate conflict-of-interest requirements on private financial firms working with the TARP program. He testified, "Conflicts of interest and collusion vulnerabilities were inherent in the design of Public Private Investment Partnership," adding that managers of the funds backed by the Treasury "will have significant power to set prices in a largely illiquid market. These vulnerabilities could result in PPIP managers having an incentive to overpay significantly for assets or otherwise using the valuable, proprietary PPIP trading information."

The TARP legislation required Treasury to send the panel any document that it requested, yet Treasury often put the panel through a slow roll or claimed that it didn't have the information, or that it contained trade secrets.

Treasury also hid behind its close partner, the Federal Reserve, over which the panel had no oversight authority. Since Bernanke and Geithner worked hand-in-glove, it was often difficult to detect which initiatives came from Treasury and which from the Fed. Among the information the panel tried and failed to get was:

- *What value did the Treasury place on the toxic assets that were clogging bank balance sheets?* Treasury either didn't know, didn't want to know, or wouldn't share the information. Warren pressed Geithner for the data at several hearings and in follow-up correspondence, but she never got it.
- *What exactly happened during September and October among Lehman, AIG, and Goldman? What were the exact terms of the derivatives entered into between AIG and Goldman? What role did Goldman CEO Lloyd Blankfein and Goldman play in meetings with Treasury and the Fed about what to do about AIG?*
- *Why did Treasury treat the huge bailout of AIG as a pass-through of tens of billions of dollars to Goldman Sachs and other banks, even though the underlying securities that were insured via AIG credit default swaps were not yet in default?* Treasury entirely stonewalled where AIG and Goldman were concerned; some information on the AIG deal eventually came out via Cuomo's investigation, press leaks, and a separate investigation by the House Government Affairs Committee.
- *What exactly was in the $306 billion of toxic assets that the Treasury had guaranteed for Citigroup as part of the November 2008 bailout? Was this figure book value or market value?* Treasury repeatedly balked. Cuomo finally obtained some of this information from Citi by threat of subpoena.
- *What formula did the Treasury use for the stress tests conducted on the nineteen largest financial institutions?* Geithner repeatedly promised this information to the panel, but ultimately he claimed that it belonged to the Federal Reserve.

In a revealing exchange between Geithner and Damon Silvers, Geithner insisted that the purpose of the stress tests was to demonstrate the true condition of the banks, in a highly transparent way, so that they could attract the additional private investment capital they needed to strengthen their balance sheets. But Silvers had a very different view of Treasury's purpose. For Silvers, the very indulgent stress tests (which, remember, nobody failed and which were anything but transparent) were Treasury's signal to the markets that the government was guaranteeing the nation's largest banks, and therefore it was safe to invest in them. That in turn almost guaranteed that private capital would come in and that bank share prices would rebound from their lows. A lot of insiders would make a lot of quick money.

At the panel's September hearing, Silvers pressed Geithner. "Mr. Secretary," Silvers asked, "how can you be certain that what you didn't really do in the stress tests was signal that you, the Treasury Department and the Fed, were not going to further hammer the capital structures of these banks and that they could be invested in because there was an implicit guarantee behind them, even though they remain at their core not really functioning institutions or, to use the graphic term, zombies?"

Geithner ducked the question. He conceded that bank lending was down, but added, "The decline in bank lending has been more than offset by the increase in borrowing in the securities markets." Of course, small and medium-size business could not get their capital from the securities market—that's why we need banks. That led to the following exchange:

> **Mr. Silvers:** Is it really a good thing that essentially credit provision has moved away from the banking system [and] that most employers, most creators of jobs, can't access the bond market?
> **Secretary Geithner:** It is an interesting question. But remember, our banking system took on too much leverage.
> **Mr. Silvers:** Unquestionably.
> **Secretary Geithner:** So, inevitably, the banking system leverage was going to have to come down. That was a necessary thing. The consequence of that is you are going to see less growth in lending by banks.

Here was another core question that divided the administration from its critics: Was the revival of the securities market a reasonable substitute for bank lending? By propping up failing banks rather than putting them through a receivership and then getting them back to normal operations, the administration believed it was hastening the recovery. But it was prolonging the agony—just as its critics warned.

Backdoor Bailouts

In addition to its explicit bailouts, Treasury found a variety of ways to subsidize the big banks indirectly. One of the oversight panel's achievements was its revelation that the Treasury had been allowing banks to buy back warrants (the right to purchase common stock at a future date) at something like 66 cents on the dollar. As a condition of receiving TARP money, banks had to give the government preferred stock (which is more like a bond and pays a fixed interest rate) but also warrants. The purpose of this was to give taxpayers some of the upside gain, as the banks recovered their footing. However, Geithner and Summers were not enthusiastic about having government exercise any of the perquisites of ownership and were pleased to allow banks to buy back their warrants as soon as they could afford to, depriving government of future gain on the risks it had incurred.

When reports first surfaced that Treasury would permit this, Warren and the oversight panel were suspicious that the price would be too low, and they retained three independent experts to review the government's pricing formula. "We jumped on that like a duck on a june bug," Warren told me.

"Because these warrants represent the only opportunity for the taxpayer to participate directly in the increase in the share prices of these banks, made possible by public money, the price at which Treasury sells these warrants is critical," Warren testified to the House Financial Services Committee on July 22, 2009. As soon as the repurchase of the warrants was consummated by an initial group of eleven small banks, Warren's outside experts reviewed the price and the way it was derived. The experts were Robert Merton, a Nobel laureate, along with Daniel Bergstresser and Victoria Ivashina—all of the Harvard Business School. The panel directed them each to review Treasury's technical valuation model and the assumptions that were built in to the model, and not to communicate with one another. All three came up with estimates that varied by only a few percent, clustering right around 66 cents on the dollar, as explained by the panel in its July 2009 report.

Had other banks been permitted to buy back their warrants at this same discount, Warren testified, the loss to taxpayers would have been about $2.7 billion. Once, that was a huge sum. Had it been misspent on some social program, conservatives would have jumped all over the misfeasance. But since the context was a multitrillion-dollar bailout of banks, it seemed like petty cash. Thanks to the panel's work, however, Treasury was shamed into using a more accurate valuation. When the next round of warrants were repurchased, large banks such as US Bancorp, JPMorgan Chase, and Goldman Sachs had to pay 100 cents on the dollar. Goldman actually paid about 101 percent of the warrants' market value.

It was the second time that the oversight panel had hired independent experts and found that Treasury was covertly subsidizing the banks. In the initial infusion of capital in fall 2008, the panel found: "Treasury made its infusions at a substantial discount. Treasury received securities that were worth substantially less than the amounts it had paid in return. In all, Treasury overpaid by an estimated $78 billion. For each $100 Treasury invested in these financial institutions, it received on average stock and warrants worth only about $66 at the time of the transaction." By a bizarre coincidence, the discount was the same in both cases—66 cents on the dollar.

The bipartisan Congressional Oversight Panel was immediately suspicious of the very generous terms granted Citigroup. In its very first report, in December 2008, the panel compared recent comparable deals in which private investors put money into shaky banks, and the terms that they negotiated. The panel noted:

> Several major TARP recipient companies have received major capital investments recently, including Mitsubishi's investment in Morgan Stanley, Warren Buffett's investment in Goldman Sachs, and the Abu Dhabi Investment Group's investment in Citigroup. On October 14, 2008, Mitsubishi UFJ (MUFJ) Financial Group of Japan invested $9 billion in Morgan Stanley. In exchange, MUFJ received a 21% stake in the company through perpetual preferred shares with a 10% annual dividend.
>
> Warren Buffett announced on September 23, 2008 that he would invest $5 billion into Goldman Sachs. In return, Buffett's company,

Berkshire Hathaway, received perpetual preferred shares with a 10% annual dividend. If Goldman Sachs wishes to buy back the preferred stock, it can do so at a premium of 10%. Berkshire Hathaway also received warrants to purchase common stock at $115 per share, up to $5 billion within the next five years.

In November 2007, the Abu Dhabi Investment Authority invested $7.5 billion in Citigroup, amounting to 4.9% of Citigroup's equity. The Abu Dhabi Investment Authority received equity units that pay an 11% annual dividend and will be converted into common stock in 2010 or 2011 at a price between $31.83 and $37.24.

By contrast, the panel noted, Treasury was getting preferred stock that paid only 5 percent, and the bank has the option to redeem the stock at its face value whenever it chooses once it has sold enough other stock to shore up its balance sheet. Treasury also gets warrants to buy common stock, but these can also be bought back by the bank at bargain terms.

Helping Banks Gouge Consumers

A related problem was the tension between the administration's strategy of rebuilding bank balance sheets and the oversight panel's commitment to ridding the system of anti-consumer abuses. For instance, hidden bank overdraft fees and extortionate credit card charges were huge profit centers for banks. As other bank earnings have fallen, those fees have been increased. To that extent, the goal of protecting consumers was seemingly at odds with the goal of getting banks back to health. Limit gouging of consumers, and you step on the banks' oxygen hose. But there was more to the story. If the administration followed the preferred course of Elizabeth Warren and FDIC chair Sheila Bair, bank stockholders and bondholders would take the big hit in receivership proceedings modeled on negotiated bankruptcies. The successor bank would have a clean balance sheet, and there would be no need to rebuild bank earnings by gouging consumers.

By protecting bank shareholders and bondholders—mostly very wealthy people who knowingly took risks as investors—the administration made it inevitable that the process of rebuilding bank profits and capital would come at the expense of ordinary taxpayers and consumers. Taxpayers and consumers were, of course, the same people—once when they filed their tax returns and again when they paid exorbitant bank charges.

The banking lobby was fiercely opposed to increased consumer protections. In early fall 2009, the big banks preemptively announced simplified credit cards and overdraft terms, in the hope of heading off increased regulation. On September 16, Bank of America, with great fanfare, unveiled a new "basic" Visa card, with just one page of explanation of terms, and "only" a $39 charge for overdrafts. Citi and JPMorgan Chase rolled out similar products. At the same time, the major banks were orchestrating a fierce lobbying campaign to kill or weaken the proposed Consumer Finance Protection Agency.

A tally of direct lobbying outlays by banks that had received taxpayer aid under TARP reveals that individual banks spent more than $12 million in the first six months of 2009 lobbying Congress and the administration to weaken rather than strengthen banking regulation. Citi and JPMorgan Chase had spent $3.1 million each. Morgan Stanley spent $1.7 million, Bank of America $1.5 million, Wells Fargo $1.4 million, and Goldman $1.3 million. This includes only explicit outlays on federally registered lobbyists; it does not include the cost of contacts by bank lawyers and executives. Gallingly, though several of these institutions literally survived only thanks to the infusion of massive funds from the Treasury and loans and loan guarantees from the Federal Reserve, the administration did not pass the word, publicly or privately, that it expected the bankers to reciprocate and to support the consumer protection bill, or at least not frontally oppose it.

Throughout the first year of the Obama administration the oversight panel continued to do the public's business, partly hamstrung by the presence of a Wall Street Democrat as the swing vote, its lack of subpoena power, and the noncooperation of the Treasury. The administration, understanding Warren as a savvy adversary who was not afraid go public, did not attempt to put pressure on her and the panel, relying on Nieman to tone things down. Warren was able to get meetings with Geithner, Summers, and Bernanke as she needed them, but there remained a huge difference in the way the two sides viewed the crisis and its resolution.

What's Right with Kansas

The most improbable progressive administration critic was Sheila Bair, a holdover appointee from the Bush administration. Her role as one of the few dissenters willing to battle fiercely inside and on occasion to go public is partly a function of the FDIC's institutional role and partly a reflection of her own personal history and character. The FDIC insures bank deposits. When a bank goes bust, its insurance fund takes a hit. The FDIC is also an independent regulatory agency with term appointees. And unlike the Treasury and the Fed, the FDIC has extensive hands-on experience with taking failed banks into receivership. On all counts, it tends to be a somewhat tougher regulator than the three other bank regulatory agencies: the Office of the Comptroller of the Currency and the Office of Thrift Supervision, which are both part of the Treasury, and the Federal Reserve, which is so captive to the banking industry. But this particular FDIC chair is something a little out of the ordinary.

Bair's own history speaks volumes about the Wall Street/Main Street divide in American financial life, a division that goes back to the nineteenth century. She was born in Independence, Kansas, near the Oklahoma border, in 1955. During college, she worked part-time for a small-town bank, and her sensibilities are very much those of a community banker. Bair's parents were progressive Republicans. Despite being a Republican, Bair has turned out to be the most assertive regulator of the Obama era.

Bair's first patron in Washington was Senator Robert Dole of Kansas. She joined his staff in 1981. Subsequently, Bair took a job with the New York Stock Exchange; in 1991, with Dole's strong backing, she was named to a seat on the Commodity Futures Trading Commission. There she became a lone voice for tougher regulation, anticipating the fight that Brooksley Born would wage a few years later under Clinton, when Born alone among Clinton officials was sounding the alarm about derivatives.

A fledgling company called Enron wanted the commission to exempt futures contracts in energy transactions from CFTC jurisdiction. It was this decision that set the stage for Enron's subsequent market manipulations and outright frauds. The CFTC obliged, in a 2–1 split vote, with Bair issuing a blistering dissent, challenging the argument that transactions between sophisticated consenting adults did not require regulation. "If we are to rationalize exemptions from antifraud and other components of our regulatory scheme on the basis of the 'sophistication' of market users," Bair wrote, "we might as well close our doors tomorrow."

Bair's manner is frank, but gentle and disarming. She comes across as a genuinely nice person. Despite her most un-Republican regulatory philosophy, Bair was appointed to a senior position at the Treasury by George W. Bush, after serving a second stint at the New York Stock Exchange. Josh Bolten, Bush's chief of staff, an old friend from her Senate days, recommended her for the job. As assistant Treasury secretary for financial institutions, Bair began noticing an alarming trend in exotic mortgage loans and sought repeatedly, with limited regulatory authority, to persuade the industry to rein them in. She also noticed that the Federal Reserve, the agency with the power to crack down on subprime, was not using it.

Then, just before the crash, Bair was named to chair the FDIC in 2006. The fact that she got the job was a fluke. Two more conventional prospective nominees had come off the rails. The second of the two, Diane Taylor, then the New York State superintendent of banks, was the companion of New York Mayor Michael Bloomberg, a nominal Republican who was deeply resented by the dominant conservative wing of the Republican Party. Working through White House political director Karl Rove, right-wing groups that had crossed swords with Bloomberg, including the NRA and the tobacco lobby, blocked the nomination.

Having pulled the plug on a woman nominee for a position that had been vacant for close to a year, the Bush people needed another woman and quickly. Bair's name surfaced, and she was not subjected to the usual ideological vetting. Having served as an assistant Treasury secretary under Bush, she seemed safe enough. Nobody took a close look at her earlier work at the CFTC or her efforts at Treasury to damp down subprime abuses.

The FDIC, as an independent agency, has a bipartisan board. The vice chairman is required to be from the opposite party. In 2006, and still at this writing, that job has been held by Martin Gruenberg, former chief of staff to Senator Paul Sarbanes, the incorruptible progressive who chaired the Senate Banking Committee during the serial Wall Street scandals of a decade ago. Gruenberg had drafted much of the Sarbanes-Oxley Act, the honest-accounting measure enacted after the Enron scandal and literally the sole piece of financial reform legislation to be passed during the Bush era. When Sarbanes retired in 2005, Gruenberg was named to the Democratic seat on the FDIC. Due to prolonged failure to find an acceptable nominee—the chairmanship was vacant for almost eight months—a progressive Democrat was in the role of acting chairman during the period just before the crash. When Bair took charge, she found the FDIC in the hands of a vice chairman who shared both her regulatory philosophy and her concerns about the subprime epidemic. Bair and Gruenberg have functioned as a close team, offering the closest thing to an axis of dissent inside both the Bush and Obama administrations.

Bair and the Old Boys' Club

The first issue that divided Bair from Paulson, and later from Summers and Geithner, was how to deal with the mounting foreclosure crisis. On July 11, 2008, Bair acted to close and seize IndyMac, a $32 billion federally insured mortgage lender that was at least $8 billion underwater. IndyMac was one of the subprime pioneers and worst offenders. In taking over IndyMac, Bair used the opportunity to design and test a strategy that she has long urged on the mortgage industry: refinancing subprime loans on terms the borrower can afford, rather than foreclosing and taking the house.

The model plan, announced in August 2008, was intended to allow at least 60,000 homeowners with mortgages serviced by IndyMac to keep their houses. The FDIC could do this because it was the temporary owner of IndyMac; and unlike the Treasury, when the FDIC recapitalizes an insolvent bank it behaves like an owner. The plan was intended by Bair to serve as a template for the broader reform that Bair has championed since the subprime crisis began. But the Treasury—under both Paulson and Geithner—had little sympathy for Bair's approach, preferring instead the voluntary plans greased by government inducement payments that have achieved such little traction.

The second big bone of contention between Bair and Paulson/Geithner was how to deal with insolvent banks. As chair of the FDIC, Bair was accustomed to a straightforward resolution process: The failed bank is seized, its management tossed out, its depositors paid off, and its assets sold, and a viable successor bank is either merged into a stronger one or run briefly by the FDIC and then sold off to new private ownership, based on an accurate and clean balance sheet. But the Treasury people preferred to use public money to prop up existing banks, bail out the shareholders, and rescue the executives who had gotten them into such difficulty.

In fall 2008, Geithner bitterly crossed swords with Bair over how to deal with two failed institutions, first Washington Mutual and then the even larger Wachovia. In both cases, Bair won the argument—and Geithner never forgave her. Washington Mutual, known as WaMu, had invested heavily in subprime mortgages. Private equity investors had put $7 billion into WaMu in April 2008 and were pressing management for their expected 15 to 20 percent rate of return. But now in September 2008, with the subprime bust and the collapse of bigger banks, WaMu was under siege. The Office of Thrift Supervision, WaMu's regulator, seized the federally insured bank and turned it over to the FDIC. Bair quickly found a buyer, JPMorgan Chase, but only after the usual FDIC resolution process—shareholders lose everything and bondholders also take a big hit. Geithner intervened on the side of Wall Street, trying to persuade Bair to rely on the emergency provision allowing special treatment of a "systemically important" institution. He wanted WaMu's investors and bondholders to get the same kid-glove treatment as Citi. He lobbied the Fed, Comptroller of the Currency John Dugan, and Bair. But to no avail. Even Bernanke was skeptical that the $307 billion WaMu was systemically significant, and Bair hung tough. WaMu was acquired by JPMorgan Chase at no cost to taxpayers, and its investors and executives learned the old capitalist lesson from Economics 101 that an entrepreneur is defined as "someone who takes a risk."

Bair got into even bigger trouble with Geithner and Paulson for blocking a sweetheart deal in which Citigroup was set to take over failed Wachovia, with support from the Treasury and the Federal Reserve. In the cascading bank collapses of September 2008, the failure of Wachovia, the nation's fourth largest bank, got less publicity than the spectacular collapses of Fannie Mae, Lehman, and AIG or the shotgun merger of Bank of America. But as the big North Carolina bank teetered on the brink of extinction, it caused great alarm to the regulators. In July, one of Paulson's closest aides, Bob Steel, took a job as Wachovia's CEO. He soon found that the bank could not survive without a white knight.

By late September, the bidding was down to two institutions, Citi and Wells Fargo. Bair initially favored the proposal from Wells Fargo, which involved the usual FDIC medicine: Shareholders and bondholders lose, depositors are protected, another bank takes it over, and there is no loss to the taxpayers. But Geithner, according to *The Wall Street Journal*'s David Wessel, "blew up," and insisted, "The policy of the US government is that there will be no more WaMu's"—meaning no more large failures where shareholders and bondholders lose all.

Bair agreed, if only because of Wachovia's huge size, that it could be designated as "systemically important," qualifying it for direct assistance from the Fed and the Treasury before it technically failed. This, in turn, made it a more attractive merger candidate for Citi, and provided a nice indirect subsidy of Citi. Since Bair, as chair of the FDIC, was the government's lead official negotiating the disposal of Wachovia, it was her call whether to give it to Citi or Wells. Very late on the night of Sunday, September 28, she agreed to go with Citi. But Tuesday morning, Richard Kovacevich, CEO of Wells, phoned the Fed and the FDIC with a better offer. He had devised a way to take over Wachovia with no government aid, and for $7 a share. A recent change in the tax law allowed Wells to take a huge and lucrative tax loss on the deal. The Wachovia board met and agreed to sell to Wells. Bair concurred. She had never been thrilled with the terms of the Citi deal, which left the FDIC to absorb any losses that proved greater than $42 billion. In Bair's view, Citi was tottering, and using public dollars to allow it to acquire another failing bank was dubious policy. Two failures did not add up to a success. Livid Citi executives, on the phone to Geithner, demanded that he block the deal, but that decision belonged to Bair, who was unmoved. Geithner was furious at Wells, but even angrier at Bair.

Geithner put out the story that Bair cared more about conserving the FDIC's insurance funds than about preventing a wider meltdown. *The Wall Street Journal*'s David Wessel, in an otherwise fine book on the serial rescues of the first year of the crisis, tells his story largely from the Bernanke-Paulson-Geithner perspective based on their cooperation with his reporting. Bair, he writes, was a "fierce and relentless defender of the FDIC fund, putting that kitty above all else, frustrating Bernanke, Geithner, and Paulson, who saw preventing the collapse of the American financial system and economy as a greater goal." Andrew Ross Sorkin's account, *Too Big to Fail,* also drew heavily on Geithner's background comments. Geithner "had always regarded Bair as a showboat," he wrote, "a media grandstander, a politician in a regulator's position whose only concern was to protect the F.D.I.C. not the entire system."

But this is a grotesque and one-sided description of what divided Bair from the old boys' club. The issue was not whether to prevent a financial collapse, but *how.* In fact, Bair tapped the FDIC insurance fund plenty and had to resort to emergency measures to replenish it. Her preference for compelling large banks to acknowledge losses and clean up their balance sheets actually would have cost the FDIC more money in the short run.

But she was much less inclined to play favorites and more insistent on replacing incompetent executives and reorganizing insolvent banks. What's excluded from these tendentious descriptions is the possibility that Bair had a principled difference with the others about how to repair the banking system.

After being appointed Treasury secretary by President-elect Obama on November 24, Geithner, according to a well-documented report by Bloomberg News, sought to get Bair fired. This would have been very difficult, since she had a term appointment with three years left to run. She also has many fans in Congress, as the sole Bush appointee who had sought to sound early alarms about the impending subprime crisis and to remedy the foreclosure crisis in its aftermath. When Geithner complained that Bair "isn't a team player and is too focused on protecting her agency rather than the financial system as a whole," the comment prompted Barney Frank, among others, to inquire, "Exactly whose team is that?" At the time Geithner made the complaint, he was part of the *Bush* team, while the Republican Bair was sounding and acting more like a progressive Democrat. Now Geithner was joining the Obama team—but continuing the Bush policies.

The set-to between Bair and the Geithner Treasury continued into 2009 and 2010. Bair, like Elizabeth Warren, had little sympathy for Geithner's entire approach, even though her FDIC was called upon to play a leading role in capitalizing some of his bailout schemes. Although she reluctantly went along with one of Geithner's deals, the so-called Legacy Loan Program that was announced in March, she scrapped most of the program in June when it became clear that few if any deals were realistic.

Bair's FDIC was also under extreme pressure because of the double standards in the treatment of big Wall Street banks and small ones. It was the small ones that were under Bair's direct jurisdiction. While the money-center banks were getting hundreds of billions in taxpayer support and enjoying regulatory indulgence, smaller banks were squeezed by worsening business conditions and got no special consideration from their bank examiners. The number of bank failures in FDIC-insured banks was more than 140 during 2009, up from 20 in 2008 and just 5 in 2007.

By September 2009, the FDIC's own insurance fund was almost out of money. The FDIC has standby authority to borrow up to $500 billion from the Treasury, but given the strained relations between Bair and Geithher, she was very reluctant to come hat-in-hand to the Treasury. Nor was Congress in a mood to provide a back-door bailout to banks. Bank lobbyists were promoting a scheme whereby the FDIC would borrow money from insured banks and pay them interest. The alternative was to increase the levy on small banks, which Bair took to be grossly unfair. She often said that small banks should not pay for the sins of the big ones that caused the collapse. Bair and the FDIC board ended up requiring insured banks to pay three years' premiums in advance, but they agreed that the payments would not be counted against the capital on their balance sheets.

Keeping Speculators Out of Commercial Banking

Bair was also in a very ticklish situation when it came to unloading the dozens of banks that the FDIC had taken into receivership as the cascade of failures continued. The FDIC has been a strong enforcer of the fundamental doctrine that you don't mix banking and ordinary commerce. The reason is simple. If a conglomerate that owns other businesses also owns a bank, it can feather its own nest by extending credit to its subsidiaries with federally insured depositor money—and thereby disadvantage competing businesses that happen not to own a bank. Transactions between banks and their customers are supposed to be at arm's length. The need to find buyers for failed banks, however, led to breaches in this doctrine.

One problematic form of hybrid business is the private equity company, which is basically unregulated and which depends heavily on borrowed money to finance takeover deals and other speculations. The private equity industry has long sought to repeal or end-run the regulations that prohibit private equity firms from owning banks. The Fed has long had a rule that 25 percent ownership in a bank is tantamount to control. A private equity company is not permitted to own a bank, because this breaches the fundamental doctrine of not mixing banking and ordinary commerce. Private equity companies got around the rule by teaming up so that no single company owned more than 24.9 percent of a senior bank. As an FDIC official puts it, "If five private equity guys get together and each take 20 percent, who are we kidding?" But faced with the absence of other buyers or merger candidates in the case of IndyMac, the largest failed bank that the FDIC had taken into receivership to date, the FDIC reluctantly permitted a sale to a consortium of several private equity companies, none of which owned more than 24.9 percent of the bank (thus violating the spirit but not the letter of its own rule). "If the Fed was doing its job of supervising the holding companies," says this official, "we wouldn't be in this mess."

Private equity's track record in operating banks does not inspire confidence. In the collapse of Washington Mutual, the Texas Pacific Group, a secretive private equity company, had invested and lost $7 billion, money invested on terms that prevented WaMu from raising needed capital elsewhere until it was too late. TPG's owners, looking for the usual outsize returns, were among the forces pressuring WaMu to take big risks.

As more and more small and medium-size banks failed during 2009, the FDIC was often hard-pressed to find buyers for failed banks even after it stepped in to compensate depositors for losses. In May 2009, four private equity firms joined forces to buy Bank United, a $12.7 billion failed Florida bank. The FDIC, with no other plausible buyers, let the consortium have the bank for $900 million and shared in 84 percent of losses, while the private equity group stood to get the entire upside gain.

Private equity companies stepped up their lobbying campaign to have the FDIC weaken its rules. According to an FDIC expert, "Private equity hopes to buy up banks at depressed, bargain prices, then either sell them in a few years at a large profit or use them as funding vehicles for their other businesses." Ideally, according to this official, "failing institutions should be acquired by other banks, and if private equity plays a role at all it should be as a passive investor. Their whole business model, with its high returns, high risks, and high leverage, is incompatible with the way a bank should be run."

In July 2009, the FDIC courageously issued for comment a draft policy statement proposing to limit the terms under which private equity companies could invest in banks. In the policy statement, the FDIC signaled that it would prefer to merge failed banks with other banks, or to find investors other than private equity conglomerates. It proposed to prohibit firms that acquired failed banks from lending to their own subsidiaries, and to exclude firms based in offshore tax havens. And if a consortium of private equity firms acquired a bank, it would be required to have much higher ratios of capital because of its inherently riskier business strategies. The company would also be prohibited from selling off the bank for at least three years. This policy approach was particularly brave and nervy, given the FDIC's own need for funds and its difficulty unloading failed banks. It contrasted dramatically with the one pursued by the Treasury and the Federal Reserve, which have viewed private equity as savior of the banks, while the FDIC sees the industry as an unsavory last resort.

The industry responded with a fierce lobbying campaign to weaken the proposed rules, and a series of leaks to the business press indicating that the FDIC was on the verge of caving. Wilbur Ross, the politically influential speculator who got Bank United for a song at taxpayer expense, told reporters and editorialists that he'd never buy a distressed bank again if the FDIC didn't ease its terms. Geithner and Summers also leaned on Bair on behalf the industry.

But for the most part, the FDIC stuck to its guns. In the final policy statement, the major provisions survived, with the exception of a modest weakening in the test of whether a bank proposed for acquisition in part by a private equity company was "well capitalized." The original proposal had defined that as a capital ratio of 15 percent—far higher than the 5 percent required of ordinary banks or the 8 percent required of newly chartered banks. In the end, the FDIC adopted a standard of 10 percent for private equity owners, enough to put them at a competitive disadvantage with conventional bank owners and to discourage private equity speculation in ownership of commercial banks.

And on January 12, 2009, by a 3–2 vote, Bair's FDIC put out for comment a rule that would penalize insured banks for excessive or unwise executive compensation. Bair specifically proposed to levy additional fees on banks whose pay packages promoted risky behavior, on the theory that this was passing along the risks to the insurance fund. Her model pay policy would reward banks that partly compensated executives in stock that could only be redeemed over several years, and whose executive pay was set by outside directors.

The timing was vintage Bair, upstaging an Obama initiative that had been widely leaked in advance, to add a small bank surtax (but not to limit executive pay). The two dissenters on the FDIC board were both presidential appointees, John Dugan, head of the notoriously pro-industry Office of the Comptroller of the Currency, which regulates national banks, and John Bowman, acting director of the even weaker Office of Thrift Supervision, which missed the subprime abuses in savings and loans. Dugan is a Bush holdover, and formerly a lawyer for big banks. It is emblematic of the politics of continuity that he has kept his job under Obama.

At the first mass public protest of the big banks' behavior, on October 26 outside the annual convention of the American Bankers Association in Chicago, exactly one senior public official had the audacity to address the protestors as well as the bankers. It wasn't Larry Summers or Tim Geithner, much less Barack Obama. It was FDIC chair Sheila Bair. "I don't see how anybody can say that we've done a good job protecting consumers and financial services," she said, to loud cheers. "No more too big to fail. No more bailouts."

A Lion in Winter

Though excluded by Summers from any position of real influence, Paul Volcker continued to be the single most respected outside voice on the banking crisis. In testimony and speeches, Volcker argued for a reform that had been explicitly rejected by Geithner and Summers—the resurrection of the Glass-Steagall Act or something very much like it. The administration, its apologists, and conservative commentators endlessly repeated the assertion that repeal of Glass-Steagall had not been responsible for the financial collapse. This was true only in the most narrow sense that originators of subprime loans were neither commercial bankers nor investment bankers. But if you trace back the linkages, repeal of Glass-Steagall is directly implicated.

The Fed and the Treasury had been granting piecemeal, ad hoc exemptions to Glass-Steagall since the early 1980s, softening the ground for its eventual outright repeal in 1999. For example, even before Glass-Steagall was officially repealed, Citi had been permitted to merge with an insurance company and a broker-dealer. If the Glass-Steagall wall had held, Citigroup never would have been allowed to become a conglomerate of commercial and investment banking.

Without Glass-Steagall repeal, Citi and the other large banks never would have bankrolled the retail mortgage companies that originated subprime mortgages, and bank-holding company affiliates would not have been able to trade in subprime securities. Investment banks such as Lehman and Bear might have taken some of these risks, but the markets for laying off these securities would have been far narrower and the subprime menace less pervasive. Even more importantly, commercial banks would not have gone in for creating and trading swaps.

Volcker kept returning to this theme in his speeches and congressional testimony. Speaking to the Association for Corporate Growth in Los Angeles on September 17, 2009, Volcker said that banks should be banned from "sponsoring and capitalizing" private equity firms and hedge funds, which have no meaningful regulation in terms of their use of leverage or disclosure of their holdings. He also said "particularly strict supervision, with strong capital and collateral requirements, should be directed toward limiting proprietary securities and derivatives trading." Calling for restoration of Glass-Steagall without quite using the words, Volcker called for restrictions on proprietary securities trading by banks.

"Extensive participation in the impersonal, transaction-oriented capital market does not seem to me an intrinsic part of commercial banking," he told the group.

Testifying before the House Financial Services Committee on September 26, in a statement largely ignored by the press, Volcker sharpened his criticism. He raised pointed questions about the negative effect of the administration's bailout program on the future behavior of financial engineers. "Will not the pattern of protection for the largest banks and their holding companies tend to encourage greater risk-taking," he asked, "especially when compensation practices so greatly reward short-term success?"

Turning to the administration's double standards between Wall Street mega-banks and the besieged community banks that serve small business, he asked, "Are community or regional banks to be deemed too small to save?" Volcker challenged the administration's tolerance of the blending of commercial banking and investment, with taxpayer guarantees. "Does not the extension of support to non-banks, and even to affiliates of commercial firms, undercut the banking/commerce divide, ultimately weakening the commercial banking system?" he asked. "The obvious danger is that with the passage of time, risk-taking will be encouraged and efforts at prudential restraint will be resisted. Ultimately, the possibility of further crises—even greater crises—will increase."

Volcker reiterated his qualms about the breaches of Glass-Steagall in a frontal challenge to the administration view. "As a general matter, I would exclude from commercial banking institutions, which are potential beneficiaries of official (i.e., taxpayer) financial support, certain risky activities entirely suitable for our capital markets. Ownership or sponsorship of hedge funds and private equity funds should be among those prohibited activities. So should in my view a heavy volume of proprietary trading with its inherent risks."

Until December 2009, the administration's strategy with Volcker continued as before. He was treated with great deference as a respected elder statesman—and his counsel was ignored. For the most part, the press missed the significance of Volcker's marginalization. *The New Yorker*'s Ryan Lizza, in an otherwise fine article in October 2009 on the roles and views of senior economic advisers in the Obama administration, wrote, "While almost all economic-policy traffic flows through the NEC [Summers's National Economic Council], the PERAB [the advisory panel that Volcker chairs] reports directly to the President." This was true, but only on paper.

In October, Volcker was the guest speaker at an event at the Harry S. Truman Presidential Library. One of his table mates at the dinner held in Volcker's honor inquired what Volcker thought of Treasury Secretary Tim Geithner. "My views of Tim Geithner," said Volcker, "are unprintable."

In December 2009, however, Vice President Biden and chief political adviser David Axelrod urged President Obama to pay more attention to Volcker. The banking system was back to its old ways, and a populist anger was on the rise. Obama's December 12 comment on CBS's *60 Minutes* that he didn't run for president in order to help out "a bunch of fat-cat bankers" was one of the first fruits of this presidential shift into more populist mode.

Volcker, meanwhile, hadn't only been speaking out with increasing bluntness. The aging lion turned out to be a formidable organizer. He reached out to the blue bloods of the banking profession to join him in a call for a restoration of the Glass-Steagall wall. Volcker's supporters included Bill Donaldson, who had served as SEC chairman under President George W. Bush; Nicholas Brady, treasury secretary under Bush I; John Reed, former CEO of Citi; and Bob Rubin's former deputy Roger Altman.

Obama met with Volcker at least twice during December, and over the objections of Geithner and Summers he decided to embrace the call for a new Glass-Steagall. The rollout was abruptly expedited after the shock of the Massachusetts election of January 19, and announced at a high-profile White House event with Volcker on January 21. Obama went out of his way to term the Glass-Steagall restoration "the Volcker Rule." Aides to Geithner, in damage-control mode, put out the word to reporters that Geithner had been for restoring Glass-Steagall all along. This was a complete fabrication.

At this writing, however, the banks are fiercely resisting this legislation, as are Senate Republicans, and it is not at all clear that it is an administration priority. It will take Obama's hands-on leadership, not just a rhetorical embrace of Volcker, to bring about this scale of reform.

The Senator from the Other Washington

In the 2000 election, one of the freshmen Democrats elected to the Senate was a technology executive named Maria Cantwell. A multimillionaire senior executive at Seattle's Real Networks, the company that pioneered Internet audio and video, Cantwell was billed as a "business Democrat." But that wasn't quite accurate. Moving to Seattle not long after college, Cantwell got into politics, winning a seat in the state legislature at the age of twenty-eight and then serving a single term in Congress. Cantwell was a civil libertarian and advocate of computer privacy. As a freshman Democrat, she blocked then Vice President Al Gore's proposal for a "clipper chip," a sliver of computer hardware designed to facilitate government snooping. In that fight, she worked with the Electronic Frontier Foundation and got to know Rob Glaser, the billionaire head of Real Networks. When she lost her House seat in the 1994 Republican landslide, Glaser hired her to the company's top marketing job. She subsequently was promoted to executive vice president and left to make her Senate run. Winning a squeaker of an election in 2000 by less than one-tenth of 1 percent to oust incumbent Senator Slade Gorton, Cantwell found herself thrown into the top issue then afflicting Washingtonians—soaring electricity rates.

Washington State, which is heavily reliant on hydropower, was one of the worst casualties of the Enron scandal. Thanks to several deregulatory measures affecting derivatives markets enacted in the 1990s and in the year 2000, Enron was able to manipulate the spot and futures market for electricity with no interference from regulators. Washington had droughts in 2000 and 2001, leaving its hydroelectric plants operating at well below capacity. Its main power companies were forced to buy supplementary electricity on the open market, just when spot prices and futures contracts had been manipulated into the stratosphere by Enron. In Seattle, electricity rates rose 60 percent. Even George W. Bush's industry-dominated Federal Energy Regulatory Commission found Enron guilty of market manipulation, though FERC declined to order rebates. In 2004, the local Public Utility District did its own investigation and found that market manipulation in the deregulated environment had cost Washington consumers $1.1 billion.

Cantwell quickly immersed herself in the details of electric power regulation, which led directly to the subject of manipulation of options and futures. So she also became a relentless and sophisticated critic of unregulated derivatives. Her championing of relief for Washington State ratepayers and sponsorship of a bill voiding Enron's fraudulent contracts helped her win reelection in 2006 with 57 percent of the vote.

In early 2009, Cantwell was stunned when the Obama administration appointed one official after another who were part of the Democratic deregulation gang of the Clinton era. She was appalled when Obama named Gary

Gensler to chair the Commodity Futures Trading Commission. "My reaction was, oh my God, not again," she told me. It was Gensler, a former Treasury official and onetime Goldman executive, who had been part of the pack that isolated Brooksley Born, and who had been a supporter of the 2000 legislation tying the CFTC's hands on regulation of over-the-counter derivatives. As a former executive of Goldman Sachs, Gensler admitted to Cantwell, he had recused himself for the first year of his tenure at the Treasury, as required by law, but subsequently he was involved in the administration's policy making on deregulation of banking and of derivatives.

After a lengthy meeting on January 15, Cantwell sent Gensler a detailed letter soliciting his views on several regulatory issues involving derivatives. His reply, dated February 11, was detailed, but it deftly fudged several crucial regulatory issues. For example, would all derivatives contracts be required to be traded on exchanges regulated directly by the CFTC, or only "cleared" in industry-sponsored clearinghouses, a softer remedy being promoted by the industry? And would there be a loophole for "customized" derivatives, a big source of industry profits (since there was no way of knowing their market price at any given moment) and hence a huge source of systemic risk? "They say that the insiders will always come up with new things, new ways of defeating regulation, new kinds of off-the-books games," Cantwell says. "That's why you need really bright lines."

Cantwell and independent senator Bernie Sanders of Vermont decided to put a hold on Gensler's nomination while they pressed both the White House and Gensler for more explicit commitments. In March, they and four other Democratic senators sought and got a White House meeting with Obama, in which they warned that his team—with Summers and Geithner present in the room—was far too soft on Wall Street. Cantwell began negotiating commitments with the administration for a radical shift in derivatives regulation. She and the small group of progressive Democratic senators, which also included Byron Dorgan of North Dakota, who had been an opponent of Glass-Steagall repeal, and Dick Durbin of Illinois, the Senate deputy majority leader, also warned Obama that if he kept turning to Wall Street for his top advisers, they would face very rough going in their Senate confirmation hearings.

This was at a moment when the number two job at Treasury, deputy secretary, was vacant, and the names of Wall Street eminences were being floated. For example, H. Rodgin Cohen, the power-lawyer who represented the biggest banks, was widely touted for the position. Cohen had helped draft every key piece of deregulatory legislation going back more than two decades, as the point man for the banking industry. He had negotiated the terms of the TARP bailouts on behalf of the banks. Now his name was leaked to the press as Obama's choice for deputy secretary. After several days of vetting and counterpressure from progressive Democrats in Congress, Cohen said he was withdrawing "for personal reasons."

In the meantime, Gary Gensler met with consumer groups, assuring them that in light of recent events he now had a much less sanguine view of derivatives. As a critic, I was startled to get a phone call, out of the blue, from a White House handler, saying that Gensler was eager to meet with me. Gensler started sounding like such an ardent, born-again regulator that even Public Citizen, the consumer group founded by Ralph Nader, put out a press release supporting his confirmation.

But Cantwell remained even more skeptical than Public Citizen. She wanted guarantees. She and Sanders kept the hold on Gensler's nomination. At a hearing she declared, "They are slow walking, thinking we're all going to forget what is needed. My patience is running out with the administration having to take five months to say that some of these things ought to be regulated and how they ought to be regulated."

Cantwell and Sanders held the line until they got some minimum assurances from the White House. After one frustrating conversation with Geithner, in which the Treasury secretary said he could not commit to the level of specificity that Cantwell was requesting, Cantwell's phone rang almost immediately. It was Summers, and he was prepared to get into whatever degree of detail was necessary to free the nomination.

Finally, in early May, Cantwell got the written assurances she was seeking, in a letter laboriously negotiated item by item with Summers and Geithner. The letter, ostensibly written by Geithner, promised that all derivatives transactions requiring large sums would have to be traded and cleared on regulated exchanges. Only narrow, genuinely customized derivatives would be permitted to be traded over the counter. This was strong stuff. Cantwell was playing the kind of hardball against Obama typically played by Republicans and center-right Democrats, but seldom by liberals. "We knew," she told me, "that if we were ever going to get something decent passed, we had to exert some leverage." Gensler's commitment would become the object of fierce industry lobbying, which in the end succeeded in watering down the reforms. Cantwell, however, felt she finally got what she needed.

Taking the Senate floor May 14, she jubilantly declared, "For months I have been urging the administration to move quickly to propose strong regulatory controls on these markets, require transparency in derivatives trading, and restrict market manipulation. With the announcement yesterday by Treasury Secretary Geithner in a letter he sent to Senate and House leaders, the administration has come down decisively on the side of imposing order on a marketplace whose collapse made this current recession so much deeper and more painful for the average American than it needed to be." And she announced that she was releasing the hold on Gensler's nomination.

But her suspicions of the administration's good faith persisted. She still voted against Gensler. As Cantwell drily said to me in an interview not long afterward, "It's not unheard of in DC to feign a commitment, and then not fight hard to have the legislation pass." That understated what was coming. Though Gensler worked hard to keep his word, he was ultimately overruled. The legislation that Geithner sent Congress in August opened significant loopholes, and these were only widened in the House Financial Services Committee, as the financial lobbies worked their will and were not resisted by the administration. An infuriated Cantwell told MSNBC, "The Treasury should be ashamed of itself." She added, "What is moving through on the House side is a bill that supposedly has a new rule, but has so many loopholes that the loophole eats the rule . . . current law with its loopholes would actually be better than these loopholes."

Gensler courageously resisted the attempts by his own administration to weaken the pending legislation. In a letter dated August 17 to Senate Agricultural Committee chairman Tom Harkin, he warned that the proposed exemption for foreign exchange "could swallow up the regulation that the Proposed OTC Act otherwise provides for currency and interest rate swaps." The exemption for deals between banks and nonbanks, he continued, "excludes a major significant class of end users from the clearing and mandatory trading requirement." And he challenged the premise that voluntary clearing of derivatives deal transactions on private clearinghouses would be sufficient.

As the fight moved to the Senate, Cantwell found herself allied with Gensler, whose nomination she had initially opposed. "They seem to think that if Wall Street gets healthy again making all this money, some of it will wash through to the rest of the economy," she told me. "Treasury has gone back on their original commitment to us. Gensler called Geithner on it. He's decided that he's going to be David to their Goliath. The battle lines have been drawn."

By early 2010, reform legislation increasing CFTC's powers still had not been approved by the Senate, and Gensler was fighting the good fight for tougher supervision using the regulatory powers that he had. But he was partly stymied by less-than-full support of his other commissioners. At least one of the commission's other senior Democrats was less than enthusiastic about Gensler's reforms. Of the commission's two Republican appointees, one is Jill Sommers, former chief lobbyist for the International Swaps and Derivatives Association, the industry lobby for the weakest possible regulation of derivatives.

Progressive Bipartisanship

Late in 2009, as the final details of the highly contentious health bill were being thrashed out in the Senate, bipartisanship seemed a quaint ideal of the past. Cantwell played a critical role on the Senate Finance Committee by offering a proposal based on a Washington State program that allows uninsured people to get insurance from private plans that are tightly regulated and certified by the state. Her surprise amendment was accepted by the entire committee. Cantwell's provision became the Senate's substitute for the more contentious public option, which had been the roadblock to Senate passage of the bill.

After this exercise in creative bipartisanship, Cantwell was surprised to get a call from one John McCain. Arizona was getting pummeled by foreclosures, bank failures, and scarcity of small-business credit. McCain was facing a difficult reelection, and his constituents were in full-throated rebellion against Wall Street banks. Cantwell was a progressive able, like Ted

Kennedy, to define areas of common ground with Republicans. At a meeting in Cantwell's office, McCain raised the subject of reviving Glass-Steagall. "It doesn't seem all that complicated to me," he said. "Banks shouldn't be speculating with government-insured money. Am I missing something?"

Other senators and bank lobbyists were stunned when a measure co-sponsored by Senators Cantwell and McCain, known as the Banking Integrity Act, was introduced on December 16 to restore the Glass-Steagall separation of commercial from investment banking. "I want to ensure that we never stick the American taxpayer with another $700 billion—or even larger—tab to bailout the financial industry," said McCain. "If big Wall Street institutions want to take part in risky transactions—fine. But we should not allow them to do so with federally insured deposits." Reporters pointed out that Glass-Steagall repeal had been sponsored by Phil Gramm, one of McCain's top advisers in the 2008 campaign. McCain responded that he and Gramm didn't agree on everything. If there is a populist, anti–Wall Street bipartisanship waiting to be born, Maria Cantwell is its natural leader.

The Righteous Right

Useful criticism also came from a small band of conservatives who took seriously the idea that capitalism depended on risk, and that if government bailed out those who had made bad bets, the entire logic of capitalism would fail. The key difference between them and their liberal counterparts was that liberals wanted to use regulation as a preventive, while conservatives were content to let the chips fall when markets made mistakes. The two ends of the spectrum occasionally converged, on their criticisms of the Treasury's bailout policy and on the need to render the Federal Reserve more democratically accountable. A majority of members of the House co-sponsored the bill originally proposed by libertarian Republican representative Ron Paul of Texas to subject the Federal Reserve to an annual audit by the GAO, and the provision survived in the final version of the reform bill that passed the House in December.

At least three presidents of regional Federal Reserve banks were highly critical of the Bernanke-Geithner-Summers view. Jeff Lacker, president of the Richmond Fed Bank, has opposed the whole approach of the Treasury bailing out specific financial institutions with backup support from the Fed, and he pressured the Treasury to sign an accord with the Fed promising to compensate the central bank for any losses. Richard Fisher, president of the Dallas Fed, regularly gave speeches warning of the dangers of using weak regulatory policy as a form of monetary policy. And the longest-serving president of a regional Fed bank, Thomas Hoenig of the Kansas City Fed, whose region's banks have been hard hit by the Wall Street/Main Street double standard, has been especially outspoken.

In a major speech in March, frontally criticizing the Bernanke approach, titled "Too Big Has Failed," Hoenig frankly called for rejecting TARP in favor of something like a new Reconstruction Finance Corporation, with power to take failed banks into receivership. He declared, "If we compare the TARP program to the RFC, TARP began without a clear set of principles and has proceeded with what seems to be an ad hoc and less than transparent approach in the case of banks judged to be 'too-big-to-fail.'" He added that in the government-mediated restructuring, "shareholders should be made to bear the full risk of the positions they have taken and suffer the resulting losses." Testifying in favor of this alternative before New York representative Carolyn Maloney's Joint Economic Committee, Hoenig was so persuasive that he had Senator Sam Brownback of Kansas, one of the Senate's most conservative Republicans, supporting the call for a new RFC.

Hoenig repeated variations of the argument in an op-ed piece in the *Financial Times*, in a New York speech, and in congressional testimony. In his *FT* article, Hoenig warned:

> Certain companies have not been allowed to fail and, as a result, the moral hazard problem has substantially worsened. Capitalism is a process of failure and renewal, and a "too big to fail" policy undermines this renewal and makes the financial system and our economy less efficient.
>
> So-called "too big to fail" firms have been given a competitive advantage and, rather than being held accountable for their actions, they have actually been subsidized in becoming more economically and politically powerful. Failing effectively to resolve these non-viable firms has long-term consequences. We have entrenched these even

larger, systemically important, "too big to fail" institutions into the economic system, assuring that past mistakes will be repeated.

These views, coming from the senior president of a regional reserve bank, were not exactly appreciated by Bernanke or Geithner loyalists. The peer pressure against Hoenig within the Fed system has been relentless. I have long had a friendly, off-the-record relationship with a senior Fed official. When I mentioned Hoenig's views as worth considering, this official stopped returning my phone calls.

It seems improbable that conservatives like Hoenig and Brownback would come out in favor of what is seemingly a more socialistic alternative of direct government receivership for failed banks. But this view is not inconsistent at all. It rejects the idea of an unaccountable agency, the Federal Reserve, playing multiple and contradictory roles as central banker, ad hoc bailout agency, and regulator inclined to play favorites and corrupt standards because of the need to assure that its bailouts succeed.

One of the intellectual leaders of this view is Walker Todd, a self-described conservative Republican, a former senior Federal Reserve official at both the Fed banks of New York and Cleveland, and a prominent historian of the RFC. Todd wrote, in a remarkably prescient research piece published in 1992, "A tendency to use central bank resources to fund a bailout increasingly politicizes the bank's monetary policy functions." He added that an RFC was the preferred course, "if the only alternative permitted by the political process is central-bank-funded rescues of politically designated target firms . . . The RFC should be funded on-budget and through regular appropriations." Justifying his support for something as "socialistic" as a new Reconstruction Finance Corporation, Todd told me, "It's far better to do this transparently by a public agency than to pervert the mission of the Federal Reserve."

For Todd and kindred monetary conservatives, bailing out individual institutions is a radical and dangerous departure from the Fed's appropriate role as the agency of monetary policy. Printing money and using it to guarantee banks rather than serving general credit conditions, Todd argues, gets the Fed into the business of fiscal policy, an area that exceeds both its mandate and its competence.

As evidence of the emerging left–right consensus on this proposition, *The*

Wall Street Journal recently ran an editorial that reads as if it could have been written by Joseph Stiglitz or Paul Krugman. "The sounder strategy," argued the *Journal,*

> is to address systemic financial problems the old-fashioned way: bank by bank, through the Federal Deposit Insurance Corporation and a resolution agency with the capacity to hold troubled assets and work them off over time. If the stress tests reveal that some of our largest institutions are insolvent or nearly so, it's then time to seize the bank, sell off assets and recapitalize the remainder. (Meanwhile, the healthier institutions would get a vote of confidence and could attract new private capital.)

Madame Speaker and Friends

Nancy Pelosi is in a ticklish position. On the one hand, she is Washington's most influential progressive legislator. On the other, her job is to hold together a fractious Democratic caucus and to get legislation through the House, often with votes hanging in the balance until the last moment. Pelosi has taken care not to criticize the president publicly and has been circumspect even privately. But behind the scenes, she has been a potent force pressing the White House to keep its commitments for fundamental reform.

Pelosi and Obama, then in high bipartisan mode, had deep disagreements about the February 2009 stimulus package. Obama, seeking to appease Republicans, wanted as much as 40 percent of the bill to be made up of tax cuts. The House bill provided a lesser amount, about one-third. But Obama's team assured Republicans that the conference bill would be closer to the 40 percent mark, and it was. For this gesture, Obama was rewarded with no House Republican votes. Pelosi began prodding the president to support repeal of the Bush tax cuts, as early as his first month in office. Not until February 2010, in releasing his budget for fiscal year 2011, did Obama agree to let the tax cuts expire.

In the fall of 2009, with unemployment at 10 percent, Pelosi and the House leadership pressed Obama to embrace a second stimulus package. The

White House, fearing a backlash against deficits, discouraged major new stimulus spending, preferring small initiatives that would not attract so much publicity and refusing to use the word *stimulus*. Obama and Emanuel told Pelosi to wait for Obama's January State of the Union address. In December, however, Pelosi and the House Democratic leadership resolved to act alone, in defiance of the president's wishes, as a way of prodding the White House, narrowly approving a $154 billion jobs initiative.

Elsewhere on Capitol Hill, two other unlikely administration critics were the new chair of the House Committee on Governmental Affairs, Edolphus (Ed) Towns, and Joint Economic Committee chair Carolyn Maloney. Towns, representing Bedford-Stuyvesant, a poor, mostly minority neighborhood of Brooklyn, did not have a distinguished prior career. Despite having a safe seat, he often voted with corporate interests, and he was richly rewarded with campaign contributions.

But when the longtime chair of Governmental Affairs, Henry Waxman, took over the House Energy and Commerce Committee, Towns succeeded Waxman. For Towns, the chairmanship of the powerful committee represented political salvation. He retained most of his predecessor Henry Waxman's investigative staff and commenced a tough series of investigative hearings. Governmental Affairs is one of the few committees with authority to issue subpoenas without the approval of the Speaker's office. Working with the committee's ranking Republican, Darrell Issa of California, Towns was not shy about embarrassing both the industry and the administration. It was Issa who first surfaced e-mails linking Tim Geithner to pressure by the New York Fed on AIG not to disclose to the SEC and its own investors the terms of the Fed's extraordinary aid.

Carolyn Maloney was also a pleasant surprise. Given the importance of the financial industry to New York's regional economy, members of the New York congressional delegation are supposed to cut Wall Street some slack. The prime role model is Maloney's Senate vice chairman of the committee, fellow New Yorker Chuck Schumer, who regularly leads the Senate in political contributions from bankers. But Maloney, whose district includes Manhattan's East Side, held one tough hearing after another, featuring critics of the Geithner-Summers approach. Maloney herself criticized the Treasury's anti-foreclosure as too little and too late. "If you don't get your hands on the downward spiral in housing prices, you are not going to get a recovery," she told me. She held that "all derivatives should be traded on regulated exchanges. I would not have any exceptions." And along with Warren and Bair, she favored a receivership approach to failed banks rather than too-big-to-fail and the slow transfusions of prolonged bailouts.

House progressives, for the most part, did not have powerful committee chairmanships that dealt directly with the financial crisis. However, Marcy Kaptur, the longtime congresswoman from Toledo, Ohio, organized subcommittee chairs and Democratic back-benchers into a de facto reform caucus. "If we don't apply some pressure on the administration and the leadership," she told me, "the banking industry will keep things just as they are and ruin our communities." Kaptur introduced legislation to democratize the Fed and suspend mortgage foreclosures, and she called on victims of the crisis to resist the foreclosure process. Speaking on the House floor, Kaptur declared:

> Don't leave your home. Because you know what? When those companies say they have your mortgage, unless you have a lawyer that can put his or her finger on that mortgage, you don't have that mortgage, and you are going to find they can't find the paper up there on Wall Street. So I say to the American people, you be squatters in your own homes. Don't you leave. In Ohio and Michigan and Indiana and Illinois and all these other places our people are being treated like chattel, and this Congress is stymied.

For the most part, Obama has taken the 200 or so House progressive Democrats for granted, pursuing alliances to their right.

Left Out

Going back through several Democratic presidencies, progressive groups to the president's left have performed a delicate balancing act, working with a president who is an ally, but also pushing him. This is invariably easier when social movements have real influence on the ground, such as the labor movement or the civil rights and antiwar movements of the 1960s and 1970s. I still have my protest button from the 1964 Democratic National Convention in Atlantic City, PART OF THE WAY WITH LBJ. That slogan was a very nice double entendre. It meant that we were with Johnson on civil rights but not on the Vietnam War; and also that Johnson's anti-poverty and racial justice initiatives—which at that point included seating an all-white Mississippi delegation with two token blacks as at-large delegates—would take us only part of the way.

With Obama, this balancing act is trickier than usual. Today grassroots progressive movements are weak. Moreover, most progressives like Obama personally, want him to succeed, and are inclined to blame the people around him rather than the president himself. More than a year into his presidency, we are still very pleased with ourselves for having elected him. Progressive activists also don't want to burn bridges. And although the administration's political strategists play all kinds of footsie with the banks and the insurance industry, they play hardball with the progressive community.

At weekly meetings held under the auspices of an outfit called Common Purpose, White House officials meet privately with leaders of liberal groups to give them the week's talking points, to solicit ideas, and to listen to criticisms that are invariably very circumspect and polite. Administration figures range from lobbyist Erik Smith to legislative director Jim Messina, and occasionally Rahm Emanuel. At one session in August, after some of the activist groups had been putting pressure on Blue Dog Democrats in the House who were blocking Obama's own health bill, Emanuel railed against the liberals in the room, calling them "fucking stupid" and "retarded" for criticizing fellow Democrats. Emanuel, protector of Blue Dogs, was annoyed that Health Care for America Now (HCAN)—ironically, the main grassroots *support* group for the Obama bill—was running ads in the districts of both Republicans and conservative Democrats who were opposed to the bill. Probably the most charming and revealing part of this story is that when an account of the meeting surfaced in *The Wall Street Journal*, Emanuel felt compelled to apologize—but not to the liberals. He apologized to Tim Shriver, chief executive of the Special Olympics, for using the word *retarded* as a slur. In Emanuel's warped world, it did not occur to him to apologize for slurring the party base.

Progressive groups have their own strategy breakfast meeting every other Tuesday. One faithful attendee is a woman named Buffy Wicks, of the White House Office of Public Engagement, who is the liberals' designated minder. For the most part, the Beltway liberals maintain their balancing act by attacking the interest groups out to defeat the administration, or occasionally some of Obama's aides—but never the president personally.

Americans for Financial Reform, the consumer coalition formed in early 2009 to fight for tough banking legislation, is a good illustration of the progressives' dilemma. AFR's strategy was to provide a counterweight to the immense influence of the banking lobby, but not to criticize President Obama or his administration. This reticence to press Obama came from several sources. Several leaders of the coalition had worked in the Obama campaign. Veteran organizer Heather Booth, its director, had just finished a successful stint working with the White House coordinating the grassroots support for Obama's efforts to get Congress to approve his budget. Many of the groups in the coalition, such as the powerful AARP, were politically moderate. Some had other fish to fry, such as the details of health reform or passage of labor law reform. Nearly all of the groups valued their access to the White House and congressional committee chairs such as Barney Frank and Chris Dodd and believed that direct criticism would risk their access. A number of other leaders of the group had worked either in the campaign or in Organizing for America, the quasi-official White House surrogate organization that replaced Obama for America, the president's lively grassroots network during campaign times.

Initially, most leaders of AFR saw it as basically a support operation for the White House, on the premise that the administration was acting in good faith to rein in the excesses on Wall Street. The group imagined a titanic battle between the White House and the financial industry, and saved its fire for the industry. Indeed, when the Treasury white paper was released on June 17, AFR initially sent out a press release praising the president in language far less qualified than much of the mainstream press commentary. But as AFR entered the fray and watched close-up the capitulations of both the Treasury and key congressional leaders, the group was shocked into a more assertive posture.

Virtually all the pro-consumer testimony and lobbying was orchestrated by

AFR, which was a shoestring operation outspent more than a hundredfold by industry lobbying. The defeat of the amendment to kill the Consumer Financial Protection Agency was very likely the result of AFR's work. The fact that the reform legislation was not even worse reflects the counterweight of the AFR coalition. Americans for Financial Reform had no campaign money to promise legislators in exchange for their votes, only the power to praise or to embarrass them. AFR had useful influence on public opinion and on final legislation, but almost none on the administration.

The labor movement, likewise, has found itself whipsawed. For more than thirty years, corporations have been busting unions and firing pro-union workers with impunity because current labor law is too weak to enforce the guarantees of the 1935 Wagner Act. Even if a majority of workers sign union cards, management can delay the certification election, issue threats, and fire organizers, and by the time the complaints are processed—often years later—the pro-union momentum has been broken. Industry treats the very modest fines as a cost of doing business.

The proposed Employee Free Choice Act would restore workers' rights by either requiring union recognition as soon as a majority have signed cards, or requiring a snap election to short-circuit management campaigns of harassment. For the labor movement, EFCA outweighs all other priorities. Labor was a decisive supporter for Obama. Union families voted for Obama by more than two to one, while demographically similar but non-union families went overwhelmingly for McCain. As sociologist and activist Peter Dreier observes,

Particularly impressive was the impact of union membership when voters' loyalties were divided between their economic and other interests. For example, 57% of white men favored McCain, but 57% of white male *union members* favored Obama. White gun owners cast 68% of their votes for McCain, but 54% of white gun owners who are also *union members* preferred Obama. Among white weekly churchgoers, McCain scored a landslide, receiving 70% of their votes. But Obama had a slight edge (49% to 48%) among white weekly churchgoers who were *union members*. Similarly, 58% of white noncollege graduates voted for McCain, but 60% of white *union members* who did not graduate from college tilted to Obama. Overall, 53% of white women cast ballots for McCain, but 72% of white women *union members* favored Obama.

Obama is nominally committed to supporting EFCA, but the White House has spent no political capital on it. Given Rahm Emanuel's tilt to the Wall Street wing of the Democratic Party, the last thing he wants is a stronger labor movement. Labor had also gotten nowhere in its efforts to shift administration policy on workers' rights in trade law.

After Rich Trumka was elected to succeed the retiring AFL-CIO president John Sweeney in September 2009, the AFL-CIO began speaking out more forcefully on issues that divide it from the administration, such as the proposed tax on high-quality health insurance premiums. But labor remains somewhat stymied, since it depends on White House goodwill for everything from unemployment compensation and jobs legislation to friendly appointments at the Labor Department and the National Labor Relations Board.

Reflecting on these scattered acts of political bravery, several conclusions emerge. First, there were available people at least as technically competent as the Summers-Geithner group, but for the most part they were neither hired nor consulted. Second, another policy path, very likely a path more conducive to faster economic recovery, was entirely possible. It was regularly articulated by well-informed critics but rejected by an administration with close ties to Wall Street.

Third, Obama's loyal opposition did not add up to a coherent faction pressing for tougher financial regulation, in the way that the House Blue Dogs functioned as a powerful pressure group for deficit reduction, or the pro–Wall Street New Democrat Coalition operated in concert with the financial industry to blunt reform. The progressive opposition was more of a pickup team. And it suffered from the absence of a broad protest movement in the country.

Finally, even a year into an administration that was not delivering, liberals were still inclined to cut Barack Obama a lot of slack, at least in their public statements. When it came to contesting powerful financial industries or exposing Republicans as toadies of economic elites, the administration fumbled. But the White House was superb at keeping its progressive critics off balance.

The overarching conclusion is that Wall Street still reigns. To alter that reality will take more acts of political bravery both inside the White House and in the streets—those with names other than Wall Street.

CHAPTER SIX

Political Malpractice

Insanity is doing the same thing over and over again and expecting
different results.

—ALBERT EINSTEIN

It was not the anniversary commemoration that the White House had been
hoping for. Precisely 364 days after President Obama took office, a year's
worth of political wishful thinking abruptly came crashing down. In the
special election to fill the Senate seat left vacant by the death of Ted Kennedy,
Republican Scott Brown, a political unknown, handily defeated Democrat
Martha Coakley. All manner of rationalizations and recriminations ensued.
Democratic leaders mourning the lost seat placed the blame on a weak
Democratic Senate candidate and a sneak attack by the Republican right.

Yet Brown's upset victory had much deeper roots. It was the consequence
of a presidency that had raised hopes of real change and then failed to deliver,
alienating both Democratic base voters and independents who had displayed
such excitement in 2008 for Obama. Democrat Martha Coakley, who lost the
race by 5 points, had made plenty of mistakes. But had there not been a more
general backlash against the Democratic incumbency, the Democrat should
have won easily.

In the deep recession that Obama inherited, a return to prosperity was
destined to take more than a year. Given strong presidential leadership and
identification with the struggles of working Americans, voters might well
have forgiven the majority party for the slow pace of recovery. What was not
excused by the voters was Obama's identification with bankers and insurance
moguls, his failure to clearly set priorities or name who was blocking a path
to recovery—or to stand up and fight. This recession belonged to Wall Street,

George W. Bush, Republican ideology, and Republican obstructionism—a point Obama seldom made. After a year, for many voters even in Massachusetts, Obama and the Democrats had become the resented status quo.

By the time Brown defeated Coakley, Obama's health proposal had become politically toxic. In a contest for Kennedy's seat, with health reform billed as Kennedy's legacy, Brown literally built his entire winning campaign around a pledge to be the forty-first Senate vote to block the bill. Can you imagine, in a hypothetical special Senate election in a liberal state, a year into the Roosevelt presidency, the Republican candidate campaigning on a pledge: "Elect me and I'll do everything I can to block the New Deal"? In March 1934, a year after Roosevelt took the oath of office, unemployment was still upward of 18 percent, but voters believed that help was on the way. And nobody could claim that FDR was in the pockets of the bankers.

Polls suggested that Brown beat Coakley not because Obama had attempted too much, but because he had delivered too little. In Massachusetts, Obama had won the support of non-college-graduates in November 2008 by 60–39; Brown won those same voters 57–37, so Democrats suffered a staggering 41 point loss among less affluent voters—those most hurt by the deep recession. In a Peter Hart poll commissioned by the AFL-CIO, voters by a margin of 61–18 said that government's policies were helping Wall Street but not the average working person. Even Massachusetts union families, who had supported Obama overwhelmingly in 2008, backed Brown by a margin of 49–46, Hart reported. Yet 47 percent of those polled said they felt the Democrats hadn't succeeded in making needed change; only 32 percent felt that they had tried to make too many changes too quickly. Even voters for Scott Brown were more concerned about the lack of change (50 percent) than about government trying to make too many changes too fast (43 percent), Hart found.

Other polling confirmed that Massachusetts voters supported that state's near-universal health insurance program, which superficially resembled Obama's, by margins of about two to one. Unlike the Obama plan, which promised a coverage ratio of about 93 percent by 2019, Massachusetts already covers more than 97 of its citizens. But though Massachusetts does include a mandate to purchase insurance, it does not include two of the other politically toxic elements of the Senate Obama's approach: There is no diversion of Medicare funds and no taxation of high-quality insurance premiums.

More Mixed Signals

In response to the lost Massachusetts Senate seat, the White House tacked in opposite, self-canceling directions. Obama's political operation concluded that the president needed to deliver a more populist stance when it came to the banks. That shift had been incubating since December when the president declared on the CBS program *60 Minutes* in carefully rehearsed language that he didn't become president to serve "a bunch of fat-cat bankers." So in quick succession the week of January 19, Obama offered a proposed surtax on banks, a surprise embrace of Paul Volcker's call to restore Glass-Steagall, and a strong affirmation of his personal support for a consumer finance protection agency. The president coupled all this with uncharacteristically hot anti–Wall Street rhetoric.

But that very week, the same populist anger that propelled Scott Brown into the Senate was threatening to derail Obama's renomination of Ben Bernanke. At the weekly meeting of the Senate Democratic Caucus, there were ominous defections. Even Democratic leader Harry Reid would not commit to back Bernanke. The White House political operation went into overdrive, bringing back several wavering Democrats, including Reid and his deputy Dick Durbin of Illinois. The embattled Fed chairman survived. But the all-out White House support for Bernanke signaled the opposite of Obama's newfound populist message on the banks. Obama's mistake was reappointing Bernanke in the first place. And in early February, he stepped on his own message, telling Bloomberg News that he did not "begrudge" the $17 million bonus awarded to JPMorgan Chase & Co. Chief Executive Officer Jamie Dimon or the $9 million issued to Goldman Sachs Group Inc. CEO Lloyd Blankfein, adding that some athletes make more money. "I know both those guys; they are very savvy businessmen," Obama said. "I, like most of the American people, don't begrudge people success or wealth. That is part of the free- market system." Yes, but massive taxpayer aid to banks is not the free-market speaking.

At the time of the Massachusetts bombshell, a debate was raging inside the White House about whether the headline in the upcoming State of the Union address, scheduled just a week afterward on January 27, should be deficit reduction or jobs. On the jobs side of the debate were Vice President

Biden, the House Democratic leadership, and some of the economic policy staff, most notably Austan Goolsbee, Jared Bernstein, and Christina Romer. On the deficit-reduction side were the usual suspects, Larry Summers, Tim Geithner, Peter Orszag, and Jason Furman. The political advisers managed to be on both sides, because polls showed that voters cared about both jobs and deficit reduction. The White House was also getting hammered by the deficit hawks in Congress and a media campaign orchestrated by the Peterson Foundation.

As details of the State of the Union address were leaked to reporters, progressive critics who had looked to the Massachusetts debacle as a possible wake-up call were ready to weep. Deficit reduction would come first. The speech would showcase hardly any new measures to create jobs.

The transparent budget gimmick that Obama's budget team had contrived was not credible as serious deficit reduction. Obama proposed a three-year "budget freeze"—which turned out to apply to only one-sixth of federal spending. The freeze, beginning in September 2010, would exclude Social Security, Medicare, military outlays, veterans' benefits, and homeland security, hitting only discretionary domestic spending. "Emergency" spending, such as the remaining stimulus outlays, would be outside the freeze. But the proposal put a damper on Obama's capacity to deliver new anti-recession spending. With unemployment still rising, the president was plainly signaling that deficit reduction now came first.

Even in its own terms, the freeze idea was a feeble sop to deficit hawks. The page-one headline in *The Wall Street Journal* for January 29 perfectly captured the unconvincing gimmickry:

BUDGET FREEZE IS PROPOSED
White House Plan Applies to Only 17% of
Spending; Small Impact on Deficit

Critics both in the Democratic base and on the Republican side were withering. "This is like announcing you're going on a diet after winning a pie-eating contest," said Michael Steel, the spokesman for House Republican leader John Boehner. Columnist Paul Krugman, who had been bending over backward to couch his criticisms in kind language, wrote

> A spending freeze? That's the brilliant response of the Obama team to their first serious political setback? It's appalling on every level.
>
> It's bad economics, depressing demand when the economy is still suffering from mass unemployment . . . It's bad long-run fiscal policy, shifting attention away from the essential need to reform health care and focusing on small change instead.
>
> And it's a betrayal of everything Obama's supporters thought they were working for. Just like that, Obama has embraced and validated the Republican world-view . . . A correspondent writes, "I feel like an idiot for supporting this guy."

Even Obama's own congressional leadership abandoned him. Though the White House sought statements of support from Capitol Hill, the offices of Nancy Pelosi and Harry Reid advised reporters that none would be forth-coming. Besides doing little for unemployment, the fervent lip service paid to deficit reduction only whetted the deficit hawks' appetite for deep cuts in social insurance. How, they argued, could the president be taken seriously when Social Security and Medicare were outside the freeze?

To further appease deficit hawks, Obama appointed a deficit-reduction commission—an idea that the Senate had just voted down. The commis-sion was designed by its advocates to bypass usual legislative procedures and compel an up-or-down vote on a deficit-reduction package widely expected to slash Social Security and Medicare spending.

This is, of course, appalling politics. It signals: We had to spend a ton of taxpayer money to rescue the banks and prop up the ruined economy. Now, gentle citizen, though you have paid once through the reduced value of your retirement plan and your house, you will pay again through cuts in Medicare and Social Security. By mid-February, punctuated by Senator Evan Bayh's surprise retirement, a story of systemic blockage (rather than Republican obstruction) and deficit reduction (rather than pocketbook help to ordinary people) was dominating the national narrative.

To offset this emphasis on the deficit, the White House cobbled together an equally feeble anti-recession program heavily reliant on tax credits. The total cost was $266 billion. Tax credits, of course, have the same effect on widen-ing the deficit as direct spending, but they appeal to Republicans—more bipartisanship. In a background briefing to reporters, a White House spokes-man actually bragged that Obama's proposed freeze would leave discretion-ary domestic spending at its lowest level in fifty years—quite a boast for a progressive Democrat in a still deepening crisis of unemployment. There was only $25 billion in relief to the states, far less than the projected shortfall in state and local tax revenues. His three-year spending freeze was scheduled to take effect in October 2010, just when unemployment was expected to peak. The Administration's own projections show unemployment remaining above 7 percent though 2013, a sure admission that the medicine is too weak.

Obama's post-Massachusetts stance tried to be all things to all people. A little populism here and a little conciliation there, a bit of deficit reduction on Mondays and Wednesdays and a little anti-recession spending on Tuesdays and Thursdays; a dose of gentle criticism of the Republicans combined with new pleas to seek common ground. It did not signal leadership.

In late January, after the Massachusetts result, Obama announced that he was bringing back David Plouffe, his 2008 campaign manager. Plouffe's assignment was to coordinate the 2010 off-year elections. After Obama's election, Plouffe, a new father who had been away from his wife for most of the grueling campaign, announced that he would take some time off rather than join the administration. Plouffe's return was heralded by an op-ed piece he wrote for *The Washington Post* on January 24, which sounded far tougher on the Republicans than anything Obama had said in his year as president. Plouffe concluded:

"Let's fight like hell, not because we want to preserve our status, but because we sincerely believe too many everyday Americans will continue to lose if Republicans and special interests win." It is a lesson his boss would do well to heed.

Where Credit Is Due

But hold on. Isn't this account too harsh on Obama? After all, he has done countless good things to restore the competent functioning of government. He has appointed people who believe in government's capacity to serve the public interest. Regulatory agencies, from the Environmental Protection

Agency to the Food and Drug Administration, that under Bush II were all but turned over to the regulated industry are back in competent hands. In Obama, we at last have a thoughtful, principled president we can be proud of.

Innumerable items buried in the budget, such as his initiatives on green energy, children's health, and high-speed rail, are making America a better place. Indeed, when the American Recovery and Reinvestment Act was approved by Congress, advocates for various liberal causes were overjoyed. For the first time, there were major increases in program categories that had been systematically starved under the Republicans. Head Start got $2 billion. Pell grants to help needy students attend college were increased by more than $600 per recipient. Entire categories of public outlay that had been neglected were jump-started—$80.9 billion in infrastructure spending, including $8 billion for high-speed rail, $10 billion for modernized drinking water and sewer systems, and $7.2 billion for broadband Internet access. Public education got $90.9 billion, a huge increase in traditional federal levels of support.

Nevertheless, the larger economic catastrophe overwhelmed the benefits of these new program outlays —and the incipient political reversal suggested that these new outlays would be short-lived. A child newly eligible for day care or Head Start services is actually worse off if her parents are unemployed and lose their home. Better sewer systems are small comfort if you lose your job. Despite the big boost in federal funding for schools, the much larger budget catastrophe of the states left public education closing schools and laying off teachers.

Even with these increases in long-deferred and badly needed categories of public investment, the events of 2009 were a net reversal for social justice. Obama's success, or failure, will depend not on incremental gains for liberal pet causes, but on whether he confronts the larger forces blocking fundamental reform and brings about a major shift in the economy and whom it serves. All of his small successes, some of them genuinely impressive, will be demolished by a continuing failure to seize the commanding heights of economics and politics to produce a broad-based recovery and majority political support.

Still, is it really fair to place so much of the responsibility on Obama *personally*? Didn't he face not just Republican obstruction but an undependable majority in his own party and corporate domination of political money?

The corporate capture indeed afflicts a major faction of the Democratic Party, not just Obama's own top economic appointees. There is nothing comparable on the Republican side, where party unity is fierce. In the House, Obama has fiscally conservative Blue Dogs and corporate-minded New Democrats in his own party. In the Senate, several key Democrats are even more inclined to seek common ground with the Republicans than he is. On many key issues, the sixty-vote "supermajority" that Obama lost with the election of Scott Brown existed in name only.

Here again, however, the responsibility of a president is to lead. Ronald Reagan and George W. Bush never had legislative majorities as large as Obama's. Yet Reagan got the electorate on his side and regularly peeled off dozens of Democratic legislators to support his program. Even Bush was often able to simulate leadership—enough to win reelection. Whatever his other shortcomings, he was able to carry out his party's agenda with a smaller majority because he and the legislative leadership achieved stunning party unity.

A disunited Democratic Party is nothing new. Roosevelt, Truman, and Lyndon Johnson all had conservative Democrats who collaborated with Republicans to block progressive reform, but these presidents were often able to build legislative majorities through a combination of legislative brokering and popular appeal. For several decades, the authoritative magazine *Congressional Quarterly* kept score of victories for what it called the "Conservative Coalition." According to *CQ*, the Conservative Coalition was at work whenever a majority of Democrats from the thirteen states of the Old Confederacy voted with a majority of Republicans against a majority of northern Democrats. In 1998, *CQ* discontinued the scorekeeping, because there were few traditional Dixiecrats and few liberal Republicans left. The conservative coalition had become the Republican Party, often joined by centrist Democrats on financial rather than racial issues.

Though the Republicans are a more cohesive right-wing party than in the past, the challenge for a progressive president who wants Congress to enact sweeping change is enduring. If anything, this challenge should be somewhat easier in a national crisis, when the public is hungering for real presidential leadership, as it was when Obama took office.

If Obama had the nerve that the moment requires, he'd be working with the Senate leadership to scrap the undemocratic filibuster rule. He'd be enlisting popular support with a much bolder vision of change. He'd be putting pressure on faithless House Democrats, LBJ-style, rather than letting Rahm Emanuel coddle them. And above all, he would be identifying the Republicans as the pure obstructionists that they are.

Affections Gained and Lost

In an economic crisis, popular frustration has to go somewhere. If progressives don't tell a coherent story about the culpability of rapacious elites and work to restore some balance to the economy, right-wing populists are happy to supply the narrative. A moment when progressives were primed to take back a majority politics has been not just lost but actually ceded to the right.

The events of 2008 portended a durable partisan realignment, comparable to the Roosevelt realignment of 1932. For nearly two decades, political scientists such as Stanley Greenberg, John Judis, and Ruy Teixeira have been credibly predicting an "emerging Democratic majority," the title of a book published by Judis and Teixeira in 2002. They based this projection on demographics, changing norms of tolerance, and the increasing pocketbook anxiety of the working and middle class.

In this analysis, the political cycle built on conservative social, racial, and cultural backlash, which had energized the Nixon, Reagan, and Bush coalitions, was winding down. It was giving way to an economic backlash that played to the natural strength of Democrats. Republicans had motivated their hard-core base with issues such as "guns, God, and gays." They put Democrats on the defensive as the party of affirmative action, race mixing, and sexual liberation. But voters were steadily becoming more tolerant. Citizens who were libertarian on economic issues were also libertarian on lifestyle ones. They might not want the government in their pocketbooks, but they didn't want the government in their bedrooms, either. Gay baiting was no longer a recipe for Republican success. Younger voters were also increasingly tolerant of racial diversity, as Obama's own election underscored. The shift in acceptance of intermarriage has been particularly dramatic. Even religious fundamentalism was not the monolithic force that was sometimes depicted. More than 30 percent of white evangelical Christians voted for Obama.

On balance, these writers demonstrated, groups that tended to vote Democratic were growing, while ones that typically voted Republican were shrinking. Young voters were increasingly inclined to support Democrats, and in 2008 they indeed backed Obama overwhelmingly. Blacks, Hispanics, and other immigrant groups leaned to the Democrats, and their share of the population was increasing, too. Better-educated and professional people tended to vote Democratic, and education levels were increasing. Women, especially unmarried women, an increasing fraction of the electorate, voted Democratic by large majorities.

Conversely, rural and small-town voters, religious fundamentalists, and native-born white Protestants tended to vote Republican. But their share of the population was shrinking. The hard-core Republican base of Limbaugh ditto-heads was still in a state of cultural rage, angrier than ever with the election of an African American president with a foreign-sounding name and the increasingly broad acceptance of nontraditional values, but that base was dwindling.

In addition, Judis and Teixeira contended, the shift was ideological as well as demographic, reflecting economic disparities. Writing in 2007, they argued:

> Voters returned to a more traditionally liberal view of the economy. Even though the economy is in better shape [early 2007] now than it was in 2002, proportionately more voters now believe that the rich are getting richer and the poor are getting poorer. The gap between those who believe this and those who don't has widened by 16 percentage points. More of today's voters believe it is the responsibility of government to take care of those who can't take of themselves. That gap has widened by 15 points.

And if you did the numbers state by state, which is how we elect presidents, these demographic and ideological shifts were putting more and more states in the blue and purple columns. Outside the Deep South, all but a handful of small states such as Idaho and Kansas were now contestable in presidential elections, and occasionally elected Democratic governors or representatives in Congress. The mountain West, which had been Democratic in the era bracketed by Franklin Roosevelt and John Kennedy, thanks to the benefits of federal development policies, had then veered heavily Republican in the late twentieth century. However, as the demographic composition of these states shifted, so did their politics. In 2008, you could go from the Canadian border at Montana to the Mexican border at Arizona and not pass through a state with a single Republican governor. Not only did Montana, Colorado, Wyoming, New Mexico, and Arizona all have Democratic governors, but—except for Wyoming—they all went for Obama, too. In the Southeast, states like Virginia and North Carolina had been lost to Democrats since Lyndon Johnson's civil rights revolution. But with infusions of politically moderate Yankees and a new mobilization of black voters, they became swing states.

In 2008, Barack Obama finally pulled together the winning coalition that the political scientists had long been forecasting. Several "red" states turned purple or blue. Republican efforts to make inroads with black and Hispanic voters failed. And the idealistic appeal of Obama produced a landslide among America's young.

If the Democrats needed one more gift, the unpopularity of the Bush administration, combined with the open disarray of the Republican Party in 2008 and early 2009, surely provided it. Sarah Palin wowed the narrowing party base, but she was an embarrassment to a majority of Americans. Meanwhile, the party of family values was the party of one tawdry sex scandal after another. The politics of penitence, in the case of sinners such as South Carolina governor Mark Sanford, Nevada senator John Ensign, and Louisiana senator David Vitter, seemed to the uninitiated less a matter of Christian forgiveness than ordinary political expediency and hypocrisy.

These trends were good news for Democrats—other things being equal. But other things were not always equal. As the elections of 2000 and 2004 showed, a feeble presidential candidate offering little to an economically anxious electorate could still lose despite auspicious demographic tailwinds. These groups, after all, did not vote for Democrats because they liked the color blue, but because of what Democrats delivered. And when Democrats failed to deliver, they easily reverted to Republican.

All of these demographic and political shifts were tentative and fragile. They gave Democrats an *opportunity* to win the affection of these groups, but they were no guarantee of durable support. Obama had won an audition among swing voters willing to give an African American and a Democrat a chance at governing; but the trust was provisional. The election of 2008 could have been one of history's great realigning elections. However, by late 2009, Obama was losing the Democratic edge among these newly affiliated supporters. And that disillusion was spilling over onto voter repudiation of the Democrats.

Back to a Republican Future?
Well before the debacle in Massachusetts, election night 2009 in Virginia suggested dashed hopes of a durable realignment. In recent years, Virginia had been trending strongly Democratic. In 2006, Virginians had elected a senator, Jim Webb, who campaigned on frankly populist economic themes. The Old Dominion had elected popular back-to-back Democratic governors, Mark Warner in 2002 and Tim Kaine in 2006, and Obama had carried Virginia by 6 points. But in 2009, Democratic candidate for governor Creigh Deeds, who ran very much as a New Democrat centrist, lost to Republican Robert McDonnell by 17 points. Even more distressingly for Obama and the prophets of red-to-blue realignment, Deeds lost big among the very groups that had broken late for Obama in 2008—young people, other first-time voters, working-class white men, and political independents.

McDonnell carried voters ages twenty-nine and under by a 54–44 margin. He carried independents by 66–33. He even carried non-college-educated voters, the hardest hit by recession, by an astonishing 62–37. Deeds, coached by Barack Obama's New Democrat advisers at the Democratic National Committee, evidently had nothing plausible to say to those in economic distress. A deep recession was demolishing people's dreams, and the incumbent Democrats were plainly not delivering enough.

Even worse, the Virginia result suggested the folly of the comforting thought that Republicans were just too far to the right to make gains even in the face of Democrats' weakness. McDonnell was no moderate. He was a protégé of televangelist Pat Robertson and a far-right religious zealot. His wacky ninety-three-page master's thesis at Regent University, Robertson's law school, contended that working women destroyed families; he even opposed a Supreme Court decision legalizing birth control for married couples. When *The Washington Post* surfaced the thesis last August, McDonnell's early lead dwindled to a near-tie. But McDonnell recovered by emphasizing pocket-book issues, sounding almost like a Democrat, and won the election going away. And when Republicans needed a fresh face to give the official response to Obama's State of the Union address, they turned to McDonnell, with no fear that he would scare off independent voters.

Like Ronald Reagan and George W. Bush, today's right-wing politicians have gotten ever shrewder at the art of speaking to their fundamentalist base in a dog-whistle language that goes over the heads of moderate voters but signals coded allegiance with the far-right family. Since the era of Reagan, the religious far right has become even crazier—but not so crazy that its candidates are guaranteed to lose elections if Democrats fail to deliver.

In Florida, for example, the tea-bagger faction of the local Republican Party is fanatically opposed to the state's popular Republican governor, moderate Charlie Crist, who was the odds-on favorite to win a Senate seat in November 2010. However, by late winter 2010, far-right challenger Marco Rubio had pulled slightly ahead of Crist in the polls, and looked as if he might win the August 24 primary. An extremist Republican candidate, seemingly, is good news for Democrats. But if their own base voters are unhappy and inclined to stay home, while swing voters are disillusioned with Obama, even hard-right candidates like Rubio can win. Indeed, because of the greater enthusiasm of the Republican base, January 2009 polls showed the far-right Rubio actually doing better against the likely Democratic candidate than the more moderate Crist.

As this book goes to press, in February 2010, the *optimists* in the Democratic Party are hoping to hold House losses in the November 2010 election to twenty-five seats, and the Senate losses to five or six. It would take a switch of thirty-nine seats for the Republicans to take control of the House and ten for Republicans to take the Senate. (In the 1994 blowout, the GOP gained fifty-two House seats. In the 1980 Reagan win, Republicans picked up twelve Senate seats.) Earlier in Obama's term, Democrats were hoping that they could hold on to their 2008 gains and even add a few seats—if Obama had delivered a credible, broadly based recovery to cement the alliance between newly converted swing voters and Democrats. In the Senate, 2010 had been shaping up to be a good year for Democrats simply because of the luck of the draw. Several Republican-held seats were up, in states that had been trending

Democratic. Ohio, where Republican George Voinovich was retiring, looked like a likely pickup. New Hampshire, which had trended strongly Democratic in 2006 and 2008 and was another likely Democratic gain with incumbent Republican Judd Gregg's decision to step down. Likewise Missouri, which had elected a Democrat in 2008 and had an open seat with the retirement of Republican Kit Bond. And in such swing states as Kentucky, New Hampshire, Arizona, Missouri, Florida, and Ohio, commentators in early 2009 gave Democrats a decent shot of taking over additional Republican seats. For their part, Democrats were defending only one really vulnerable seat—Blanche Lincoln's in Arkansas.

But by early 2010, that calculus had been upended. Byron Dorgan's surprise retirement in North Dakota in the face of stronger-than-expected opposition made that seat a near-certain Republican pickup. Chris Dodd, also facing a very tough race, abruptly retired in favor of a stronger candidate, Connecticut attorney general Richard Blumenthal, whose election was by no means assured. In Delaware, the popular attorney general, Beau Biden, abruptly pulled out of the Senate race for the seat that his father formerly held, leaving the likely front-runner Republican Michael Castle. In February, Indiana's Evan Bayh, the classic centrist Democrat, at age 54 announced his surprise retirement, bemoaning an excess of "brain-dead partisanship" (rather than the pure Republican obstructionism.) Eleven Democrat-held seats, in Arkansas, California, Colorado, Connecticut, Delaware, Illinois, Indiana, New York, North Dakota, and Pennsylvania, as well as Majority Leader Harry Reid's own seat in Nevada, are now rated as vulnerable. If nine of these went Republican, the Democrats' majority status would depend on the whims of Joe Lieberman. If ten flipped, the GOP would take the Senate. Indeed, if Massachusetts could fall to the Republicans, hardly any incumbent Senate seat was entirely safe.

The Wrong Populism

In 2009, something new appeared in American life—right-wingers taking to the streets. Until the Obama era, with the exception of demonstrations and occasional violence directed at abortion clinics, and mass prayer meetings that were also quasi-political events, the organized right did not go in for street activity. That was stuff for lefties. The right, rather, used radio talk shows, Fox TV news, blogs, magazines, think tanks, lobbyists, and campaign money.

But in 2009, the far right was literally on the march. The Tea Party movement began in a classic moment of faux populism, when CNBC's Rick Santelli, reporting from a Chicago trading floor, denounced mortgage relief for "losers" and proposed a "Chicago tea party." How fitting that a right-wing populist revolt was initiated by a TV financial commentator, to a background of cheering stock traders. By late February, dozens of anti-tax tea-party events had materialized, promoted by far-right talk shows. The Tea Party movement spread to right-wing shock troops shouting down congressmen attempting to hold town meetings on health reform. Gun fanatics brought assault weapons to political rallies, relying on laws in some states that allow weapons to be openly carried, and dared the Secret Service to intervene. In several states, far-right opponents of President Obama tried to block him from disseminating an anodyne back-to-school classroom address urging kids to work hard and stay in school, on the grounds that the president of the United States was subjecting their schoolchildren to "socialist indoctrination." Many local school officials were intimidated and hesitant to intervene to defend Obama's right to speak.

An anti-Obama protest on the National Mall on September 12, the day after the 9/11 commemorations, drew tens of thousands of protestors. The mood was carnival. The far-fringe right mingled with mainstream Republican politicians. Demonstrators carried placards accusing the president, however inconsistently, of communism and of Nazism. Many of the posters featured a whiteface, minstrel-style doctored photo of Obama as "the Joker," the character in the 2008 Batman movie.

These movements rely on a seemingly spontaneous right-wing populism, and some of the participants are anxious, previously apolitical citizens. However, much of the street action, from the Tea Party movement to the confrontations at congressional town meetings, is organized and underwritten by financial elites. Investigative work by the Center for American Progress revealed that the health insurance lobby, the Association of American Health Plans (AHIP), while supposedly working on a consensus program of reform in partnership with the White House, also organized some 50,000 of its member companies' employees to pack congressional town meetings. The behind-the-scenes work for many of the Tea Party demonstrations was financed by the FreedomWorks Foundation, which is headed by former House Republican Leader Dick Armey and is a coalition of some three dozen conservative organizations, including several financed by large wealthy donors and corporations such as the anti-tax "Club for Growth." These rallies, in turn, were promoted by conservative talk shows. Though some Republican elected officials periodically disavowed the fringe, behind the scenes they worked hand-in-glove.

The Tea Party revolt, the disappointment with Obama, and the voter backlash against the health-care bills came together in the Massachusetts special election. Though Republican Scott Brown seemed to come out of nowhere, in fact his campaign was built substantially on the strategic, beneath-the-radar efforts of the Tea Party movement. FreedomWorks employs a director of state campaigns, a man named Brendan Steinhauser. Noticing the potential for an upset, Steinhauser in December recruited Tea Party organizers from all over America to come to Massachusetts. Meanwhile, the National Republican Senatorial Committee, in a poll taken December 16, showed Brown down by 16 points, but by only 3 points among likely voters. Both the NRSC and the Tea Party organizers kept a very low profile, but made sure Brown had both money and ground troops. As he campaigned, his crowds were unexpectedly large; more than 1,000 appeared in a parade in the town of North Andover, for instance, with ranks swelled by the Tea Party mobilization.

FreedomWorks and its Tea Party also adopted an uncharacteristic stance of pragmatism, even excusing Brown's abortion rights stance, a deal-breaker for the far right in most circumstances. All this suggests that Democrats underestimate both the flexibility and political skill of the far right. When the institutional Republican Party tries to make the Tea Party movement part of its own organization, the movement insists on its independence, but it is nonetheless able to work tactically with Republicans on the ground when circumstances are opportune.

Studios and Streets
The echo chamber of right-wing media reinforced the fervor of the ground troops and gave them a coherent ideological narrative. In the Obama era,

America had supposedly put racism behind. But if you listened to right-wing media, race was alive and well. Obama's health program was going to tax your premiums to pay for insurance to unemployed blacks. He was using your tax dollars to bail out deadbeats who had taken out mortgages that they couldn't afford, many of them presumably minorities.

In the absence of compelling progressive narrative and policies to match, talk-show hosts like Rush Limbaugh and Glenn Beck provided a nicely simplified one: The frustrations of regular Americans were the result of the incursions of big government and high taxes; the erosion of traditional values of work, family, and religion; and the invasion of millions of illegal aliens. Liberals and Democrats, as the sponsors of expensive government programs, amnesty for illegal immigrants, and acceptance of cultural and sexual minorities, were the instruments of this deterioration. Obama, they charged, was a dangerous radical. Often, the lunatic version of this message melded into that of the mainstream Republican Party and of more moderate-sounding commentators like CNN's Lou Dobbs, now a exploring a new career in politics. Mercifully, Rush Limbaugh will never be an instrument of majority politics. But listen to the more urbane Dobbs, and you will get a sense of what might capture the mainstream if Obama fails: a glib but nasty politics that defines the crisis as the fault of an ill-defined brew of government, bankers, liberals, and foreigners—a familiar populism of the right slouching toward Washington to be born.

Saturday Night Live, as it often does, captured the damage to Obama with perfect pitch. In early October, as accusations of Obama's alleged radicalism were being repeated in talk shows and street demonstrations, the opening *SNL* skit showed Obama sitting stiffly behind his presidential desk "rebutting" the right-wing accusations. He begins,

> There are those on the right who are angry. They think I am turning this great country into something that resembles the Soviet Union or Nazi Germany . . . But when you look at my record, it's very clear what I've done so far is . . . nothing. Nada. Almost one year, and nothing to show for it.

Obama then pulls out a checklist of campaign promises, and none of them have been achieved. He continues:

So I just don't understand why the right is so riled up. I mean, how do you think the left feels? So please stop saying that this country is on the road to socialism. If that were actually the case, I'd be making some real changes. Instead, it took me four months to pick out a dog.

Conclusion: Glenn Beck and the far right are wrong. Obama is not fascist, only feckless. Small comfort.

Bryan or Roosevelt?

Elite commentators routinely disparage "populism" as a know-nothing spasm of class resentment. William Jennings Bryan is routinely trotted out to demonstrate that populism is not only misguided but politically doomed. As *New York Times* columnist David Brooks wrote, in an emblematic column titled "The Populist Addiction," populists "can't seem to grasp that a politics based on punishing the elites won't produce a better-educated work force, more investment, more innovation or any of the other things required for progress and growth."

But in fact, there are times when economic progress precisely requires displacing the malign influence of economic elites. What these broad-brush critiques invariably miss is the fact that there is an ugly version of populism that scapegoats foreigners, blacks, Jews, homosexuals, and others, and a constructive one that correctly identifies powerful economic forces that are blocking reform. Bryan had elements of both. But Roosevelt and Truman offered a progressive brand of populism, which was successful politics as well as economics.

The history of the past century shows all too vividly that when progressive reformers fail to address popular pocketbook grievances, the right fills the gap. It doesn't matter that their diagnoses make no sense or that their remedies fail. Anxious and frightened people seek scapegoats and simple explanations. The charge that Obama was a dangerous radical was preposterous, yet it resonated in part because of his failure to use a little constructive radicalism on behalf of popular frustrations.

In 2008 and 2009, America's economically stressed voters were up for grabs ideologically and politically, just as they were in 1932 and 1933. They were not at all sure of the cause or cure of their deteriorating pocketbook condition, who to blame, or who to trust to provide remedies. In these murky currents, several contradictory story lines were contending for attention. Obama's job was not just to fashion bold policies; it was to create a persuasive narrative. Thus far he has failed on both counts, because of his reluctance to take on and displace powerful economic elites.

Here again, the comparison is with FDR. Unlike Obama, Roosevelt was not afraid to take on Republicans for fear of being called a partisan. Nor was he reluctant to take on Wall Street for fear of being called radical. Roosevelt was not intimidated by claims that drastic reforms would "unsettle" financial markets, which were already unsettled to the point of collapse. The point of the New Deal was not to appease money markets, but to remake them— which Roosevelt did. The strategy was not to conciliate the Republican Party, but to outvote it. Virtually all of Roosevelt's major reforms were enacted over the strenuous opposition of both Wall Street and Republicans in Congress. But it didn't matter, because the reforms served the people and the goal of a broad recovery. Roosevelt didn't aspire to consensus at all costs but to help people, and that proved to be astute politics. Despite the hysterical opposition from the Republican Party and Wall Street, the people reciprocated. In his 1936 reelection campaign, Roosevelt carried forty-six states.

During that campaign, Roosevelt brilliantly framed the battle as one of the people versus the selfish special interests. He could do this with credibility because his policies were bold enough to yield concrete benefits in people's lives. There were plenty of right-wing populists around, but once the idiosyncratic Huey Long fell to an assassin's bullet in 1935, there were no reactionary populists attracting significant support because it was hard to argue that Roosevelt was not serving regular Americans. Far-right movements trying to rally desperate people kept bumping into folks who loved Roosevelt, because Roosevelt had tangibly improved their lives. Socially conservative citizens who did not think much of Roosevelt's relatively liberal views on race, his appointment of the first woman to the cabinet, or his Jewish advisers nonetheless supported him in droves.

In 2008, just enough working-class Americans in rural Pennsylvania or depressed Ohio, and even in predominantly white areas of Virginia and North Carolina, voted for Barack Obama, despite their hesitations about his racial background or his liberal social views, because they saw in him economic hope. It is not clear that they will vote for him again.

Nothing in the Republican program addressed any of the real sources of economic unease. The Republican Party had no serious program to remedy the financial collapse, except for more tax cutting and more deregulation. It had no believable program to put Americans back to work at good jobs, and no strategy to deal with the increasing insecurity of health care, or the deeper problems such as the vulnerability of the dollar or the collapsing retirement system. The efforts of its younger intellectuals to fashion an ideology that somehow combined support for individual incentives with government help in the form of tax credits fell apart on close inspection, because the proposed level of subsidy was too paltry to make much of a difference. Nor did it have plausible national leaders. The party chairman, Michael Steele, kept tripping over his own rhetoric and embarrassing other Republicans. Unlike in past years, the Republican bench was fairly thin when it came to potential presidential nominees. But none of that mattered. If the in-party fails to perform well in a crisis, the out-party gains.

Ill Health

The administration's inept strategy on health reform was an unfortunate bookend to its failed effort on financial reform. In both cases, the administration was far too closely aligned with industry special interests, rather than rallying the people against the elites. And in both cases bad policy turned out to be worse politics.

Obama and his advisers wanted to get health reform done in the first year as a signature initiative. Their premise was that this breakthrough would demonstrate the new president's effectiveness as a leader and deliver tangible and valued benefits to the citizenry. But their pursuit of health reform was a textbook example of how not to proceed. By the time the upset in the Massachusetts special Senate election provided the explanation point, many Democrats felt they were walking a political plank on behalf of a deeply unpopular bill.

Rahm Emanuel, Obama's chief of staff, was at first skeptical of the idea of doing comprehensive health reform. He favored a more modest, bipartisan bill. But once Obama opted for a major bill, Emanuel became the quarterback. As former political director to Bill Clinton and later a Democratic member of

Congress, Emanuel drew three lessons from Clinton's humiliating and politically disastrous failure to get his health plan enacted, all of them misplaced.

First, get it done early before the honeymoon wears off. (Clinton had relied on a complex task force that took several months to render its proposal.) Second, let Congress lead. (Clinton had naively dropped a massive, fully baked proposal onto Congress, rather in the manner of a British prime minister delivering a Royal Commission report, and expected Congress to dutifully enact it.) Third, and perhaps most important, don't get on the wrong side of politically powerful industries. (Clinton thought that by allowing a major role for private health insurers in his proposed expansion of health coverage, he would co-opt their support or at least their neutrality. He was wrong. The industry launched a massive and successful media and lobbying campaign to kill the proposal, most famously through the "Harry and Louise" ads.)

All three of Emanuel's lessons from the Clinton debacle backfired. The health bill, which consumed the attention of Obama and his legislative staff for a full year, was a huge distraction. The president passed up opportunities to rally citizens against special interests on the more pressing imperatives of economic recovery, mortgage relief, and financial reform. Letting Congress lead ate up time, and left the president looking like someone who had abdicated leadership.

Cutting a deal with the insurers and drug companies, not exactly candidates to win popularity contests, associated Obama with profoundly resented interest groups. This was exactly the wrong framing. This battle should have been the president and the people versus the interests. Instead more and more voters concluded that it was the president and the interests versus the people.

As policy, the interest-group strategy made it impossible to put on the table more fundamental and popular reforms, such as using federal bargaining power to negotiate cheaper drug prices, or having a true public option like Medicare-for-all. Instead, by embracing a deal that required the government to come up with a trillion dollars of subsidy for the insurance industry, Obama was forced to pursue policies that were justifiably unpopular—such as taxing premiums of people with decent insurance, or compelling people to buy policies that they often couldn't afford, or diverting money from Medicare. He managed to scare silly the single most satisfied clientele of our one island of efficient single-payer health insurance—senior citizens—and to alienate one of his most loyal constituencies, trade unionists. By September, *The Economist* magazine's polling unit reported that 47 percent of the elderly strongly opposed the health reform, while only 29.6 percent strongly supported it.

The bill helped about two-thirds of America's uninsured, but it did almost nothing for the 85 percent of Americans with insurance that is becoming more costly and unreliable by the day—except frighten them into believing that what little they have is at increased risk of being taken away. Emanuel grossly underestimated the political damage of his alliances and the compromises they would require. By late 2009, polls showed that most Americans doubted Obama's health reform would do anything positive for them, and the bill only became more unpopular over time both with his base supporters (who wanted a single-payer plan) and with the general public.

The damage extended to Democrats in Congress. When North Dakota Democrat Byron Dorgan made his surprise announcement in January that he was retiring from the Senate, his home-state press cited the extreme unpopularity of the Obama health plan as the prime reason. At the beginning of 2009, Dorgan was considered a shoo-in for reelection. A DailyKos/R2K poll showed Dorgan trouncing his most likely opponent, Republican governor John Hoeven, 57 percent to 35 percent. But in the last Rasmussen poll taken just before Dorgan decided to hang it up, voters preferred Hoeven by a margin of 58 to 36. What had changed? The monumental unpopularity of the Obama health plan, which, by then, 64 percent of North Dakotans opposed.

In my earlier book, *Obama's Challenge*, published in August 2008, I wrote,

> Many observers have assumed that Obama would make health reform one of his first and highest-profile initiatives. That, in my view, would be a mistake . . . Health reform will be one of [the] most politically difficult of all of Obama's challenges. He may only get one shot at it. He should take a little more time until he has the stature to prevail and the plan to get reform right. It would be a huge risk . . . to stake the prestige of his entire presidency on health reform at the outset, as Bill Clinton disastrously did.

I think events have proven me right.

Harry, Louise, and Barack

Throughout 2009, Obama's strategists, led by Emanuel, worked to keep the insurance and drug industries in their coalition. The key industries, in turn, worked to make sure that any bill would subsidize the status quo rather than supplanting it with public insurance or robust regulation and cost containment. In a May 11 memo, the insurance, drug, hospital, and medical-device industry lobbyists delivered a proposal to the White House promising to voluntarily cut costs in return for a White House plan they could live with. They were told by Emanuel and aides to Senate Finance Committee chair Max Baucus that a deal was contingent on their not attacking the White House plan or joining with Republicans to target vulnerable House Democrats.

On July 6, the White House made a deal with the hospital industry committing to cut projected costs by $150 billion over a decade. On July 7, Billy Tauzin, a former Republican congressman now heading the drug lobby Pharmaceutical Research and Manufacturers of America (PhRMA), took five drug company CEOs to the White House to seal their part of the deal at a meeting with Emanuel, his deputy Jim Messina (former aide to Baucus), and Nancy-Ann DeParle, director of the White House Office of Health Reform. The centerpiece of the deal was no price controls on drugs. In return, the drug firms promised to cut costs by $80 billion over a decade—a small fraction of their profits.

For Emanuel, former head of the Democratic Congressional Campaign Committee (DCCC), the motivation in these deals was as much partisan and financial as legislative. If he could keep the insurance, drug, medical-device, and hospital industries from aligning themselves with the Republicans, he could keep industry money from flowing to Republican challengers in the 2010 election. So while Obama was talking a language of sweet bipartisanship, Emanuel was doing what he could to neuter the institutional Republican Party. Industry lobbyists were given explicit warnings not to get in bed with Republicans, either financially or in their messaging, if they wanted the deal to hold. In a scathing letter to his former colleague Tauzin, leaked to *The Wall Street Journal*, House Republican leader John Boehner excoriated Tauzin, declaring that he had "betrayed" the true interests of the pharmaceutical industry by aligning PhRMA with Obama rather than his Republican opponents. As the summer and fall wore on, Americans were treated to the odd spectacle of industry groups underwriting a national advertising campaign to support a health reform sponsored by a liberal Democrat.

Ammunition for the Far Right

As Emanuel worked his deals with the drug and insurance industries, the Republican right took full advantage of the confusion by making preposterous allegations about the plan. One provision in the House bill provided payment for end-of-life counseling. This became the basis for a notorious Big Lie, popularized by Sarah Palin, that the Obama plan would create "death panels" to decide which elderly patients should receive care and which should be left to die. Palin wrote, on her Facebook page, "The America I know and love is not one in which my parents or my baby with Down Syndrome will have to stand in front of Obama's 'death panel' so his bureaucrats can decide, based on a subjective judgment of their 'level of productivity in society,' whether they are worthy of health care."

The provision that Palin distorted beyond recognition was actually sponsored by a Georgia Republican, Senator Johnny Isakson, who is an advocate of end-of-life planning. Isakson told *The Washington Post*'s Ezra Klein, "How someone could take an end-of-life directive or a living will as that [death panels] is nuts. You're putting the authority in the individual rather than the government." Isakson added, "I've seen the pain and suffering in families with a loved one with a traumatic brain injury or a crippling degenerative disease become incapacitated and be kept alive under very difficult circumstances."

The death panel canard, however, was repeated endlessly on right-wing talk shows, and versions of it seeped into mainstream Republican commentary. On the Senate Finance Committee, even Republicans such as Mike Enzi of Wyoming, who often worked with the late Ted Kennedy, and Charles Grassley of Iowa, a sometime ally of committee chair Max Baucus, were alleging that the bill did in fact give bureaucrats life-and-death powers.

Enzi declared in a radio address in late August that Democrats are "cutting hundreds of billions from the elderly" and plan "to limit or deny care based on age or disability of patients." Grassley, speaking in the town of Winterset, Iowa, on August 12, during a week when the death panel hysteria was at its peak, said, "There's some people that think it's a terrible problem that grandma's laying in the bed with tubes in her . . . We should not have a government program that determines whether you're going to pull the plug on grandma." He subsequently clarified his remarks to say that he was not accusing the administration of planning to pull the plug on Grandma, but in late August, Grassley signed a fund-raising letter exhorting Republican donors to "help stop 'Obama-Care.'" Obama's people were indignant about the misrepresentations—but so traumatized that they directed support for end-of-life counseling to be stricken from the bill. The efforts at bipartisanship yielded nothing, other than a waste of precious time and momentum.

The Vanishing Public Option

In addition to the fateful question of whether to treat the insurance and drug industries as allies or targets, any reformist president faces another core political conundrum: how to get the desperate uninsured and the anxious insured into the same coalition. In 2001, Yale University political scientist Jacob Hacker devised an elegant strategy. Suppose the government gave non-elderly people the option to join Medicare, a plan that he termed Medicare-Plus? And suppose government used general tax revenues to subsidize the premiums so that they would be affordable, just as government does with the current Medicare program for the elderly? This strategy, Hacker thought, neatly solved four problems.

First, it would create a viable coalition. People who liked their current insurance could keep it, while the uninsured would gain coverage. Second, the proposed hybrid system was a way of moving gradually to single-payer. Over time, the superior efficiency of a public system would attract more and more people and crowd out its less efficient private insurance competitors. Third, as a stepping-stone to single-payer, it would gain the enthusiastic support of liberals who were lukewarm about subsidizing the existing, inefficient existing private insurance system. And finally, by delivering care more efficiently, the plan would lead to enough cost containment to pay the costs of covering the uninsured.

In his 2001 version of the idea, Hacker wrote,

> [A]pproximately 50 to 70 percent of the non-elderly population would be enrolled in Medicare Plus . . . [C]ritics will resurface

whatever the size of the public plan. But this is an area where an intuitive and widely held notion—that displacement of employment-based coverage should be avoided at all costs—is fundamentally at odds with good public policy. A large public plan should be embraced, not avoided.

Key liberal advocacy groups including the Economic Policy Institute, the Campaign for America's Future, and Families USA embraced Hacker's strategy. In an amplified 2007 version of the idea, renamed the Health Care for America Plan, Hacker wrote, "Through it, roughly half of non-elderly Americans would have access to a good public insurance plan . . . A single national insurance pool covering nearly half the population would create huge administrative efficiencies."

This meant that Medicare-style public insurance would cover about 130 million people, dwarfing the 45 million currently covered by Medicare itself. In 2007, EPI raised money to have health-consulting firm the Lewin Group cost out such a program. The Lewin Group reported back that a program like this one would cost about $100 billion in the first year but produce net *savings* of a trillion dollars over a decade because of its superior efficiencies and bargaining power over price. The key to the savings was the large scale of people in a single, government-organized pool. The liberal groups widely disseminated these findings.

Next, the advocacy groups went about selling the approach to each of the leading Democratic presidential campaigns. Eventually, primary candidates Hillary Clinton, John Edwards, and Barack Obama all embraced slight variations on the Hacker plan. Of the three, Obama's was most cautious, and stopped short of true universal coverage. The liberal groups eventually mounted a $40 million support campaign known as Health Care for America Now (HCAN). In Obama's version, the Medicare buy-in idea was changed to a "Medicare-like program," and eventually dubbed "the public option." The liberals took the position that having the right to select public insurance was an essential ingredient to the success of the plan and to their support.

Obama's aides crafted a bill that nominally included a public option, but they pursued a very different political strategy. In order to make their deal with the drug and insurance companies, the White House had to sacrifice a true public plan as part of the bargain. Obama and his legislative aides let it be known that a public option was something the president favored, but failure to include it would not be a deal-breaker. In the bill reported July 14 by three key House committees, a much-reduced public option was available mainly to the uninsured. Citizens who had coverage through large employers, however lousy or unaffordable, could not shift to the public option. At most, according to the Congressional Budget Office, 11 or 12 million people might participate in the public plan by the time it was fully implemented in 2015, a far cry from Hacker's 130 million—and most of the efficiency or bargaining advantage of a single large purchasing pool would vanish.

CBO director Douglas Elmendorf, after a review of the bill, testified, "We do not see the sort of fundamental changes that would be necessary to reduce the trajectory of federal health spending by a significant amount." So the government would have to finance the net new cost of the plan, $1.042 trillion over a decade in the House bill, some other way. Different versions of the Obama plan proposed to find the money via a "play-or-pay" tax on employers who did not provide coverage, income surtaxes on the wealthiest, taxation of so-called Cadillac plans, plus hundreds of billions in savings in Medicare.

Frightening Natural Allies

Alliance with the status quo health complex led to a bizarre and self-defeating politics in which the industry was sometimes painted as the problem and sometimes as the solution, and ordinary voters became increasingly suspicious of Obama and his mixed messages. By late 2009, Obama was fighting simultaneously on several flanks. Republicans were opposing the bill wall-to-wall. Liberals were insisting the bill was dead without a public option, though they didn't really mean it. Conservative Democrats wanted more severe cost containment but were also protective of Medicare reimbursements to doctors and hospitals. The one Republican most likely to vote with the Democrats to break a filibuster, Senator Olympia Snowe of Maine, was objecting to the large fines that Obama wanted to charge people who failed to buy insurance, while the insurance industry was objecting that the Snowe amendment, reducing the fines, would deplete the new customer base they had been promised.

In the Senate, the endgame came down to doing whatever was necessary to keep Joe Lieberman and Ben Nelson on board. For Nelson, it was all about strengthening the bill's anti-abortion provisions. But Nelson, a fiscal conservative, also insisted that the bill tax high-end insurance policies. For Lieberman, the price was rejecting a last-minute compromise provision fashioned by Majority Leader Harry Reid jettisoning the public option but allowing an optional buy-in to Medicare for people over fifty-five. In some ways, this was more radical reform than the already enfeebled public option and would have covered a lot more people. The fact that fifty-nine senators were prepared to support it suggests that Medicare-for-all was not that far-fetched. But Lieberman, who had supported just such an idea himself as recently as 2005, pronounced it a deal-breaker, in part because the liberals liked it so much and the insurance companies didn't. Rahm Emanuel instructed Reid to do whatever it took to get Lieberman's support, and the Medicare-at-fifty-five option was killed.

Nelson soon faced a backlash of Nebraska voters that went far beyond the bill's abortion provisions. As one of the Senate's last Democratic holdouts, Nelson had used his leverage to bring home some pork for Nebraskans, including a deal to have the federal government pick up all the costs of expanded state Medicaid. Yet the plan, widely ridiculed as Nelson's Cornhusker Kickback, was nonetheless monumentally unpopular with Nelson's own constituents as an emblem of backroom corruption. Nelson would not have to face the voters again until 2012, but polls taken in December 2009 showed him losing by more than 20 points. Nelson began running commercials in Nebraska that declared, among other things, that the Obama plan was "not run by the government."

Nothing more clearly demonstrated the political costs of the path Obama chose. Medicare, the government-run health insurance plan for the elderly, is exceptionally popular. It is so popular that Republicans, who blast government-run health care in one breath, outdo the Democrats in the next breath proclaiming their undying defense of Medicare (which is, of course, *government-run health care*). Yet the Obama strategy was so much of a mixed message that it made *government* a dirty word.

"Not run by the government" is a sad slogan for a party that relies on democratically elected government to offset the insecurity, inequality, and insanity generated by private commercial forces. If not-run-by-government is the Democrats' credo, why even have a Democratic Party?

So we went from a politics in which government is necessary to provide secure health insurance—because the private insurance industry skims off outrageous middleman fees and discriminates against sick people—to a politics in which Democrats, as a matter of survival, feel they have to apologize for government. Thank you, Rahm Emanuel.

The deficit-obsessives around Obama had insisted that most of the bill not take effect until 2013 in order to postpone the impact of the costs. This was pure political malpractice. All of the worries about the bill raising costs or cutting benefits would fester for three years before most people saw any benefit. At a time when costs are rising and benefits getting cut due to other factors, the health plan gets set up to take the blame. Lyndon Johnson's far more revolutionary Medicare program, in an age before computers, became effective within a year.

If Obama's approach to financial reform and health reform united the right in opposition and kept regular Americans wondering which side he was on, these measures badly split his strongest supporters. Throughout late 2009, debate raged among progressive activists and health policy experts, on blogs, in the liberal press, and across kitchen tables about whether the health bill was an incremental step forward, the best available under the circumstances— or worse than nothing. It did, after all, insure more than 30 million more Americans, though if it kept an inefficient private system basically intact.

On the eve of the Massachusetts bombshell, presidential historian Robert Dallek, in a mash-note to Obama published in, of all places, *The Wall Street Journal's* op-ed page, wrote effusively, "However the political future unfolds, the Obama White House can take great satisfaction from winning passage of a reform on a par with Franklin Roosevelt's 1935 Social Security law, and with Lyndon Johnson's 1964 Civil Rights bill, and the 1965 Medicare and federal aid to education laws."

This encomium will doubtlessly be good for a state dinner invitation or two, but it is a gross exaggeration. The Social Security and Medicare laws created *public* social insurance to compensate for the failure of the commercial economy to provide adequate retirement in the first instance and affordable health insurance in the second. These landmark programs reinforced the sense among the people that government was on their side, and that it took compassionate government to address needs that private markets could not supply. The

Obama health reform, by contrast, muddled that message, ideologically and institutionally. It used taxpayer resources to subsidize badly flawed and inefficient commercial providers of insurance, tempered by only modest regulation.

We will never know whether a more robust approach might have commanded legislative support, because it was never tried. Had Obama started with Medicare-for-All (a partial variant of which, remember, attracted fifty-nine supporters in the Senate), Republicans and conservative Democrats would have been in the position of opposing a popular and easily understood reform. Had he made the resented insurance companies his nemesis instead of his partner, the lines would have been clearly drawn, with Obama on the popular side.

As for increasing coverage, the devil was in the details. Yes, more than 30 million previously uninsured people stood to gain coverage (or pay a fine), but for many the coverage would be unaffordable. Even with the premium limits in the Senate bill, MIT health economist Jonathan Gruber, an adviser to the administration, calculated that a family of four at about $60,000 income would have to pay fully 20 percent of their income in premiums and out-of-pocket charges. The vast majority of Americans—who still get coverage as a fringe benefit of their jobs—get no assistance and remain subject to the vagaries of employer-provided insurance, which increasingly offers unaffordable premiums, deductibles, and co-pays.

Because the plan left the system of private insurance largely intact, its promise of more efficient use of medical resources and cost containment was mostly a fantasy. More likely, the system would continue to contain costs the same way it has done in recent decades—by shifting them to consumers. Had the bill passed, we were on track to trade a crisis of un-insurance for one of under-insurance, in which people are nominally insured—but when they become seriously ill they can't afford care.

Trade unionists, who were among Obama's most loyal supporters in the primary and the general election, were furious at the tax on so-called Cadillac policies. In early January, Obama, meeting with House and Senate leaders, singled out the tax on expensive premiums as something he specifically wanted to remain in the bill, as a form of both revenue and cost containment. But decent health benefits, especially in collectively bargained plans, were something that unions had fought for, often as an alternative to wage increases. By taxing them, Obama was specifically going back on his pledge not to raise taxes on anyone who made less than $250,000 a year. Moreover, the "Cadillac" label was a misnomer. Many of these plans had costly premiums mainly because they covered companies with aging employees, or because of the inefficiency of the insurance companies that provided them. They were Chevrolet policies with Cadillac sticker prices.

Because the tax threshold was not to be adjusted for inflation, the proposed tax crept up on the middle class by stealth. Within six years, the tax would hit about 20 percent of households earning between $50,000 and $75,000 annually. AFL-CIO president Rich Trumka, in a blistering speech at the National Press Club, declared, "Instead of taxing the rich, the Senate bill taxes the middle class," adding that "most of the 31 million insured who would be hit by the tax are not union members." Trumka warned that Obama and the Democrats risked losing the support of working people who supported him overwhelmingly in 2008: "Politicians who think that working people have it too good—too much health care, too much Social Security and Medicare, too much power on the job—are inviting a repeat of 1994."

This was the same Rich Trumka who had been one of Obama's earliest and most energetic supporters, going on the road again and again in the summer and fall of 2008 to surface the hidden issue of race and urge workers to vote their pocketbook interests. In his standard stump speech, Trumka bluntly declared, "There are a thousand good reasons for any worker, particularly a union worker, to vote for him. There is only one very bad reason not to and that is because he is not white."

Along with Trumka's public tongue-lashing came a private warning. Trumka was working hard to keep some of his member unions from working to block the entire health legislation. And if Obama persisted in his plan to tax workers' premiums, he could forget about serious labor financial support in the fall. It was the rare moment in the Obama presidency when progressives talked tough, meant it, and got results.

Just hours after Trumka's public warning at the press club, Obama met privately with trade union leaders and agreed to reduce the tax on workers' insurance premiums as well as exempting collectively bargained plans for five years. But it was not clear that Obama would make it a priority to deliver on this bargain.

Some critics, such as former Democratic Party chairman Howard Dean, concluded that the bill was so badly flawed both as politics and as policy that it should be voted down. "If I were a senator," Dean wrote in a *Washington Post* op-ed, "I would not vote for the current health-care bill. Any measure that expands private insurers' monopoly over health care and transfers millions of taxpayer dollars to private corporations is not real health-care reform."

Mercifully perhaps, these intramural arguments were suddenly sidetracked on January 19, 2010, when Scott Brown's victory cost the Democrats their sixtieth Senate vote. It remains to be seen whether this defeat is a political blessing in disguise.

The Bipartisan Fantasy

Barack Obama came to Washington pledging both to change the tone of partisan acrimony and to work for substantive change in a politics that had brought America to the brink of a second Great Depression. In that bipartisan spirit, he named two Republicans to his cabinet, Bush's defense secretary Robert Gates and Representative Ray LaHood as secretary of transportation. He added hundreds of billions of dollars to the stimulus bill in tax cuts demanded by Republicans, and was rewarded with not a single House Republican vote.

It was noble of Obama to seek to end the partisan rancor and to pursue new areas of consensus, but it was obvious as early as February 2009 that nobody in the Republican camp cared to be the other party to that bargain. Yet a year later, in much the spirit of Einstein's definition of insanity, Obama was still pursing the same elusive bipartisanship. As Senator Bernie Sanders of Vermont memorably put it, "In order to dance, you need a dance partner, and there ain't no dance partner out there."

It remained an article of faith at the White House that Obama had won the affections of independent voters because they hated partisan acrimony. Therefore, to attack Republicans supposedly would alienate the independents who had put Obama in the White House. When Republicans won November 2009 governors' races in New Jersey and Virginia and then the

Senate seat in deep blue Massachusetts, it was political independents who massively defected to the GOP. The national Republican Party had displayed the opposite of bipartisanship—but independent voters evidently did not hold that against Republican candidates.

In his State of the Union address, Obama declared, "What the American people hope—what they deserve—is for all of us, Democrats and Republicans, to work through our differences, to overcome the numbing weight of our politics." But why ascribe symmetrical blame to the two parties—to himself and his opposition? The problem isn't "the numbing weight of our politics." It's the persistent power of free-market ideology and the sheer obstructionism of the Republican right. Lines like this buttress the view that the problem is generic gridlock and the incompetence of "government." By using this kind of language, Obama reinforces the right's story and communicates weakness as a leader.

Two days after his State of the Union address, Obama went to Baltimore as the guest of the Republican House Caucus Retreat. He spoke and took questions, again pleading for bipartisanship. Even after a year of pure Republican obstruction, Obama and his political tacticians were proceeding on a model of change that had already been overtaken by events. The assumption was that he will win approval for delivering on his pledge of civility, while Republicans will reap the public's scorn for their refusal to meet him halfway. Then he will gain some leverage to pressure the Republicans to at least find some areas of common ground.

Except politics doesn't work that way. The Republicans get far more mileage out of continuing to block him at every turn. And his increasingly plaintive pleas only make the president look weak.

At the Republican retreat, insisting that he was open to good ideas from any quarter, Obama even declared: "I am not an ideologue. I'm not."

But then, why bother? Ideology is not some arbitrary penchant for clinging to stale ideas. It is a principled set of beliefs about how the economy and society work, and should work. To be a conservative Republican is to believe that markets work just fine, people mostly get what they deserve, and government typically screws things up. To be a liberal Democrat is to believe that market forces are often cruel and inefficient; that the powerful take advantage of the powerless; and that there are whole areas of economic life, from health care and Social Security to regulation of finance, where affirmative government is the only way to deliver defensible outcomes for regular people.

That's an ideology, one that progressives are proud to embrace. So why does Obama think it virtuous to disclaim ideology in general? The problem afflicting America is not "ideology." It's the hegemony of *right-wing* ideology. And given presidential leadership, most working Americans—most voters—would identify with the progressive view of how the world works, especially in an era where conservative ideology has produced financial collapse.

In late January, the White House sense of how to proceed was spinning like a broken compass. Obama's Baltimore meeting was immediately followed by two sessions where he sounded almost truculent. Speaking to a town meeting in Nashua, New Hampshire, he insisted that the health bill was alive, with or without Republican support. "We're in the red zone," he insisted. "We've got to punch it through." And at a Democratic Party fund-raiser, he demanded, "How can the Republicans on the Hill say, 'We're better off just blocking anything from happening?'" But the same week, White House aides were discussing a new outreach effort to find areas of collaboration with Republicans.

Obama's strategists went back and forth between seeking a minimal health bill that Republicans could support and a Democrats-only plan proposed by Speaker Nancy Pelosi to pre-negotiate changes to the Senate bill acceptable to House Democrats. The fixes could then be approved by both houses with a simple majority as part the budget process, and the House could use the Senate-passed bill as a vehicle to send to the president's desk. As the White House agonized over whether to do health reform as weak bipartisan token-ism or a go-for-broke Democrats-only bill, a senior Democratic aide was quoted comparing Obama to a dithering driver in a traffic rotary unable to decide which road to take. "We're still going around the circle," he said. "You run out of gas at some point."

It may be, as was said of Obama during the campaign, that he is playing chess while everyone else is playing checkers. On February 8, in a surprise appear-ance on the CBS show *60 Minutes,* just before the Super Bowl, Obama revealed something of his hand. He called for a half-day, televised bipartisan "summit" with Democratic and Republican congressional leaders, February 25, to force the Republicans to reveal what they were offering to solve the health care crisis. The move came after weeks of White House tacking in opposite directions.

237er, warned that the president was playing a double game—that he was already planning a Democrats-only deal and that the February 25th summit was just for show. Said Boehner, "We now know that instead of starting the 'bipartisan' health care 'summit' on Feb. 25 with a clean sheet of paper, the president and his party intend to arrive with a new bill written behind closed doors exclusively by Democrats."

Finally, on March 3, Obama spoke for twenty minutes from the Oval Office, urging the passage of his bill. "At stake right now is not just our ability to solve this problem, but our ability to solve any problem." Belatedly, he had given up the fantasy of bipartisanship, at least on health care. Obama asked House Democrats to approve the Senate-passed bill, and differences would be ironed out in the "reconciliation" process requiring only 51 votes. Republicans squawked, but the sky did not fall. However, so much damage had been done along the way, that it was not clear whether House Speaker Nancy Pelosi could round up the necessary 218 House votes.

It remains to be seen whether Obama is truly abandoning the illusion that today's Republicans are potential partners. Getting the Democrats to pass even a flawed health bill would be a victory for Obama's leadership, but the bill itself still produces collateral political damage. And a win on health care would be only the beginning of a long road back to presidential leadership and economic recovery.

The Road from Here

If you reread Barack Obama's youthful autobiography, *Dreams from My Father*, in light of his first year as president, you appreciate that here is a man who spent his entire life reinventing himself. I don't say that disparagingly; nothing is more quintessentially American. As a child he was effectively deserted by both his parents and raised by his maternal grandparents. He went from being Barry Obama, a highly assimilated scholarship student at an elite prep school in Hawaii, to the Barack Obama who gradually rediscovered himself as an African American at Occidental College in Los Angeles and then at Columbia University on the edge of Harlem. He reinvented himself again as a community organizer on Chicago's South Side, then went back east to another elite experience at Harvard Law School, where he became president of the *Harvard Law Review*. He then returned to Chicago as a downtown lawyer and then a law professor, and he became a Christian, a member of Michelle Robinson's extended family, and a politician. Obama has always navigated between the black community and the broader American experience. Had he not, he never would have been elected president.

One could say of such a man, uncharitably, that he has a facility for trying on masks. A kinder reading of his books, speeches, and personal history suggests an integrity at the core of a quest for selfhood, and a self-confidence that sometimes borders on complacency. "My wife will tell you," he writes in *The Audacity of Hope*, "that by nature I'm not somebody who gets real worked up about things."

In all of these personal quests, the search for common ground has been a constant. The success of his presidency may well depend on what lessons he learns from his first year, and whether Barack Obama can reinvent himself once more—as a fighter.

CHAPTER SEVEN

Change We Can Believe In

Don't speak too soon. For the wheel's still in spin.

—Bob Dylan

Next January, the 112th Congress will take office. It will almost surely have fewer Democrats than the Congress elected with Barack Obama in November 2008. But whether the election is a blowout or a modest shift depends substantially on President Obama. If he can recover his footing as a champion of ordinary Americans, he will minimize his party's losses and be a more effective president in 2011 and 2012 as he faces his own reelection. The longer he waits, the more on the defensive he will be.

At various points in this book, I have invoked Franklin Roosevelt as the model of a president who seized a moment of economic crisis to rally the people to support transforming change. Given Obama's failure to follow the Roosevelt example during his first year, a different role model comes to mind for his path forward: Harry Truman.

When Republican obstruction of Truman's policies was unrelenting and Truman's own popularity was near an all-time low, he recovered by becoming an effective partisan. He not only saved his own presidency in the great election upset of 1948 but enabled Democrats to take back Congress in one of the largest vote swings in American political history. With the 1948 election, the House went from 244 Republicans and 188 Democrats to 263 Democrats and 171 Republicans, a net pickup of 75 seats for the Democrats.

In Obama's conciliatory gestures toward the Republicans, his own impulse is less Truman than Bill Clinton. This predisposition is reinforced by the Clinton veterans around Obama. President Clinton did manage to win reelection, but at great cost to American progressivism and to the Democrats as a majority party.

Truman or Clinton?

Clinton did not have a very happy first two years. He did reduce the huge deficits he inherited from his two Republican predecessors, and without raising taxes on the bottom 98 percent of Americans. But he did not deliver much on his highly effective campaign promise to reward people "who work hard and play by the rules." From his very first address to Congress, according to his political adviser Stan Greenberg, there were fierce arguments over whether even to use the words *working people*. Clinton's top economic adviser, Robert Rubin, won the political argument within the administration: Clinton would not talk about social class, lest financial markets be upset.

Clinton, like Obama, spent a lot of political capital on health reform, and came up empty.

His ambiguous moves to the left on social issues, most notably on gay rights, offended both social conservatives and many social liberals, while his lackluster performance on pocketbook issues failed to offset the damage with downscale voters. He badly split his own party by embracing the North American Free Trade Agreement negotiated by Bush I. NAFTA passed Congress with most Democrats voting no. When the November 1994 elections came, Republicans took control of the House, vowing to resist Clinton at every turn.

Clinton went on to win reelection in 1996 by moving to the right and positioning himself as a president above party. The strategy, devised by two pro-corporate advisers, Dick Morris and Mark Penn, was known as Triangulation. He distanced himself from congressional members of his own party as well as from the Republicans. "Congress," rather than Republican obstructionism, became the newly defined problem. For the most part, Clinton tried to meet the Republicans halfway or better so that he could get legislation enacted, which meant that he embraced many conservative proposals. Occasionally he pushed back, as when Republicans refused to pass a budget in 1995 and Clinton essentially dared Speaker Newt Gingrich to shut down the government. All non-essential services were shut down twice over the coming months, but Gingrich blinked first. Still, in general Clinton's efforts to move to the center, like Obama's, were not reciprocated. The Republican strategy was to take no prisoners.

Clinton signed several really awful Republican bills. He vetoed others, some of which were passed over his veto. And while there was political genius in his initial approach to welfare reform, true reform failed to materialize as he capitulated to Republicans. Clinton's original impulse was to take welfare off the table as an issue where Democrats were seen as rewarding idleness, and to substitute a framing that rewarded work. But as his own task force on welfare reform found, to execute this reform properly cost money. People moving from welfare to work needed child care, training, and wage subsidies, and they still required a safety net for periods of high unemployment. Republicans were delighted to "end welfare as we know it," but with draconian time limits and only the most meager work supports.

Clinton did not get welfare reform done in his first two years, as he had hoped. After the Republicans took over Congress, he rejected two drafts of a Republican bill. But eventually he agreed to sign a bill that was still highly punitive: It cut benefits and kicked people off the welfare rolls with only minimal transitional supports. That action—over the strenuous objections of two of his top political advisers, Stan Greenberg and James Carville, as well as Health and Human Services Secretary Donna Shalala—led to protest resignations by the three Clinton sub-cabinet officials who had worked most intensively on the substance of welfare reform.

But he did manage to salvage his own presidency. He was reelected in 1996 by about 8 points. Part of the reason was that Clinton simply got lucky, drawing a very weak Republican opponent in Robert Dole. In hanging on to office, Clinton created a lot of collateral damage for his own party and for American liberalism. By positioning himself above party, he wasted few opportunities to suggest that the Democrats were somehow too liberal. In embracing a combination of budget balance and financial deregulation as the preferred economic strategy—Rubinomics—he set in motion a boom that turned out to be a bubble. He failed to rekindle the image or reality of the Democrats as the party of working Americans, or of the value of affirmative government. He helped push the entire center of gravity of American politics to the right.

This is not a record for Obama to emulate. Even so, many political commentators are already urging Obama to govern more in concert with his Republican adversaries. And if Republicans make big gains in the November 2010 midterm elections, you can count on the usual pundits to declare that Obama tried to do too much too soon, and that he needs to acknowledge the shift to the right in the electorate by moving closer to the GOP as Clinton did after 1994.

But as we have seen, today there is no middle ground to occupy. Congressional Republicans, even more than in 1994, want a far-right program or nothing. Their main goal is to destroy Obama. With a jobs recession still raging, the Republican program has little that would revive the economy. So Obama has neither a political nor a substantive reason to meet the Republicans halfway. Unlike Clinton, who at least had a relatively prosperous economy in 1996 at his back, an Obama who moved closer to the Republicans after 2010 would have almost nothing to offer voters when he stands for reelection in 2012.

Give 'Em Hell

Harry S. Truman redeemed his presidency in a very different fashion. As a senator from border-state Missouri, Truman during the 1930s had tacked back and forth between supporting Roosevelt's New Deal some of the time, and occasionally siding with southerners and Republicans who opposed it. Elected to the Senate in 1934 as a product of Kansas City's corrupt Pendergast machine, Truman first came to national prominence as head of the wartime Senate Special Committee to Investigate the National Defense Program, soon known simply as the Truman Committee.

The committee's investigations of waste and corruption in military contracts saved the taxpayers an estimated $15 billion. His role also gave Truman his first populist edge as the scourge of corrupt war profiteers. The Truman Committee investigated scandals where shoddy contractors cost the lives of American servicemen, a theme immortalized in Arthur Miller's *All My Sons*. Truman could attack big business for contract abuses but also criticize big labor when unions went on strike in violation of the wartime pact of labor peace. And Truman was also prudent in whom he criticized. His biographer Alonzo Hamby writes that the Truman Committee "never went after Franklin Roosevelt. The last omission left Truman well positioned for higher office."

In that era, despite the overwhelming popularity of President Roosevelt, other party figures had far more influence than their counterparts do today. Vice President Henry Wallace, a darling of the labor left but a quirky personality, had managed to alienate key figures in Congress, the administration, and the Democratic Party. By early 1944, it was clear that he would be dumped at the party's July nominating convention. Senator Jimmy Byrnes of South Carolina seemed to be the front-runner to replace Wallace, but the party's liberal and labor leaders made it clear that they could not live with the segregationist Byrnes. After a brief boomlet for Supreme Court Justice William O. Douglas, Truman emerged as the compromise candidate and was nominated to succeed Wallace. He had no real working relationship with FDR. Upon Roosevelt's death in April 1945, Truman found himself president of the United States only months after being sworn in as VP. He was totally unprepared. He had not even been briefed on the atomic bomb.

For the party's liberal wing, Roosevelt's death was a crushing loss, and Truman was a poor successor. Not only did he lack FDR's stature, but he was far more centrist. In 1945 and 1946, Truman was preoccupied with foreign and military policy. On domestic affairs, he replaced several leading New Dealers with more orthodox figures. Truman presided over what was then called "re-conversion"—the shift of the wartime economy back to a peacetime footing, with the huge challenge of absorbing 12 million vets and millions more idled war-production workers. That transition was very tricky to accomplish without kindling either unemployment or inflation.

Liberals criticized Truman for abandoning wage and price controls too quickly. When unions, which had been docile during the war effort, pressed for deferred wage increases, Truman worried about the effect on inflation. In several high-profile conflicts, he seized factories and broke strikes in industries as diverse as coal, oil, steel, and railroads, invoking emergency wartime powers still on the books. He enraged Roosevelt's close ally, CIO president Philip Murray, by supporting legislation authorizing an anti-strike injunction.

Initially, Truman also lacked Roosevelt's sensitivity on race. When the Daughters of the American Revolution refused to allow pianist Hazel

Scott, wife of Harlem congressman Adam Clayton Powell, to perform at Constitution Hall, in an echo of the famous Marian Anderson incident of 1939, Powell asked the first lady, Bess Truman, to boycott a tea that the DAR has arranged in her honor. Mrs. Truman refused, leading Powell to blast her as "the last lady of the land." Liberals objected that Eleanor Roosevelt never would have attended.

Truman signed the Employment Act of 1946, which had begun as a far more robust piece of legislation—a commitment to full employment. The watering down of the bill was not mainly Truman's fault, but he was bitterly criticized for not fighting harder for the original version. Liberals hoped that the newly created Council of Economic Advisers would be staffed by Keynesians, but Truman picked a more centrist group, with Edwin Nourse of the moderate Brookings Institution as its first chairman. On a number of fronts, liberals felt that they had lost a champion in the White House.

By the eve of the 1946 midterm elections, Truman's popularity rating was just 33 percent. He was widely viewed as a little man far out of his depth. A popular one-liner had it that "To err is Truman." To nobody's great surprise, Republicans took control of Congress.

It was then that Truman rediscovered his New Deal roots. Far from accommodating himself to the Republicans, Clinton-style, he fought them at every turn. Despite his own bitter battles with labor just months earlier, he vetoed the Republican-sponsored anti-union Taft-Hartley Act, which he termed a "slave labor act." The act was passed over his veto. He was more successful in vetoing several other Republican bills. Truman emulated Roosevelt in championing public power. He nominated the revered New Dealer, David Lilienthal, former head of the iconic Tennessee Valley Authority, to chair the new Atomic Energy Commission, battling successfully to win his confirmation by the Republican Senate. And he emerged as a somewhat improbable champion of civil rights, appointing a President's Committee on Civil Rights that delivered a landmark manifesto, "To Secure These Rights," and addressing the National Association for the Advancement of Colored People (NAACP) convention in June 1947, the first president do so. There he delivered a tough speech promising the extension of basic rights "to all Americans." The black press even compared Truman favorably to the beloved Roosevelt. "We cannot recall," editorialized the flagship *Pittsburgh Courier*, "when the gentleman who now sleeps at Hyde Park made such a forthright statement against racial discrimination."

The Life of the Party

With pundits predicting a landslide Republican win in 1948, a famous memo authored by advisers Clark Clifford and James Rowe in November 1947 urged Truman to double down on his New Deal liberalism. In June 1948, he used an invitation to accept an honorary degree at Berkeley to make a two-week whistle-stop rail tour of the American heartland. He began abandoning his rather stiffly delivered prepared texts and speaking off the cuff. He made a few impromptu gaffes, but audiences warmed to him. He covered 9,505 miles, delivering seventy-three speeches to an estimated 3 million people. A new persona emerged: Truman as a plainspoken man of the common people.

Truman also began accepting more ideas from his left, another important history lesson for the redemption of the Obama era. At the party's Philadelphia convention in July, delegates from the newly created Americans for Democratic Action, led by Hubert Humphrey, pushed through a very strong civil rights plank for the party platform. Truman had initially favored a much milder statement on civil rights explicitly designed not to alienate the white South, but he didn't actively oppose the stronger one. Truman was now a civil rights president. He would later desegregate the armed services by executive order.

With the Cold War percolating, ADA had been founded as the voice of the noncommunist New Deal left, in contrast with the Wallace wing of the party that accepted the support of the far left. ADA for a time wanted to dump Truman, beseeching Dwight Eisenhower to run as a Democrat, but as Truman became more of a progressive the ADA became his fervent supporter. Without the pressure of both the ADA and the Wallace forces farther left, Truman would have been much more inclined to seek the safe center. The passage of a strong civil rights plank was the final straw that led to a convention walkout of key southerners, who formed their own States' Rights Party with Senator Strom Thurmond of South Carolina as nominee. Farther to the left, the newly created Progressive Party, made up of people who rejected Truman's Cold War policies, nominated former vice president Henry Wallace.

With defections on both his left and right, commentators were convinced that Truman was doomed. It was at the party convention that Truman announced the brilliant tactic of calling Congress back into session so that he could dramatize the stark differences between Republican policies and his own. His call electrified the convention. According to historian David McCullough, "The cheering and stomping in the hall was so great he had to shout to be heard." Truman then sent Congress a Rooseveltian package of legislation, on housing, aid to education, a higher minimum wage, development and reclamation programs for the South and West, increased Social Security, and expanded public power, knowing that it stood little chance in the present Congress. Biographer Hamby writes, "[T]he objective was not to achieve compromise legislation that all sides would consider flawed. It was to underscore ideological differences for a presidential campaign. In achieving this goal, Truman was extraordinarily effective. The dozen or so significant vetoes he issued in 1947 and 1948 underscored differences between Democrats and Republicans on issues such as income equity, labor–management relations, regulation of business, and the New Deal welfare state."

The observation bears repeating. *Truman's strategy was not to achieve flawed compromise legislation but to underscore differences*—differences that would play to Democrats' latent strength as the party of the common people. Truman's strategy, in short, was 180 degrees opposite from the one that Obama has been pursuing. In no major case did Obama introduce the bill that he really wanted, to emphasize party differences and to embarrass Republicans into either casting an unpopular vote or backing legislation that they didn't want. In countless cases, Obama's objective was precisely to achieve legislative compromise, often badly flawed. He would be wise to read up on Truman.

Truman's attacks on the "do-nothing 80th Congress" created the lasting image of "Give 'Em Hell Harry," friend of the common American. Meanwhile, the timing of the Soviet Union's Berlin blockade and the coup in Czechoslovakia, both in early 1948, undermined the credibility of Wallace's peace campaign, while Truman's strong support for civil and labor rights prevented most black and trade union voters from defecting to Wallace. Several leading southern moderates refused to join the Dixiecrats, while the Republican nominee, Governor Thomas Dewey of New York, succumbed to front-runner disease and ran a safe, lackluster, and uninspiring campaign.

In September, Truman decided to complete an extended version of his earlier two-week tour across America, traveling by presidential railcar, the armor-plated *Magellan*. This time, he would spend a total of thirty-three days and cover 21,928 miles. With each stop, his attacks on the Republicans grew more scathing, and his subject was nearly always the economy and the Republicans' role as the party of obstruction and privilege. In Dexter, Iowa, he told a crowd of some 90,000 people,

> I wonder how many times you have to be hit on the head before you find out who's hitting you? . . . The Democratic Party represents the people . . . These Republican gluttons of privilege are cold men. They are cunning men . . . They want a return of the Wall Street dictatorship . . . I'm not asking you to vote for me. Vote for yourselves.

Speaking in Denver, he told a crowd of 25,000 people in front of the state capitol,

> I'm not talking about the average Republican voter . . . individually, most Republicans are fine people. But there's a big difference between the individual Republican voters and the policies of the Republican Party. Something happens to Republican leaders when they get control of the Government . . . Republicans in Washington have a habit of becoming curiously deaf to the voice of the people. They have a hard time hearing what the ordinary people of the country are saying. But they have no trouble at all hearing what Wall Street is saying.

Imagine if Barack Obama spoke like that. As McCullough summarized the trip, Truman "was cheerful, friendly, and full of fight." In his standard speech he had favorite lines: "In 1946, you know, two-thirds of you stayed home. You wanted a change. Well, you got it . . . Now, use your judgment, keep the people in control of the government."

Speaking in Sam Rayburn's hometown of Bonham, Texas, Truman said,

> Some things are worth fighting for . . . Our primary concern is for the little fellow. We think the big boys have always done very well,

taking care of themselves . . . It is the business of government to see that the little fellow gets a square deal . . . Ask Sam Rayburn how many of the big money boys helped when he was sweating blood to get electricity for the farmers and the people in the small towns.

This was a language of populism, even of class warfare. But this language accurately describes the relationship of Wall Street to Main Street, in 1948 and in 2010. It turned out to be winning politics not because it was cheap demagoguery but because there were real differences between the parties, and major public issues at stake whose resolution one way or the other would benefit different classes of voters. Billionaire Warren Buffett once quipped that there is class warfare in America, "but it's my class, the rich class, that's making war, and we're winning." It is astonishing how the commentators who cluck about the perils of mentioning class routinely ignore endemic class warfare from the top.

In September 1948, *Newsweek* polled fifty leading political journalists to see who they thought would win. All fifty predicted Governor Thomas E. Dewey. A tiny handful of journalists traveling with Truman sensed the change in public opinion. "There is an agreeable warmheartedness and simplicity about Truman that is genuine," Richard Strout wrote in his *New Republic* column. Three months earlier, on the eve of the Democratic Convention, the same magazine had run a cover piece on other possible Democratic nominees to save the party from certain defeat, headlined, "Truman Should Quit."

Today's conventional wisdom would say that with a president's ratings in the 30s and the Republican Party controlling Congress, the obvious strategy was for Truman to embrace the Republican ideology and program. Thank God Truman was not being advised by Mark Penn and Dick Morris!

Historical parallels can only be stretched so far. Today's voters do not remember Herbert Hoover, but they certainly remember George W. Bush and the collapse of 2008. With a little presidential reminding, they would come to reject the House and Senate Republicans in the House and Senate as the Party of No.

Emulating Truman would seem to make a lot more sense than copying Clinton. Obama's ratings in terms of his effectiveness have been falling, but he remains personally popular. Most Americans want him to succeed. Why not lambaste the Republicans for their negativity and obstructionism? And why wait until a midterm defeat? Why not become a fighter for ordinary Americans right now?

It is too easy to contend that Truman did not have the 24/7 news cycle to reckon with, and could speak directly to the people. Ronald Reagan, after all, was president in an age of media saturation, when liberal press voices were stronger than they are today and when there was no Fox News. Yet Reagan was superb at taking his case directly to the people and using media against itself. People who did not like his individual policies nonetheless supported the whole package because Reagan offered a convincing narrative. Obama, with his mixed messages, is losing control of his narrative and letting his opposition define him.

Obama's political aides, including Rahm Emanuel, seem to be in denial mode. Supposedly, the sheer extremism of the current Republican Party will bring middle-of-the-road voters back to the Democrats. But this is wishful thinking. We have been here before. In 1980, a lot of Democrats convinced themselves that Reagan's extremism was sufficient to protect Jimmy Carter. It wasn't. Political scientists are fond of observing that American presidential elections are referenda on the incumbent administration. Presidents who fail to deliver, especially in crises, risk defeat. The extremism of the opponent is no protection.

Thinking Big

To create the political and legislative space to achieve the strong recovery that America needs, Obama has to begin delivering more for working Americans—now. Politically, he needs to more clearly articulate who is the source of economic woes and who is blocking reform. Instead of bending over backward to meet Republicans halfway, he needs to force them to take vote after vote that demonstrates just how little they have to offer non-rich American families, and how closely aligned they are with financial elites. And it would be salutary for Obama to distance himself from those elites himself.

Unlike Truman or Clinton, who both presided over relatively good economic conditions, under the best of circumstances the economy of late 2010 and 2011 will still be very fragile. At this writing, in early 2010, the administration's projections are for unemployment to stay around 10 percent for most of this year, and above 9 percent in 2011. That's all the more reason for Obama to promote a much more aggressive program of practical help, and dare the Republicans to block it—beginning now, while he can still count on Democratic control of both houses of Congress.

It's true that some Democrats in both houses of Congress often vote against the president. Truman had exactly the same problem. His famous veto of the Taft-Hartley bill weakening trade unions was subsequently overridden by the required two-thirds margin. But Republicans did not have two-thirds of either house. They were helped by anti-union southern Democrats. Yet that and similar votes did not prevent Truman from branding Republicans as his main opposition.

The risk of a jobs recession and a prolonged period of slow growth requires Obama to think big. But his actual policies have often fallen far short of his rhetoric. Roosevelt, as we have seen, was finally able to get the level of public spending necessary to break out of the Great Depression only via World War II.

How to have the national commitment that a war engenders, but without the war? Only a president can summon a generation to greatness, by defining the nature of a national emergency and using his powers of persuasion. Lyndon Johnson was able to do that, in the absence of an economic crisis, by defining poverty and racism as a moral emergency. Today we have no shortage of worthy causes, from ending the threat of global climate change to the challenge of putting Americans back to work. Both the stimulus package of February 2009 and Obama's attempt to reposition himself in his 2010 State of the Union address stopped short of being a summons to national purpose. The tone of the administration was almost apologetic for having to spend so much money.

A more serious round of new public outlay should be understood not as an emergency onetime stimulus but as a down payment on adequate levels of social investment to rebuild a decent and secure society. To coin a phrase, Obama needs to articulate a plausible politics of tax-and-spend—or more precisely tax-and-invest.

Investing in Families and Workers

Economic balance requires sustained public outlay in human needs and working families. After 1968, the task of aligning America's social investment with the needs of a changing society was short-circuited. The elderly had gotten Social Security and Medicare. But we never completed the task of investing socially in working-age families—programs of comprehensive early-childhood education, paid family leave, high-quality day care, affordable higher education, and universal health care, and programs for a well-qualified and well-compensated workforce.

These outlays make the economy more competitive as well as more just. And of course they reinforce that virtuous circle of government delivering for people, and people valuing government. Once government really delivers, the more that Republicans scream about tax-and-spend, the better.

It is important for government to improve the quality of jobs, not just the quantity. Government has unused executive power, as regulator and contractor. It should be national policy that no private company that does business with the federal government be a low-road employer. In recent years, there has been an epidemic of what's known as "misclassification." Permanent jobs are misclassified by employers as contract positions or temp jobs, so that management can avoid paying unemployment taxes or health benefits, and workers are not able to organize unions. Obama, by executive order, could specify that no company that misclassifies workers is eligible for a government contract.

During World War II, Roosevelt used government's power as a contractor to insist on decent working conditions not just in war-production plants but in all facilities of a corporation that did any contract business with the government. In the 1960s, when civil rights legislation was being blocked by racist Dixiecrat committee chairmen, Presidents Kennedy and Johnson invented the concept of affirmative action by requiring any company that had a defense contract to fashion an affirmative action program to recruit minority employees throughout its operations.

If we are going to use government to deliver all the things that markets can't, it's time for the president of the United States to use his exceptional narrative skills to explain why markets alone can't do the job. Obama has intermittently invoked the power of government to make the society more just and the economy more efficient, but he hasn't connected that rhetoric to programs at an adequate scale. He has also been intimidated by the fear-mongering about deficits.

A Fiscal High Road

Most of the current deficits are the result of the recession itself, which dramatically reduced tax receipts because of depressed economic activity. The deficits were compounded by President George W. Bush's policy of cutting taxes and increasing military spending for two wars. When Obama took office, the deficit for Fiscal Year 2009, which began in October 2008, was already projected at more than 9 percent of GDP.

There are really four distinct issues here that need to be disentangled rather than conflated: What's the best recovery strategy? How much government outlay do we need over the long term? What should government spend money on? And how do we reconcile adequate public spending with a sound long-run budget policy?

Despite the fiscal irresponsibility of the last three Republican presidents, the corporate right has nearly succeeded in monopolizing the franchise on fiscal prudence. For a progressive Democrat, there is a far better alternative: Use large deficits now to produce a recovery. Then increase progressive taxes on the top 2 percent of the population once we have a recovery, and use the proceeds both for fiscal balance and for increased public outlay. With adequate revenues, we do not need to choose between a responsible budget policy and the social investment America needs.

During the thirty years prior to the Bush tax cuts, federal revenues averaged just under 19 percent of GDP while federal outlays were about 21 percent, leaving deficits averaging about 2 percent. That meant the economy was growing at a more rapid rate than the national debt, and so the debt was not a problem. But the United States ranked near the bottom of the advanced countries that are members of the OECD in its spending on labor-market policies, publicly funded health insurance, early-childhood education and child care, paid parental leave, unemployment compensation, and other basic social outlays. According the American Society of Civil Engineers, we also have a backlog of spending on basic public infrastructure of better than $2.2 trillion.

Once the recession is truly over, a sensible strategy would be to increase taxes so that we can spend about 26 percent of GDP on federal outlays, while we collect about 24 percent in revenues. That would restore the annual deficit to about 2 percent of GDP and cause the debt ratio to steadily decline as it did after World War II. The Congressional Budget Office projects that the deficit will decline from its current peak to less than 4 percent of GDP by the middle of this decade, and the ratio of public debt to GDP will stabilize at below 80 percent. That's well under the post–World War II peak. By raising additional revenues, it's possible both to increase social investment and to reduce the debt ratio.

What taxes should be enacted? Here are some good candidates that together would bring in close to a trillion dollars a year, all of which would fall on the upper brackets:

- Rescind the 2001 and 2003 Bush tax cuts for people earning more than $250,000.
- Restore the estate tax to the pre-Bush levels.
- Add a transfer tax on very short-term financial transactions.
- Tax short-term capital gains at the same rate as ordinary income.
- Remove the tax deductibility of interest used to finance corporate takeovers.
- Close loopholes that allow domestic firms to incorporate in tax havens for tax purposes.
- Make offshore tax evasion an enforcement priority.
- Add interest, dividend, and capital-gains income to the Medicare tax base.
- Add a special surtax on all incomes over $1 million a year.
- Close other narrow-interest loopholes.

Walking the Talk

It is not sufficient simply to get the economy out of recession and then go back to business as usual. It would be a travesty to avert a second Great Depression, only to return to the precarious economy of 2006. That economy of increasing inequality and insecurity, artificially pumped up by debts and bubbles, was never sustainable, was never defensible, and is no longer available.

Obama's recent speeches have been filled with rhetorical acknowledgment of the need for big dreams, but not backed up by policies to match. Here is an emblematic passage from the 2010 State of the Union address.

> From the day I took office, I've been told that addressing our larger challenges is too ambitious . . . that our political system is too grid-locked, and that we should just put things on hold for a while.
>
> For those who make these claims, I have one simple question: How long should we wait? How long should America put its future on hold?
>
> You see, Washington has been telling us to wait for decades, even as the problems have grown worse. Meanwhile, China is not waiting to revamp its economy. Germany is not waiting. India is not wait-ing. These nations—they're not standing still. These nations aren't playing for second place. They're putting more emphasis on math and science. They're rebuilding their infrastructure. They're making serious investments in clean energy because they want those jobs.

This observation is spot-on, as far as it goes. The problem is that Obama's actual program doesn't go far enough to challenge Germany or China for industrial leadership.

Once recession is truly behind us, and the Federal Reserve returns to some-thing like a normal monetary policy, interest rates and inflation are both likely to rise. On top of that is the challenge of reconciling a prosperous economy with an environmentally sustainable one. All of this creates the imperative of a very strong recovery, so that these challenges are not exac-erbated by slow growth and chronically high unemployment. This, in turn, requires redefining America's place in the world, so that we pay our way with balanced trade accounts.

In the face of these challenges, there is a relentless stream of commentary from the right and the center that "we" have lived beyond "our" means and now we need to tighten "our" belts. This formulation is one of the very few in which Wall Street seems willing to grant that America is a collectivity. The fact is that most Americans have not lived beyond our means. Productivity has doubled in the thirty years since the late 1970s, while earnings for the bottom 70 percent of Americans have been flat or declining. The bottom 95 percent have suffered income declines for a decade, and the rate of decline worsened in 2007. But the top 1 percent have made out like bandits. Whose belts are to be tightened?

It is insulting for a president governing during a period of severe recession to tell the American people that what awaits them after recovery is a prolonged period of austerity. But this is precisely the Wall Street message—and Obama would be wise to distance himself from it. The alternative is a summons to a new period of American economic greatness.

Redefining Globalization, Restoring Manufacturing

For thirty years, globalization has been constructed on terms congenial to financial elites but corrosive to the living standards of ordinary people. Administrations of both parties have promoted a design for global trade that displays a studied indifference to the fate of US manufacturing and a willful ignorance of the fact that other governments promote their domestic manufacturers though industrial policies and varying degrees of mercantilism. Supposedly, we didn't need manufacturing because we could live in a service economy. But the most lucrative services turned out be financial services built on speculation that ended with a crash.

Why would the US government, which has not been shy about defending the nation's military security, be such a pushover when it comes to trade and industry? The Cold War, paradoxically, is a major explanation. After World War II, the United States was industrially preeminent, and we were also building an alliance system against the USSR. We had our own vast, unacknowledged system of industrial planning, research, and development. It was called the Pentagon. American industry was enjoying huge spillovers from technologies created by military agencies, as well as the pure research spending of the National Science Foundation and the National Institutes of Health that subsidized our great universities as incubators of industry.

In the meantime, countries such as Germany, France, Korea, and Japan explicitly practiced a somewhat different form of capitalism, namely state-led economic development—a concept we thought far inferior to our laissez-faire approach. Yet we were hypocrites. We talked free markets, but we had our own closet industrial policy—though it was not coherent or strategic, and it has withered over time.

We were also mistaken in our premise that foreign mercantilism could not succeed. By the 1980s, the state-led industrial development of nations such as Japan had become more than a minor pinprick. Europe had recovered, with no small dose of planning. The Cold War was ending, and China was knocking on the door. Entire US industries were being displaced. The role model for newly emergent nations was not the laissez-faire model touted by the United States but rather the frankly mercantilist forms of capitalism such as those of Korea and Brazil, and in more extreme fashion China.

It would have made sense for our leaders to realize that we were no longer in the cozy womb of 1950s industrial supremacy. We might have initiated a new round of trade talks intended to clarify which policies of industrial aid, applied research-and-development assistance, wage subsidies, regional policies, domestic content requirements, and other forms of mercantilism are legitimate tools of economic development and which ones are predatory. We might have created robust tribunals to identify and punish illicit behavior. We might have used our still-substantial economic leverage to deny market privileges to flagrant and chronic violators. We might have devised an industrial policy of our own.

But we did none of the above. The reason for this seemingly irrational trade diplomacy was one part military goals crowding out industrial ones, one part ideology, and one very large part the increasing influence of Wall Street. Free-trade economists provided intellectual cover, but the push for ever-"freer" trade mainly came from the influence of the US financial industry seeking global reach and from allied industries eager to produce in the cheapest possible location and to use global trade to undercut all forms of domestic regulation.

When China applied for membership in the World Trade Organization in 1998, at a time when China was a lot weaker economically and financially, and the stench of the Tiananmen massacre was still fresh, the United States had far more diplomatic leverage than the rather pitiful show of humility befitting a debtor nation displayed on President Obama's maiden trip to Beijing. But as the memoirs of both Robert Rubin and Joseph Stiglitz confirm, that leverage was used mainly to gain access for US banks, and not to require China to modify its system of predatory industrial mercantilism. For now, the moment has passed. The longer we delay using our leverage against the Chinese, the weaker is our hand.

Today most American multinational companies, largely abandoned by their government, have been left to make a separate peace with foreign mercantilist practices. That means accepting foreign offers to shift research, technology, and production offshore, sometimes with the benefit of explicit subsidies of land, plant, equipment, and R&D, and the implicit subsidy of very low-wage and docile workers and weak environmental or safety requirements. At other times, the terms of the deal are more stick than carrot: If you want to sell here, you must manufacture here. Or even worse, you can manufacture here but only for re-export to your own domestic market and not for local sale.

In this fashion, we are losing industry after industry. The ranks of the companies that behave like patriots have dwindled. Most big multinationals are now too cozy with foreign mercantilists to put up much of a fuss anymore. It has fallen to smaller companies, trade unions, and a few large firms such as Corning and US Steel that are still committed to producing domestically to fight the good fight.

In the meantime, the promise of an industrial renaissance spearheaded by the Obama administration's investment in green energy or mass transit or high-speed rail or a smart electricity grid is not translating because there are just too many products that we no longer make, too many foreign links in the industrial supply chain, and an ideological aversion to a true industrial policy. It will not do to have made-in-America mean only final assembly while the engineering and advanced manufacturing repose abroad. We need a comprehensive industrial strategy to reclaim manufacturing, and a companion trade policy to make sure that foreign producers do not capture advantage by placing thumbs on the scale, or by manipulating their currencies as the Chinese do. It is better to have this showdown with China sooner rather than later.

Putting Finance in Its Place

In earlier chapters, I have suggested the elements of an effective program of financial reform. The bottom line is that the entire business model of the financial industry needs to be drastically simplified, so that banking reverts to its proper role of providing credit and capital to the rest of the economy, and no financial product is too complex for regulators to grasp. This will require not just the tougher rhetoric we have lately seen, but a concerted regulatory push relying on all the powers of the presidency. Some of this requires new legislation, but much of it can be accomplished by executive action, as Sheila Bair of the FDIC has demonstrated.

It is simply a myth that the complexity adds to the economy's efficiency, or that these are financial products required or demanded by bank customers. Paul Volcker memorably quipped that the only recent financial innovation that truly added value was the ATM machine.

Not long ago, I found myself speaking at a conference at the United Nations. One of my co-panelists was Dr. Yaga Reddy, who had just retired from his post as governor of the Bank of India, the counterpart of Fed chairman Ben Bernanke. India somehow missed the consequences of the toxic products invented and exported by US financial institutions. It had no financial crisis.

Chatting at a panelists' lunch before the program began, I asked Dr. Reddy how India managed to dodge the financial bullet. "We don't understand these complex instruments," he told me with a smile, "so we don't permit them. We leave them to the advanced nations like you." Barack Obama should hire this man.

My reporting has confirmed that Dr. Reddy stood firm in the face of intense pressure from the governments of Britain and the United States, as well as the world's large banks and their Indian affiliates. He was attacked as old-fashioned and rigid. But the Indian central bank under his leadership persisted in using reserve requirements to make it unprofitable for Indian banks to create and gamble in the kind of exotic derivative securities that crashed the American system. India sailed through 2009 with 8 percent growth, and Dr. Reddy's banking colleagues belatedly thanked him. India's banking system does its job of collecting savings and channeling the capital to productive investments.

In the United States, the historic task of this era of reform is to shrink the financial sector back down to an efficient size with a transparent business model. The absence of sweeping reform leaves us with a bloated financial sector that constitutes a large tax on the rest of the economy. Banks are often described as financial intermediaries. They are paid to hold deposits and make informed judgments on credit risks. In the healthy years of the post-war boom, when the financial system was well regulated, the real economy thrived and the banking sector was more like a public utility. It was simple and transparent enough to regulate.

There were no collateralized debt obligations, no credit derivatives. Nobody was too big to fail. Commercial banks and thrift institutions took in deposits and made loans. The more entrepreneurial parts of the financial system, such as investment banks and venture capitalists, used money not tacitly backed by government and channeled risk capital for new enterprises and corporate expansions. The real part of the economy got the capital it needed, and the financial sector itself consumed only a small share of total corporate profits. From the 1950s through the early 1980s, banks and other financial institutions accounted for between 8 and 16 percent of total corporate profits. By 2006, the figure was more than 40 percent.

Those who defended the bloating of the financial sector argued that the innovation on Wall Street, by definition, was good for the real economy. Year after year, Alan Greenspan and others kept giving speeches, writing academic papers, and testifying before Congress on how newly created instruments helped disseminate capital and spread risk. But the test of that should be increasing productivity or GDP growth. We now know that the new financial economy *concentrated* risk and spread contagion. The banking sector became an end in itself. All of this functioned at the expense of the real economy.

A New Economic Team

Early in 2009, I was invited to a two-day retreat of union organizers. My assignment was to discuss the rising levels of unemployment and the challenge of financial reform. The speaker who was on just before me was a man named Mike Kruglik, who had worked with Barack Obama as an organizer on the South Side of Chicago. Kruglik began a long conversation with the union organizers about the nature of power by asking, "Do you think Barack

Obama wants power?" For Kruglik, the right answer was, "Of course Barack Obama wants power." It was a variation on training sessions that Kruglik has done hundreds of times, in the manner of his mentor Saul Alinsky, raising questions of how to shift power from economic elites to regular people. He used Obama as an example of someone who has successfully sought and gotten political power, hopefully to be used for the common good.

At one point in the conversation, Kruglik, emphasizing the importance of toughness, reminded his listeners how quickly and unsentimentally during the campaign Obama had distanced himself from the Reverend Jeremiah Wright, a onetime father figure and spiritual mentor whose inflammatory comments had become an embarrassment. Kruglik added, "There are perhaps six or seven people who Barack Obama would die for. Anyone else, he would throw under a bus if it became necessary to preserve his power."

This was hyperbole to make a point. But when his close friend and adviser Tom Daschle turned out to have misreported expenses on his income taxes, Obama did not hesitate to jettison Daschle's nomination as secretary of health and human services, overnight. And when it came out that Van Jones, a very talented environmental leader appointed to a White House post on green jobs, had once signed a foolish statement implying that President Bush might have had advance knowledge of the 9/11 attacks, Jones was dispatched in a day. White House Counsel Greg Craig was a very close friend of the Clintons going back to their Yale Law School days; he had deserted Hillary Clinton's candidacy to support Obama. But when Craig crossed swords with Rahm Emanuel, he was gone. Craig's sin was to take literally Obama's rhetoric that the United States should never again be complicit in torture. That threatened to embarrass the CIA, even to expose some of its agents and senior officials to prosecution. CIA chief Leon Panetta, in an earlier incarnation, had been Bill Clinton's chief of staff, and had rescued the career of the young Rahm Emanuel from a series of missteps. Emanuel owed Panetta, and now Panetta needed Emanuel's help in getting Craig to back off. Soon Craig was squeezed out.

Obama needs to direct this resolve at the failures of his economic team. There are several key members who are not serving his interests—or the country's. They richly deserve to be thrown under the proverbial bus. We'll see whether Obama can muster the nerve.

Barack Obama is a man of many parts. He is above all a learner. As Doris Kearns Goodman reminds me, Lincoln had to go through several generals before he finally found a competent commander in Ulysses S. Grant. Will Obama rediscover that audacious self that attracted so many Americans during the campaign, and save his presidency?

It Takes a Movement

In the 2008 campaign, Obama demonstrated a stunning capacity to inspire Americans who were cynical after decades of dashed hopes and failed politicians. He combined an idealistic personal appeal with an organizing machine seldom seen in presidential politics. But once the campaign ended, the grassroots organizing machine, Obama for America, was neutered into Organizing for America. This was intended to keep Obama's volunteers engaged, but OFA was quickly downgraded into a rather mechanical support group that the White House and the Democratic National Committee hoped could be activated on command to support presidential initiatives. The idea of a real social movement, sparked by a progressive president, to contest entrenched elites was dead. The elites were now inside the government. The Web site and events orchestrated by Organizing for America were uninspired, lackluster affairs, and few people showed up. The White House seemed afraid of anything smacking of a mass movement that the administration might not totally control.

In September 2009, a frustrated Marshall Ganz, the veteran organizer who had brilliantly directed Camp Obama, where campaign organizers were trained, wrote with Peter Dreier in *The Washington Post:*

> Since January, most advocacy groups committed to Obama's reform objectives (labor unions, community organizations, environmentalists and netroots groups such as MoveOn) have pushed the pause button. Organizing for America, for example, encouraged Obama's supporters to work on local community service projects, such as helping homeless shelters and tutoring children. That's fine, but it's not the way to pass reform legislation.
>
> One Obama campaign volunteer from Delaware County, Pa.,

put it this way soon after the election: "We're all fired up now, and twiddling our thumbs! . . . Here, ALL the leader volunteers are getting bombarded by calls from volunteers essentially asking 'Nowwhatnowwhatnowwhat?'"

Meanwhile, as the president's agenda emerged, his former campaign volunteers and the advocacy groups turned to politics as usual: the insider tactics of e-mails, phone calls and meetings with members of Congress. Some groups—hoping to go toe-to-toe with the well-funded business-backed opposition—launched expensive TV and radio ad campaigns in key states to pressure conservative Democrats. Lobbying and advertising are necessary, but they have never been sufficient to defeat powerful corporate interests.

In short, the administration and its allies followed a strategy that blurred their goals, avoided polarization, confused marketing with movement-building and hoped for bipartisan compromise that was never in the cards. This approach replaced an "outsider" mobilizing strategy that not only got Obama into the White House but has also played a key role in every successful reform movement, including abolition, women's suffrage, workers' rights, civil rights and environmental justice.

But, as Ganz and Dreier add, you would not really expect the White House to be the primary engine of a social movement. In every important progressive era, social movements that were organized outside electoral politics have put constructive pressure on presidents and on Congress. Since Reagan, the right has been brilliant at using its period in office to deliver resources and ideological support to the mass movement of the grassroots right, such as the Christian fundamentalist right, the gun lobby, and the anti-abortion movement. The Reagan and Bush White House political operations understood that these mass movements were their base. Democratic presidents, by contrast, have been far more ambivalent about using the power of public office to help progressive movements such as the labor and environmental movements become more powerful forces that might at times push them from the left.

At the end of the day, it is up to progressive activists to build movements that could move this president to a more progressive course, and not expect Obama to do the job for them. Indeed, if you look at the great successes of social change in the past century, you appreciate that every one of them required a social movement. In two crucial cases, Roosevelt's strategic alliance with the labor movement during both the 1930s and World War II, and Lyndon Johnson's encouragement of Dr. King and the civil rights movement in 1964 and 1965, there was a potent alliance between a popular movement and a committed president. And in both cases, the president started out more conservative and became more progressive in office, sometimes working with the movement for change, sometimes pushing back on it, often being pushed by it.

In all the instances of progress on social reform, the movement came first. Typically, political radicals were the instigators, norms gradually changed, and once-radical views became mainstream. Half a century ago, anyone who proposed that interracial marriage, much less gay marriage, was no big deal would have been dismissed as far-fringe. Today a majority of Americans under fifty tell pollsters they have no qualms about marriage across races, and large majorities consider homosexuality a private matter.

It took a more than a century of a women's protest, ridiculed both in the era of the crusaders for women's suffrage (who were put down condescendingly as suffragettes) and among the second-wave feminists (who were dismissed as "bra-burners") before mainstream politicians took women's rights seriously.

Beginning with the spontaneous Stonewall protests of 1969, and the earlier, very polite Mattachine Society dating to the 1950s, it took the bravery of gay activists, the movement to encourage gays and lesbians to come out to their friends and family, the enlistment of sympathy rather than scorn for the HIV epidemic, and candidates running as openly gay and getting elected, before straight public opinion very gradually acknowledged that homosexuals were human beings and gay baiting retreated to a fringe viewpoint.

The disability rights movement seemingly came out of nowhere and persuaded a Republican president, George H. W. Bush, to sign the sweeping Americans with Disabilities Act in 1990. But the movement was the result of extensive and sophisticated peer consciousness raising and organizing.

The one quasi-economic movement that made some incursions on power-ful corporate elites, the movement to save the planet, was also the result of on-the-ground organizing and changes in popular consciousness. There was no latter-day Teddy Roosevelt in the White House leading the charge. The people led, and the politicians followed.

And of course, it took the sheer radicalism of the early civil rights protest-ers to build a movement for justice so powerful that two presidents, Kennedy and Johnson, had to pay attention. Very gradually, despite continuing skir-mishes about affirmative action, racial tolerance in the minds of the people grew to the point where America could elect an African American president.

Three conclusions emerge from this history. First, with the partial excep-tion of the environmental and civil rights movements, every one of the successful postwar social movements has been primarily about something other than economic issues. The movements for women's, black, gay, and disability rights were demands by oppressed groups for inclusion. They were secondarily about economic justice, since the inferior civil status of these groups had a significant economic dimension—blacks and women were systematically relegated to inferior jobs and opportunities; gays could not acknowledge their real sexual identity without wrecking careers; and handi-capped people were widely assumed incapable of doing real work and were relegated to low-status jobs. The connection of rights to economics was vividly underscored by Dr. King's last march, the one where he was assas-sinated. He was marching with the janitors of Memphis on a strike for better wages. Even so, these movements were primarily demands by out-groups for full membership in the American dream. None was per se an economic movement.

Second, while the past half century, beginning with the civil rights move-ment, has shown surprising progress in both changed laws and changed norms on issues of social inclusion, it has been a period of retrogression on purely pocketbook issues. Economic security and opportunity have been worsening for three decades. Blacks and women are now part of the civic and economic mainstream, but that mainstream is filled with shoals. The public instruments for promoting opportunity and redressing inequality—regula-tion, progressive taxation, and social investment—have all been weakened. With concentrated economic wealth has come concentrated political power.

The one social movement that is explicitly about pocketbook aspirations, the labor movement, has been on the defensive since the late 1960s.

One must infer from this reality that in America, with its ideal of *E Pluribus Unum*, inclusion is a less arduous crusade than economic justice. When you consider the implications, that is truly remarkable. After all, to recognize full civil rights for African Americans required the overthrow of an entire system of white privilege. In the Deep South especially, it was extremely convenient and economically rewarding to whites that blacks were available to do all the drudgery (and at very low wages) while the economic rewards, plum jobs, and best land went entirely to Caucasians. By the same token, it was very handy for men that women just happened to be suited to keeping house and raising children. It took a social revolution, both in private lives and in public policies, to shift assumptions that have been nearly universal for millennia. These movements were far from easy. They took extraordinary struggle. And judging by persistent white–black and male–female income gaps, as well as largely unchanged statistics on who does most of the house-work and who has to make career sacrifices for the sake of raising families, these social revolutions are still unfinished.

But while the ruling white and male elites were substantially displaced in the late twentieth century to make room for the aspirations of blacks and women, nothing comparable happened with *financial* elites. On the contrary, even after a financial collapse, these elites emerged stronger than ever, with two nominally progressive governments—Clinton's and Obama's—as their close allies. You might think that aspirations of working Americans in general for a decent share of the economic pie would be an easier cause to achieve than the demands of out-groups to be included as full members of civil society. That's especially the case since the accommodation of blacks and women required displacement of deeply entrenched system of privilege. You might also think that a collectivity that represented, say, the bottom 80 percent of the income distribution—those who have been losing out since the 1970s—would be a mighty force. Yet in an era when movements for social justice have successfully knocked down one improbable barrier after another, there has been no comparably successful movement for economic justice. And that has to say something about the hegemonic power of finan-cial elites.

The third conclusion is that while social movements are the prime engine of change, it does matter whether they have the president of the United States on their side. Some of this is a matter of sheer luck, personality, and circumstance. Had a chief executive less friendly to the labor movement than Franklin Roosevelt been president of the United States in the 1930s and early 1940s, he might not have made as close an alliance with organized labor. The Wagner Act, committing the government to enforce the right of workers to bargain collectively, mattered; so did the organizing efforts of workers on the ground. Even more than these, the institutional power of the postwar labor movement was built on Roosevelt's decision in World War II to use the power of government contracting to compel even the most anti-union bosses such as Henry Ford and Sewell Avery of Montgomery Ward to come to terms with unions. Nothing comparable happened during World War I. Woodrow Wilson did not give a damn about unions or workers' rights. In the same way, Lyndon Johnson personally helped make the civil rights movement on the ground into an irresistible legislative force for reforms that had been considered politically inconceivable even a year earlier.

What is dismaying is that Barack Obama, a onetime community organizer, has shown little appreciation for the power of social movements as necessary allies for radical social and economic change, and has done even less to help them. On the contrary, his message has been to cool it, and his strategy has been to damp it down.

Democratic power brokers have increasingly relied on independent-expenditure organizations, so called Section 527 groups, named for the section of the revenue code that permits them. These groups raise money on an ad hoc basic for advertisements, direct-mail pieces, and other forms of political advocacy. They are not, however, grassroots movements, and the use of Section 527 organizations diverts a lot of money from true social movements. One activist told me, "They use 527's because they don't want to strengthen independent progressive groups."

Obama relied heavily on both the financial contributions and on-the-ground campaigning of the labor movement to get elected, yet he did not set as a priority enactment of the Employee Free Choice Act, restoring organizing rights that workers have had in principle since the 1935 Wagner Act. This was the fourth time since the Johnson administration that a Democratic president with a working legislative majority failed to put the full force of the presidency behind labor law reform, thus weakening America's most effective grassroots movement for economic justice as well as a movement on which Democratic candidates rely in every election. We can only conclude that the White House alliance with capital trumps its appreciation of the practical support of labor.

Since the late nineteenth century, the overarching premise of progressives in America and social democrats in Europe has been that the prime counterweight to the excesses of the capitalist market has been a mobilized citizenry using the instruments of the democratic state, especially the state in friendly hands. Unlike corporations, which are (imperfectly) accountable to shareholders and financial traders (who are evidently accountable to no one but their own propensity to incur highly leveraged risks) states via their elected leaders are accountable to democratic electorates. In the twentieth century, especially in the period from the 1940s through the 1960s, states on both sides of the Atlantic fought markets to a draw. Thanks to the tight regulation of financial markets, the use of progressive taxation, the expansion of social insurance, the state as partner in economic development, and the empowerment of workers and unions, economies grew at an impressive clip while the income distribution became steadily more egalitarian.

But what you do when the state falls into unfriendly hands? More frustratingly, what do you do when nominally progressive parties and leaders are substantially captured by the same elites represented by conservative parties?

This has been the trend for more than three decades, both in the United States, where the Democratic Party has increasingly been captured by financial elites, and also in Europe, where nominally center-left parties like the British Labour Party and the German Social Democratic Party have bought most of the center-right recipe of deregulate, privatize, and prune back the welfare state and the bargaining power of trade unions and wage earners generally.

What you do is organize a movement. Rekindling a movement for sweeping economic change in the face of a Democratic administration disappointingly allied with the financial status quo is an even heavier lift than, say, under a Clinton or a Carter because progressive groups find it hard to outflank Obama and even harder to criticize him directly.

From Confederation to Majority

American progressivism, in its activist incarnation, is an archipelago of many thousands of organizations. As the political scientist Karen Paget has long observed, it is a series of movements that doesn't add up to a *movement*. One reason is that progressive activists typically operate in single-issue silos. Another is that many of them are nonprofit, tax-exempt organizations that are prohibited from explicitly engaging in electoral politics. As seekers of foundation funding, many liberal groups go to great lengths to differentiate themselves from one another—they need to persuade funders that some distinction makes them novel or special, which creates fragmentation. As a consequence, there are jillions of groups, many of them doing very useful work, but in a posture of friendly rivalry to kindred groups. And few foundations support direct, on-the-ground organizing. Today's typical liberal group, as Harvard's Theda Skocpol has observed, is more likely to be a letterhead organization, comprising a professional staff and a mailing list, than a genuine grassroots enterprise of the sort that flowered a century ago. There are exceptions to this generalization, but they face uphill battles.

Sometimes, however, the dream of progressive issue organizing, popular mobilization, and influence in electoral politics actually comes together. Perhaps the most powerful example in recent years is the living-wage campaign.

This campaign began in 1994, when the grassroots organization BUILD (Baltimoreans United in Leadership Development) worked with AFSCME (American Federation of State, County and Municipal Employees) to enact a living-wage ordinance in Baltimore, requiring all contractors with the city to pay a living wage well in excess of the federal minimum wage. From that local beginning, the living-wage movement has spread, organized by a very broad coalition of groups including ACORN (Association of Community Organizations for Reform Now) and the labor movement, especially the Service Employees International Union. Living-wage laws have been passed in very unlikely places, suggesting a latent support for economic populism. They are now in force in more than 150 cities and counties, as well as one state (Maryland). These include such liberal redoubts as New York, Los Angeles, San Jose, Portland, Detroit, Milwaukee, St. Louis, Minneapolis, Cleveland, Toledo, Madison, San Francisco, and Boston. But living-wage laws were also enacted in less likely places including Tucson, Duluth, San Antonio, Des Moines, Omaha, Dade County, Denver, Buffalo, and Rochester.

In 2004, an increase in the minimum wage was placed on the Florida ballot. It carried every Florida county, winning statewide by a margin of 71 to 29. It collected far more votes than George W. Bush did. In the presidential race, Bush beat Democrat John Kerry in Florida by some 381,000 votes. The minimum-wage boost won by more than 3 million votes. Had Kerry been on Florida street corners with local organizers agitating for a hike in the minimum wage, he might have won Florida and the presidency.

In 2006, organizers for successful living-wage ballot initiatives strategically targeted swing states where progressive candidates were on the ballot for senator or governor. The initiatives increased turnout among lower-income voters and identified the Democratic candidates with practical help for economically stressed citizens. As Peter Dreier, a public policy professor and activist, recounts the story,

> In November 2006, ACORN led successful ballot measures to raise the minimum wage in four other states (Missouri, Ohio, Colorado, and Arizona), while unions led similar successful campaigns in Montana and Nevada. In each state, they forged broad coalitions between community groups, clergy and churches, unions, and other constituencies. They mobilized effective voter registration and get-out-the-vote campaigns.

In all of these states, the Democrat won. So it is possible for grassroots mobilization around economic issues to influence both the stance of Democratic candidates and election outcomes.

One other place where progressive activists would do well to focus their energies is in Democratic primaries. As I noted in chapter 1, in 2006 and 2008 progressive Democratic candidates won primary and general elections in more than a dozen swing states. There is a latent populism crying out for articulation by believable leaders. If the president of the United States is not yet that sort of leader, others can partly fill the vacuum. Obama has been partly stymied by corporate Democrats who hold upward of fifty House seats. These House members often vote against the economic interests of their constituents. Some primary battles would be salutary. The current labor secretary, Hilda Solis, came to political prominence when she challenged a conservative Democratic incumbent in a working-class Hispanic district in East Los Angeles. Another rising star in the House, Donna Edwards of Prince Georges Country, Maryland, ran a grassroots campaign to displace a Democratic incumbent who was far more conservative than his district. In the Arkansas Democratic primary, the popular lieutenant governor, progressive Bill Halter is challenging the pro-corporate and vulnerable incumbent, Blanche Lincoln, in a campaign backed by MoveOn. Halter has a better shot at representing the interests of ordinary Arkansans—and holding the seat. Had a credible populist run to fill Ted Kennedy's seat, it would not have gone Republican. Senator Bernie Sanders of Vermont did not get elected because that state is a hotbed of socialism, but because he articulates the pocketbook needs of ordinary voters.

The value of enlisting organizers and activists in Democratic primaries has multiple dimensions. It uses people power to offset corporate power. It increases the ranks of progressives in Congress. The process itself rekindles civic life and hones a common progressive ideology. Paradoxically, it was the excitement of a series of Democratic primary and caucus contests that enlisted millions of volunteers and propelled Barack Obama to the presidency, though Obama has disappointed much of his base. This progressive energy must not be reserved for presidential years.

Though some Democratic elected officials do behave like Republicans, especially when it comes to coddling Wall Street, most Democrats are basically progressives. Some more victories in primaries would reinforce the party's identity and legislative representation as a progressive one. A president such as Obama would have an easier time governing as a progressive, and the party rank and file could better hold him accountable.

Tough Love for Obama

Interacting with a president who has been a source of both great hope and disappointment is a tricky affair. For the most part, liberals have continued to be very protective of Obama. I interviewed a progressive elder states-man, who prefers to remain anonymous. We had been talking about the differences between Obama and Bush. He said, "The history of the world is largely a history of governments that are awful—and Obama is not awful. So I'm going to defend a disappointing administration because it's not awful." I take the point, but that is a pretty low bar. "Not awful" isn't what we voted for, and it is hardly sufficient to win reelection during a severe recession.

If Hillary Clinton were engaging in the capitulations that Obama has brought us, progressives would be giving her a much rougher time. If you look at the testimony, the Web sites and blogs, and the speeches of leading progressive leaders and progressive journals, the criticism has been polite and oblique. The tone has been, *We love and appreciate you, President Obama, but couldn't you try a little harder?*

Bill Moyers, America's preeminent progressive broadcast journalist, speaking on the eve of the Senate health insurance showdown, closed his September 4 broadcast respectfully and almost imploringly:

> Come on, Mr. President. Show us America is more than a circus or a market. Remind us of our greatness as a democracy. When you speak to Congress next week, just come out and say it. We thought we heard you say during the campaign last year that you want a government-run insurance plan alongside private insurance—mostly premium-based, with subsidies for low- and moderate-income people. Open to all individuals and employees who want to join and with everyone free to choose the doctors we want. We thought you said Uncle Sam would sign on as our tough, cost-minded negotiator standing up to the cartel of drug and insurance companies and Wall Street investors whose only interest is a company's share price and profits.

Two months later, when I appeared on his show, Moyers had lost patience. He said,

> Something's not right here. One year after the great collapse of our financial system, Wall Street is back on top while our politicians dither. As for health care reform, you're about to be forced to buy insurance from companies whose stock is soaring, and that's just dandy with the White House.

Truth is, our capital's being looted, Republicans are acting like the town rowdies, the sheriff is firing blanks, and powerful Democrats in Congress are in cahoots with the gang that's pulling the heist.

We need more progressives to lose patience.

Potential left-of-center groups have also been neutralized because they need Obama, in the same way that Martin Luther King needed Lyndon Johnson and the CIO of the 1930s needed Franklin Roosevelt. The movement groups of the 1930s and 1960s were a lot less reticent about criticizing the presidents who were their sometime allies—and these presidents delivered a lot more. AFL-CIO president Rich Trumka's threat to withdraw support is a welcome sign of toughness.

At the same time, challenging a president to live up to his promise is not simply a matter of criticizing him. As Marshall Ganz observes, "The left is so used to a politics of disappointment that their critical faculties are over-developed. They have a distant early warning system for signs of betrayal. It requires more courage to see opportunities and to act on them than just to stay on the sidelines and criticize."

If Barack Obama, as organizer Mike Kruglik observed, understands how to use power, he also reacts to power. For now, nearly all the power has been coming from financial and economic elites—bankers, health insurers, financial traders, drug companies. In the occasional cases recounted in this book where power is displayed courageously by reformers, such as a Sheila Bair, an Elizabeth Warren, a Maria Cantwell, a Gary Gensler, a Rich Trumka, Obama has given ground and rediscovered his reformist side. If there were real social movements in high gear, as well as isolated brave individuals, Obama is capable of further movement himself.

Once a president chooses a particular path, it is not easy for that path to change. The path is reinforced by legions of advisers who have vested interests in not departing from it. But there are plenty of precedents. They include not just Truman's rediscovery of the New Deal, but Lincoln deciding that the Civil War was not just about preserving the Union but about freeing the slaves; John Kennedy moving from a candidate hawkishly railing about a missile gap to the president who began détente; and Lyndon Johnson shifting from the southern moderate who brokered between the Dixiecrats and the liberals to the president who redeemed the promise of Lincoln. Presidents grow in office, and they grow when they are pushed. They also grow when they face the prospect of humiliating defeat.

So I remain an optimist. Despite a year of disappointment and disillusion, we have three things on our side. We have reality—most people are not experiencing the economic recovery being enjoyed on Wall Street. We have a clever but empty opposition—a right-wing Republican Party offering nothing to solve this severe crisis. And, in Barack Obama, we have a president who has only begun to realize his full potential as a leader. Whether he does will be a test of his character—and ours.

Endnotes

Front Matter

ix **"I have spent my entire"** www.nytimes.com/2008/04/29/us/politics/29text-obama
.html?pagewanted=all.

ix **"I did not run for office"** www.cbsnews.com/video/watch/?id=5975092n&tag=mncol
;lst;10.

ix **"You can always count"** http://en.wikiquote.org/wiki/Winston_Churchill.

Introduction: The Man and the Moment

xi **"We will need to remind"** Barack Obama, *The Audacity of Hope* (New York: First Vintage
Books Edition, 2008), 31.

xii **"Instead of establishing a twenty-first-century"** Robert Sheer, "Why the Rush on
TARP 2?" *The Nation,* January 14, 2009, www.thenation.com/doc/20090126/scheer.

xii **"If there's a child"** www.washingtonpost.com/ac2/wp-dyn/
A19751-2004Jul27?language=printer.

xiv **"He's taking over the auto industry"** Author's interview.

xiv **"and now I'm sitting on my hands"** Author's interview.

xiv **"total disgust"** Jonathan Weisman, "Gloom Spreads on Economy, but GOP Doesn't
Gain," *The Wall Street Journal,* October 28, 2009, http://online.wsj.com/article/
SB125667589615011225.html.

xvi **"stridency and hardball tactics"** Obama, *Audacity,* 48–49.

xvi **"A lot of us thought"** Author's interview.

xvii **"Barack Obama is widely regarded"** Cass Sunstein, "The Visionary Minimalist," *The New
Republic,* January 30, 2008, www.tnr.com/article/the-visionary-minimalist.

xvii **"transactional leaders who thrive"** James MacGregor Burns, *The Power to Lead* (New
York: Simon & Schuster, 1984), 16.

xx **"lost the narrative"** www.ft.com/cms/s/0/4853d25e-1a5b-11df-a2e3-00144feab49a.html.

xxii **"In the New Deal era"** Author's interview.

xxiii **"I would advise that we try"** http://abcnews.go.com/WN/Politics/
president-obama-scott-brown-massachusetts-victory/story?id=9611222&page=2.

xxiii **"want a fight, it's a fight"** www.msnbc.msn.com/id/34967521.

xxiii **history failed to turn** A. J. P. Taylor, *The Course of German History* (London: Routledge,
1988), 35.

1. The Politics of Capture

1 **"Increasingly, I found myself"** Barack Obama, *The Audacity of Hope* (New York: First
Vintage Books Edition, 2008), 136–7.

2 **"Under Republican and Democratic"** www.nytimes.com/2008/03/27/us/
politics/27text-obama.html?pagewanted=all.

2 **"We need to regulate institutions"** Ibid.

3 **"This was not the invisible"** Ibid.

5 **"The Committee to Save the World"** www.time.com/time/covers/0,16641,19990215,00
.html.

6   **liquidity put** Carol Loomis, "Robert Rubin on the Job He Never Wanted," *Fortune,* November 28, 2007 http://money.cnn.com/2007/11/09/news/newsmakers/merrill_rubin.fortune/index.htm.

6   **"Mr. Rubin, whose contract"** Eric Dash and Louise Story, "Rubin Leaving Citigroup; Smith Barney for Sale," *The New York Times,* January 9, 2009, www.nytimes.com/2009/01/10/business/10rubin.html.

8   **"Oh my goodness"** Author's interview.

9   **"Eisenhower Republican"** Bob Woodward, *The Agenda: Inside the Clinton White House* (New York: Simon & Schuster, 2005), 161.

10   **"one of the more thoughtful"** Obama, *Audacity,* 206.

10   **"I tend to be cautiously optimistic"** Ibid., 207.

11   **"Rubin now freely acknowledges"** William Greider, "Born-Again Rubinomics," *The Nation,* July 13, 2006, www.thenation.com/doc/20060731/greider/single.

11   **Greider asked Rubin lots** www.thenation.com/doc/20060731/greiderweb.

12   **"[O]ne of us (Mr. Bernstein)"** www.nytimes.com/2008/11/03/opinion/03rubin.html?pagewanted=print.

13   **"The public financing of presidential"** www.msnbc.msn.com/id/25259863.

14   **"She's going to raise more money"** Ben Smith, "Clinton Fundraising in Overdrive," *Politico,* February 7, 2007, www.politico.com/news/stories/0207/2670.html.

14   **"I've never had a higher hit ratio"** Kristin Jensen and Christine Harper, "Obama Top Fundraiser on Wall Street," *The Washington Post,* April 18, 2007, www.washingtonpost.com/wp-dyn/content/article/2007/04/17/AR2007041701688.html.

15   **"to build suspense"** David Plouffe, *The Audacity to Win* (New York: Viking, 2009), 52.

16   **"My key mandate"** Kim Chipman and Matthew Benjamin, "Obama Names Rubin Ally Furman to Economic Policy Post," *Bloomberg Press,* June 9, 2008, www.bloomberg.com/apps/news?pid=20601103&sid=acigw2e6gl8Y&refer=us.

17   **"Oh, stop it"** www.youtube.com/watch?v=NmcupSmgraw.

18   **"The Secretary is authorized"** www.nytimes.com/2008/09/21/business/21draftcnd.html.

20   **"That must have been some stemwinder"** http://online.wsj.com/article/SB123905884295394797.html.

22   **"Larry," Barro said, "He's right"** Author's interview.

22   **"breaching my fiduciary duty"** Author's interview.

24   **Harvard locked in future interest** Michael McDonald, John Lauerman, and Gillian Wee, "Harvard Swaps Are So Toxic Even Summers Won't Explain (Update 3)," Bloomberg.com, December 18, 2009, www.bloomberg.com/apps/news?pid=20601087&sid=aHQ2Xh55jI.Q.

24   **"The growth in the global economy"** http://blogs.ft.com/economistsforum/2008/04/america-needs-to-make-a-new-case-for-trade.

25   **"Elizabeth Warren gets up"** Author's interview.

27   **"Rahm was no financial genius"** Author's interview.

28   **"You can't understand utility transactions"** Michael Luo, "In Banking, Emanuel Made Money and Connections, *The New York Times,* December 3, 2008, www.nytimes.com/2008/12/04/us/politics/04emanuel.html?_r=1&pagewanted=1.

28   **As head of the DCCC** This account draws on my own reporting and that of Rick Perlstein, "Plan of Attack," *The New Republic,* November 8, 2006, http://downwithtyranny.blogspot.com/2006/11/new-republic-gasp-gets-it-right-but-i.html.

28   **"Rahm recruited a lot"** Author's interview.

32 **"genuinely impressed"** Monica Langley, "Volcker Makes a Comeback as Part of Obama Brain Trust," *The Wall Street Journal,* October 21, 2008.

35 **"You cannot have a strong"** www.cbsnews.com/stories/2009/01/30/politics/100days/economy/main4764111.shtml.

36 **"Hyman Minsky (1977) and Charles Kindleberger (1978)"** www.nber.org/papers/w1054.

37 **"I do not deny"** Ibid.

38 **"The correct interpretation of the 1920s"** www.federalreserve.gov/BoardDocs/Speeches/2002/20021015/default.htm.

39 **"In the area where"** Edmund L. Andrews, "Bernanke Says Fed 'Should Have Done More,'" *The New York Times,* December 3, 2009, www.nytimes.com/2009/12/04/business/economy/04fed.html.

40 **"Following our economic collapse"** http://topics.npr.org/quote/0afpbK222VeQe.

40 **"For the first time in history"** www.msnbc.msn.com/id/34749128/ns/msnbc_tv-the_ed_show.

2. Continuity and Collusion

42 **"My Administration is the only thing"** Eamon Javers, "Inside Obama's Bank CEOs Meeting," *Politico,* April 3, 2009, http://news.yahoo.com/s/politico/20090403/pl_politico/20871.

42 **"We had to struggle"** http://docs.fdrlibrary.marist.edu/od2ndst.html.

44 **"What if Ben Bernanke had not"** David Wessel, *In Fed We Trust: Ben Bernanke's War on the Great Panic* (New York: Crown Business, 2009), 275.

44 ***Time* magazine named Bernanke** www.time.com/time/specials/packages/article/0,28804,1946375_1947251,00.html.

45 **"What if, amid all their missteps"** www.nytimes.com/2009/08/08/business/08leonhardt.html.

47 **"selling a car with faulty brakes"** www.fcic.gov/hearings/pdfs/2010-0113-Transcript.pdf.

48 **"about two million homeowners have already suffered foreclosure"** Calculations provided by Professor Alan White of Valparaiso University Law School, relying on data from Mortgage Bankers Association and Fannie Mae.

48 **"The Debt-Deflation Theory of Great Depressions"** Irving Fisher, "The Debt-Deflation Theory of Great Depressions," *Econometrica,* 1:4, October 1933.

48 **61 percent of securitized subprime loans** www.calculatedriskblog.com/2010/01/option-arm-recast-update.html.

48 **Moody's Economy.com projected that** http://topics.nytimes.com/top/reference/timestopics/subjects/f/foreclosures/index.html.

48 **Deutsche Bank estimated** Al Yoon, "About Half of U.S. Mortgages Seen Underwater by 2011," Reuters.com, August 5, 2009, www.reuters.com/article/idUSTRE5745JP20090805.

49 **34 percent of the modifications** Alan M. White, "Deleveraging the American Homeowner: The Failure of 2008 Voluntary Mortgage Contract Modifications," *Connecticut Law Review* 41, 2009, 1107.

49 **HOPE for Homeowners** http://cop.senate.gov/documents/cop-030609-report.pdf.

51 **"The rules by which servicers"** www.bos.frb.org/economic/ppdp/2009/ppdp0904.pdf.

52 **"Data on delinquencies"** Peter Goodman, "Lucrative Fees May Deter Efforts to Alter Loans," *The New York Times,* July 29, 2009, www.nytimes.com/2009/07/30/business/30services.html?sq=taking%20control%20of%20houses%20and%20selling%20them&st=cse&scp=1&pagewanted=all.

52 **Alfred Crawford of Los Angeles** Peter S. Goodman, "Homeowners and Investors May
Lose, but the Bank Wins," *The New York Times*, July 29, 2009, www.nytimes.com/
2009/07/30/business/30serviceside.html.

53 **As of December 2009** http://blogs.abcnews.com/theworldnewser/2009/12/only-31000
-americans-entered-into-mortgage-modifications-for-obamas-housing-help-program.html.

54 **Eileen Ulery** Peter S. Goodman, "Promised Help Is Elusive for Some Homeowners," *The
New York Times*, June 2, 2009, www.nytimes.com/2009/06/03/business/03mortgage.html.

54 **Jaime Smith** Rabbi Shmuley Boteach, "Mortgage Ignominy at JPMortgage Chase,"
Huffington Post, January 6, 2010, www.huffingtonpost.com/rabbi-shmuley-boteach/
mortgage-ignominy-at-jp-m_b_414206.html.

54 **Treasury quietly admitted** Shahien Nasiripour and Jeff Muskus, "House Passes Wall
Street Reform Bill with Zero GOP Votes," Huffington Post, December 11, 2009,
www.huffingtonpost.com/2009/12/11/house-passes-financial-re_n_389267.html.

55 **"the banks are not doing"** Peter Goodman, "U.S. Will Push Mortgage Firms to Reduce
More Loan Payments," *The New York Times*, November 28, 2009, www.nytimes
.com/2009/11/29/business/economy/29modify.html.

55 **"firms ought to be embarrassed"** Ibid.

55 **"fat-cat bankers"** www.cbsnews.com/video/watch/?id=5975092n&tag=mncol;lst;10.

55 **"the people on Wall Street still don't get it"** www.cbsnews.com/video/watch/?id=
5975092n&tag=mncol;lst;10.

61 **"shock and uh"** Edmund L. Andrews and Stephen Labaton, "Bailout Plan: $2.5 Trillion
and a Strong U.S. Hand," *The New York Times*, February 10, 2009, www.nytimes
.com/2009/02/11/business/economy/11bailout.html?pagewanted=1.

61 **"had likewise offered to raise"** Andrew Ross Sorkin, *Too Big to Fail: The Inside Story of
How Wall Street and Washington Fought to Save the Financial System—and Themselves* (New
York: Viking Penguin, 2009), 516.

63 **"nationalization"** Author's interview.

67 **"Japanese authorities pinned"** http://cop.senate.gov/documents/cop-040709-report.pdf.

67 **"The consensus view among economists"** Ibid.

71 **Jesse Jones** Jesse H. Jones, *Fifty Billion Dollars: My Thirteen Years with the RFC* (New York:
Macmillan, 1951), 7–8.

74 **Center on Budget and Policy Priorities** www.cbpp.org/research/index.cfm?fa=
topic&id=29.

77 **Birmingham, Alabama, cannot afford** Shaila Dawan, "Alabama Area Reeling in Face
of Fiscal Crisis," *The New York Times*, July 31, 2009, www.nytimes.com/2009/08/01/
us/01alabama.html?scp=2&sq=+birmingham+bury&st=nyt.

79 **"The last thing we would want"** www.huffingtonpost.com/robert-kuttner/
a-tale-of-two-obamas_b_382061.html.

82 **"entirely consistent with the approach"** www.reuters.com/article/
idUS210981+28-Oct-2009+PRN20091028.

83 **"a third of US multinational profits overseas"** Author's interview.

83 **Goldman Sachs set aside** http://online.wsj.com/article/SB10001424052748704281204575
003351773983136.html.

85 **"Given population growth"** Heidi Shierholz, "Labor Market Closes 2009 with No Sign
of Robust Jobs Recovery," Economic Policy Institute, January 8, 2010, www.epi.org/
publications/entry/jobs_picture_20100108.

3. Missing a Rendezvous with Reform

88   **"The Obama plan is little more"** www.nytimes.com/2009/06/18/business/18nocera.html.

88   **"a sweeping overhaul"** www.whitehouse.gov/the_press_office/Remarks-of-the-President-on-Regulatory-Reform.

88   **"Credit conditions have improved"** Author's interview.

89   **"Remember that Cooper Union speech?"** Author's interview.

93   **"The approach proposed"** www.house.gov/apps/list/hearing/financialsvcs_dem/volcker.pdf.

95   **"There are two reasons"** Author's interview.

97   **"The spread of unsustainable"** www.financialstability.gov/docs/regs/FinalReport_web.pdf.

97   **"The CFPA's strong rules"** Ibid.

98   **"We propose that the regulator"** Ibid.

98   **"We propose that the government"** Ibid.

99   **"The economy has made it tough"** Michael Kranish, "Business Takes Aim at Proposed New Rules," *The Boston Globe,* September 19, 2009, www.boston.com/business/personalfinance/articles/2009/09/19/white_house_rails_against_ad_protesting_new_consumer_agency.

99   **"The Federal Trade Commission has a clear mission"** www.financialstability.gov/docs/regs/FinalReport_web.pdf.

100   **"No 'Plain Vanilla' Requirements"** http://blog.prospect.org/blog/weblog/FrankCFPAMemo.pdf.

104   **"The undersigned companies"** http://big.assets.huffingtonpost.com/finalcoalitionletter.doc.

108   **"I don't see a Goldman"** www.cftc.gov/ucm/groups/public@newsroom/documents/file/transcript072909.pdf, quote at page 137.

108   **"literally worse than nothing"** Author's interview.

110   **In a series of closely orchestrated** www.house.gov/apps/list/press/financialsvcs_dem/pressotc_100209.shtml.

112   **of the 253 current and former** Ryan Grim and Arthur Delaney, "The Cash Committee: How Wall Street Wins on the Hill," Huffington Post, December 29, 2009, www.huffingtonpost.com/2009/12/29/the-cash-committee-how-wa_n_402373.html.

114   **"Under this amendment"** www.c-spanarchives.org/congress/?q=node/77531&id=9078982.

114   **"We believe that if we ban"** www.c-spanarchives.org/congress/?q=node/77531&appid=595067179.

115   **"Doing financial reform in 2009"** Author's interview.

116   **"seemed to many to be transparently political"** Jim Kuhnhenn, "Obama Banking Plan Complicates Regulatory Bill," *The Boston Globe,* February 2, 2010, www.boston.com/news/local/connecticut/articles/2010/02/02/dodd_complains_obama_banking_plan_complicates_bill.

4. Crony Capitalism

118   **"Barack Obama ran"** "Reflections on Economic Policy in a Time of Crisis," www.whitehouse.gov/administration/eop/nec/speeches/reflections-on-economic-policy-in-time-of-crisis.

119   **"The audacity of that prick"** William D. Cohan, *House of Cards* (New York: Doubleday, 2009), 115.

120   **"Chuck was totally new"** See Eric Dash and Julie Creswell, "Citigroup Saw No Red Flags Even as It Made Bolder Bets," *The New York Times,* November 22, 2008, www.nytimes .com/2008/11/23/business/23citi.html?pagewanted=all.

122   **"Citi got the money"** Author's interview.

123   **government-guaranteed toxic stew** www.bloomberg.com/apps/news?pid= 20601087&sid=aWRQBVRCi6G0.

124   **"Sandy Weill paid Bob Rubin"** Author's interview.

125   **Global Transaction Services** David Enrich, "Citi Unit Grows—with Feds' Help," *The Wall Street Journal,* January 12, 2010, http://online.wsj.com/article/SB126317001431624045 .html.

126   **Andrew Cuomo revealed** Andrew Cuomo, "No Rhyme or Reason: The 'Heads I Win, Tails You Lose' Bank Bonus Culture," July 30, 2009, www.scribd.com/doc/17850928/ Andrew-Cuomo-Bonus-Report.

129   **"I think in some cases"** www.cbsnews.com/blogs/2009/12/13/politics/ politicalhotsheet/entry5975318.shtml.

130   **"We don't make the determination"** www.huffingtonpost.com/2009/12/17/ treasury-official-blames_n_396211.html.

132   **"This big bonus season"** http://transcripts.cnn.com/TRANSCRIPTS/1001/10/ sotu.04.html.

133   **Feinberg devised what might be** Steven Brill, "What's a Bailed-Out Banker Really Worth?" *New York Times Sunday Magazine,* December 29, 2009, www.nytimes .com/2010/01/03/magazine/03Compensation-t.html?pagewanted=all.

134   **It fell to Warren Buffett** Andrew Ross Sorkin, *Too Big to Fail: The Inside Story of How Wall Street and Washington Fought to Save the Financial System—and Themselves* (New York: Viking Penguin, 2009), 473.

134   **The intrepid Gretchen Morgenson** "Paulson's Calls to Goldman Tested Ethics," *The New York Times,* August 8, 2009, www.nytimes.com/2009/08/09/business/09paulson.html.

135   **When Special Inspector General Barofsky** "Factors Affecting Efforts to Limit Payments to AIG Counterparties," November 17, 2009, www.sigtarp.gov/reports/audit/2009/ Factors_Affecting_Efforts_to_Limit_Payments_to_AIG_Counterparties.pdf.

136   **The SEC has determined** Gretchen Morgenson and Louise Story, "Testy Conflict with Goldman Helped Push AIG to the Edge," *The New York Times,* February 6, 2010, www .nytimes.com/2010/02/07/business/07goldman.html?ref=business&pagewanted=all.

137   **According to Greenberg** Holman W. Jenkins Jr., "Can AIG Be Saved?" *The Wall Street Journal,* January 9, 2010, http://online.wsj.com/article/SB10001424052748704130904574644 4693895033518.html.

138   **had reaped close to $3 million** http://online.wsj.com/article/SB124139546243981801 .html

138   **"the kind of person we needed"** Kate Kelly and Jon Hilsendrath, "New York Fed Chairman's Ties to Goldman Raise Questions," *The Wall Street Journal,* May 4, 2009, http://online.wsj.com/article/SB124139546243981801.html.

139   **the case of Gene Sperling** www.bloomberg.com/apps/news?pid=20601087&sid= abo3Zo0ifzJg.

141   **"It gives comfort to our clients"** Eric Lipton and Michael J. de la Merced, "Wall Street Firm Draws Scrutiny as U.S. Adviser," *The New York Times,* May 18, 2009, www.nytimes .com/2009/05/19/business/19blackrock.html?_r=1&dlbk=&pagewanted=all.

142 **"They have access to information"** http://dealbook.blogs.nytimes.com/2009/05/19/in-advising-us-blackrock-thrives-in-uncertain-times.

143 **"In other words, the conflict"** SIGTARP, *Quarterly Report to Congress,* April 21, 2009, www.sigtarp.gov/reports/congress/2009/April2009_Quarterly_Report_to_Congress.pdf.

143 **"[C]entral banks do liquidity"** Cohan, *House of Cards,* 441.

145 **the SEC sued Bank of America** www.sec.gov/litigation/complaints/2010/comp21377.pdf.

146 **"a bargaining chip"** http://online.wsj.com/article/SB124466361157703247.html.

147 **"[T]his interaction among Treasury"** http://cop.senate.gov/documents/letter-051909-geithnerbernanke.pdf.

148 **73 percent reported an increase** http://agriculture.house.gov/testimony/111/h061109sc/Bauer.doc.

149 **an analysis by Dean Baker** www.cepr.net/index.php/press-releases/press-releases/taxpayer-subsidizing-banks.

149 **The August 2009 report** http://cop.senate.gov/documents/cop-081109-report.pdf.

150 **"a very harsh examination"** http://banking.senate.gov/public/index.cfm?FuseAction=Files.View&FileStore_id=cede97ec-ba28-42d5-8404-2b86554b6973.

150 **"The banks that behaved well"** Author's interview.

151 **"more than 150 examiners"** www.federalreserve.gov/newsevents/speech/bernanke20090507a.htm.

152 **"moved securities from their trading account"** http://financialservices.house.gov/cop-081109-report.pdf.

157 **"We cannot and must not"** www.nytimes.com/2009/03/30/us/politics/30obama-text.html.

157 **"[A] group of investment firms"** Ibid.

157 **Tom Lauria** http://blogs.abcnews.com/politicalpunch/2009/05/bankruptcy-atto.html.

159 **"The challenges the United States faces"** www.theatlantic.com/doc/200905/imf-advice.

5. Obama's Loyal Opposition

162 **"Too big to fail has failed"** www.kc.frb.org/speechbio/hoenigpdf/omaha/03.06.09.pdf.

163 **She wrote a popular book** Elizabeth Warren and Amelia Warren Tyagi, *The Two-Income Trap: Why Middle-Class Mothers and Fathers Are Going Broke* (New York: Basic Books, 2003).

164 **"People like my grandparents"** Author's interviews.

168 **"TARP has become"** www.sigtarp.gov/reports/testimony/2009/Testimony_Before_the_House_Committee_on_Oversight_and_Government_Reform.pdf.

169 **exchange between Geithner and Damon Silvers** http://cop.senate.gov/hearings/library/hearing-091009-geithner.cfm.

171 **"Because these warrants"** www.house.gov/apps/lkist/hearing/financialsvcs_dem/elizabeth_warren_oversight_subcom_7-22_testimony_final.pdf.

172 **Treasury was covertly subsidizing the banks** http://cop.senate.gov/documents/testimony-033109-warren.pdf.

172 **"Several major TARP recipient companies"** http://cop.senate.gov/reports/library/report-121008-cop.cfm.

174 **A tally of direct lobbying outlays** www.boston.com/business/articles/2009/09/27/bailed_out_banks_battle_to_reshape_bills.

176 **"If we are to rationalize"** Quoted in Ryan Lizza, "The Contrarian," *The New Yorker,* July 6, 2009, www.newyorker.com/reporting/2009/07/06/090706fa_fact_lizza?currentPage=all.

179 **"no more WaMu's"** David Wessel, *In Fed We Trust* (New York: Crown, 2009), 223.

179 **"fierce and relentless defender"** Ibid., 219–20.

180 **"Bair as a showboat"** Andrew Ross Sorkin, *Too Big to Fail: The Inside Story of How Wall Street and Washington Fought to Save the Financial System—and Themselves* (New York: Viking Penguin, 2009), 296.

180 **Geithner . . . sought to get Bair fired** www.bloomberg.com/apps/news?pid= 20601087&sid=aTFflUwD.Qbg.

182 **"If five private equity guys"** Author's interview.

182 **"Private equity hopes to buy up"** Author's interview.

183 **a draft policy statement proposing** www.fdic.gov/news/board/jul2sop.pdf.

183 **excessive or unwise executive compensation** www.fdic.gov/news/news/press/2010/ pr10005.html.

184 **"I don't see how anybody"** www.huffingtonpost.com/2009/10/26/showdown -in-chicago-sheil_n_333969.html.

185 **"sponsoring and capitalizing"** http://online.wsj.com/article/SB125313031639216991 .html.

185 **"Will not the pattern"** http://house.gov/apps/list/hearing/financialsvcs/ dem_volcker.pdf.

186 **"While almost all economic-policy"** Ryan Lizza, "Inside the Crisis," *The New Yorker,* October 12, 2009, www.newyorker.com/reporting/2009/10/12/091012fa_fact_lizza.

189 **His reply, dated February 11** www.prospect.org/cs/articles?article=wall_street _meets_its_match.

190 **"They are slow walking"** http://seattletimes.nwsource.com/html/ businesstechnology/2009281564_born31.html.

191 **"The Treasury should be ashamed"** www.huffingtonpost.com/2009/10/16/ sen-maria-cantwell-savage_n_323868.html.

191 **"could swallow up the regulation"** http://sifma.org/uploadedFiles/Government _Affairs/OTC/Gensler_to_Harkin_Chambliss_Aug_17_2009.pdf.

194 **"If we compare the TARP"** www.kc.frb.org/speechbio/hoenigpdf/omaha/03.06.09.pdf.

194 **"Certain companies have not"** www.ft.com/cms/s/0/46e2f784-380b-11de-9211 -00144feabdc0.html.

195 **"A tendency to use"** https://clevelandfed.org/Research/Review/1992/92-q4-Todd.pdf.

196 **"The sounder strategy"** http://online.wsj.com/article/SB124027165661037073.html.

198 **"Don't leave your home"** www.govtrack.us/congress/record.xpd?id=111-h20090115-29.

199 **"retarded"** Peter Wallsten, "Chief of Staff Draws Fire from Left as Obama Falters," *The Wall Street Journal,* January 26, 2010, http://online.wsj.com/article/SB10001424052748703 80890457502503038469515 8.html.

201 **"Particularly impressive was the impact"** Peter Dreier, unpublished research paper, cited with permission of the author.

6. Political Malpractice

204 **"Insanity is doing the same thing"** www.quotationspage.com/quote/26032.html.

205 **In a Peter Hart poll** www.aflcio.org/issues/politics/upload/mass_elections.pdf.

206 **CBS program *60 Minutes*** www.cbsnews.com/video/watch/?id=5975092n.

207 **page-one headline** http://online.wsj.com/article/SB10001424052748703808904575024772 877067744.html.

207 **"This is like announcing"** Eve Conant, "This Week in Conservative Media: Should Conservatives Rally Behind Obama's Budget Freeze," *Newsweek,* January 27, 2010, http:// blog.newsweek.com/blogs/thegaggle/archive/2010/01/27/this-week-in-conservative -media-should-conservatives-rally-behind-obama-s-budget-freeze.aspx.

208 **"A spending freeze?"** Paul Krugman, "Obama Liquidates Himself," *The New York Times,* January 26, 2010, http://krugman.blogs.nytimes.com/2010/01/26/obama-liquidates-himself.

209 **"Let's fight like hell"** David Plouffe, "November Doesn't Need to Be a Nightmare for Democrats," *The Washington Post,* January 24, 2010, www.washingtonpost.com/wp-dyn/content/article/2010/01/22/AR2010012204216.html.

210 **A huge increase in traditional** http://projects.nytimes.com/44th_president/stimulus.

211 **"Conservative Coalition"** Arthur C. Paulson, *Electoral Realignment and the Outlook for American Democracy* (Evanston, IL: Northeastern University Press, 2007), 142–44.

212 **"emerging Democratic majority"** John B. Judis and Ruy Teixeira, *The Emerging Democratic Majority* (New York: Simon & Schuster, 2002).

213 **"Voters returned to a more"** www.prospect.org/cs/articles?article=back_to_the_future061807.

215 **McDonnell carried voters** www.nytimes.com/interactive/2009/11/04/us/politics/1104-va-exit-poll.html.

215 **wacky ninety-three-page master's thesis** www.washingtonpost.com/wp-dyn/content/article/2009/08/29/AR2009082902434.html.

217 **"brain-dead partisanship"** http://abcnews.go.com/GMA/Politics/evan-bayh-assails-senate-congress-partisanship-denies-presidential/story?id=9849082.

218 **CNBC's Rick Santelli** www.cnbc.com/id/15840232?video=1039849853.

218 **In several states, far-right opponents** Matthew Shaer, "Conservatives Wave Red Flags Over Obama School Speech," *Christian Science Monitor,* September 2, 2009, www.csmonitor.com/USA/Politics/The-Vote/2009/0902/conservatives-wave-red-flags-over-obama-school-speech.

219 **Steinhauser in December recruited** www.nytimes.com/2010/01/21/us/politics/21reconstruct.html.

220 *Saturday Night Live* www.huffingtonpost.com/2009/10/04/snl-obama_n_308979.html.

221 **"can't seem to grasp"** David Brooks, "The Populist Addiction," *The New York Times,* January 25, 2010, www.nytimes.com/2010/01/26/opinion/26brooks.html.

225 *Economist* **magazine's polling unit** http://media.economist.com/media/pdf/tabs20090916.pdf.

225 **"Many observers have assumed"** Robert Kuttner, *Obama's Challenge: America's Economic Crisis and the Power of a Transformative Presidency* (White River Junction, VT: Chelsea Green, 2008), 166.

226 **Billy Tauzin** Paul Blumenthal, "The Legacy of Billy Tauzin: The White House–PhRMA Deal," Huffington Post, February 12, 2010, www.huffingtonpost.com/paul-blumenthal/the-legacy-of-billy-tauzi_b_460358.html.

226 **Boehner excoriated Tauzin** http://realclearpolitics.blogs.time.com/2009/08/18/boehner-pops-tauzin-in-the-nose.

227 **a notorious Big Lie** www.facebook.com/note.php?note_id=113851103434.

227 **"How someone could take"** http://voices.washingtonpost.com/ezra-klein/2009/08/is_the_government_going_to_eut.html.

227 **Enzi declared in a radio address** Jonathan Wiseman and Janet Adamy, "Democrats Try Tougher Tone on Health Plan," *The Wall Street Journal,* September 2, 2009, http://online.wsj.com/article/SB125184862134977755.html.

227 **"There's some people that think"** http://interact.stltoday.com/blogzone/political-fix/political-fix/2009/08/grassleys-grandma-remark-re-ignites-debate.

228 **Grassley signed a fund-raising letter** http://voices.washingtonpost.com/ezra-klein/grassleyfundraising.pdf.

228 **Jacob Hacker devised** www.rwjf.org/files/research/hacker.pdf.

229 **"roughly half of non-elderly Americans"** www.sharedprosperity.org/bp180/bp180.pdf.

229 **bargaining power over price** www.sharedprosperity.org/hcfa/lewin.pdf.

230 **"We do not see"** http://online.wsj.com/article/SB124775966602252285.html.

231 **"not run by the government"** www.journalstar.com/news/state-and-regional/govt-and-politics/article_19bc53c8-f4e8-11de-ab34-001cc4c002e0.html.

232 **"However the political future unfolds"** Robert Dallek, "Obama's Historic Health-Care Victory," *The Wall Street Journal,* December 29, 2009, http://online.wsj.com/article/SB10001424052748703278604574624123140468430.html.

233 **Jonathan Gruber** Jonathan Cohn, "Recognizing Reform," *The New Republic,* December 21, 2009, www.tnr.com/article/health-care/recognizing-reform.

234 **"Instead of taxing the rich"** www.aflcio.org/mediacenter/prsptm/sp01112010.cfm.

234 **"There are a thousand"** www.huffingtonpost.com/richard-trumka/dont-let-our-opponents-di_b_119606.html.

235 **"If I were a senator"** Howard Dean, "Health-Care Bill Won't Bring Real Reform," *The Washington Post,* December 17, 2009, www.washingtonpost.com/wp-dyn/content/article/2009/12/16/AR2009121601906.html.

235 **"In order to dance"** www.nytimes.com/2010/01/31/weekinreview/31quotation.html.

237 **"We're in the red zone"** www.washingtonexaminer.com/opinion/blogs/beltway-confidential/Obama-on-health-care-Were-in-the-red-zone----weve-got-to-punch-it-through-83369397.html.

237 **"We're still going around"** Robert Pear and David M. Herszenhorn, "Democrats Ask, Can Health Care Bill Be Saved," *The New York Times,* February 5, 2008, www.nytimes.com/2010/02/06/health/policy/06health.html.

238 **"We now know"** http://thehill.com/blogs/blog-briefing-room/news/81023-boehner-slams-healthcare-summit.

239 **"My wife will tell you"** Barack Obama, *The Audacity of Hope* (New York: First Vintage Books Edition, 2008), 27.

7. Change We Can Believe In

244 **"never went after Franklin Roosevelt"** Alonzo L. Hamby, *Man of the People* (New York: Oxford University Press, 1995), 259.

245 **"last lady of the land"** Ibid., 365.

245 **Truman's popularity rating** http://webapps.ropercenter.uconn.edu/CFIDE/roper/presidential/webroot/presidential_rating_detail.cfm?allRate=True&presidentName=Truman.

245 **"We cannot recall"** William C. Berman, *The Politics of Civil Rights in the Truman Administration* (Athens: Ohio University Press, 1970), 64.

246 **a famous memo** Hamby, *Man of the People,* 430–32.

247 **"The cheering and stomping"** David McCullough, *Truman* (New York: Simon & Schuster, 1992), 643.

247 **"[T]he objective was not"** Hamby, *Man of the People,* 433.

248 **"I wonder how many times"** McCullough, *Truman,* 658–59.

248 **"I'm not talking about"** Ibid., 660–61.

248 **"was cheerful, friendly"** Ibid., 662.

248 **"Now, use your judgment"** Ibid.

248 **"Some things are worth fighting for"** Ibid., 677.

249 **"but it's my class"** www.nytimes.com/2006/11/26/business/yourmoney/26every.html.

249 **"There is an agreeable warmheartedness"** McCullough, *Truman*, 664.

255 **2010 State of the Union address** www.whitehouse.gov/the-press-office/
remarks-president-state-union-address.

258 **that leverage was used** Robert E. Rubin, with Jacob Weisburg, *In an Uncertain World*
(New York: Random House, 2003); Joseph Stiglitz, *The Roaring Nineties* (New York: W. W.
Norton, 2003).

260 **From the 1950s through** Simon Johnson, "The Quiet Coup," *The Atlantic*, May 2009,
www.theatlantic.com/doc/200905/imf-advice.

262 **"Since January, most advocacy groups"** www.hks.harvard.edu/news-events/news/
commentary/we-have-the-hope.

269 **it is a series of movements** Karen Paget, "Many Movements. No
Majority," *The American Prospect,* Summer 1990, www.prospect.org/cs/
articles?article=citizen_organizing_many_movements_no_majority.

269 **As Harvard's Theda Skocpol has observed** Theda Skocpol, *Diminished Democracy*
(Norman: University of Oklahoma Press, 2003).

270 **"In November 2006, ACORN led"** Peter Dreier, unpublished research paper, cited with
permission of the author.

272 **"Come on, Mr. President"** www.truthout.org/090609Z.

272 **"Something's not right here"** http://digg.com/educational/
Bill_Moyers_Journal_Something_s_not_right_here.

ACKNOWLEDGMENTS

A great many of the people from the Obama Administration, the Federal Reserve System, and the Congress who helped me with both the reporting of this book and with explanations of highly technical issues cannot be properly acknowledged, because they were kind enough to speak to me on background. Those whom I can thank include: Damon Silvers, Elizabeth Warren, Maria Cantwell, Marcy Kaptur, Rob Johnson, Michael Greenberger, Joseph Stiglitz, Heather Booth, George Goehl, Mike Elk, Dana Chasin, Rob Weissman, David Arkush, Travis Plunkitt, Ellen Harnick, Rich Ferlauto, Matt Stoller, Heather Slatkin, John Taylor, Tom Hoenig, Alan White, Jane D'Arista, Robert Pollin, Jerry Epstein, David Moss, Richard Parker, Robert Borosage, Roger Hickey, Larry Mishel, Ross Eisenbrey, Ron Blackwell, Stephen Lerner, Stephen Abrecht, Janet Shenk, Chris Slevin, Joel Merkel, James Galbraith, Dean Baker, Theda Skocpol, Larry Jacobs, Greg Anrig, Dan Geldon, Scott Paul, Leo Hindery, Barry Zigas, Ellen Seidman, Alex Burden, Andrew Rich, Bill Black, Henry Berliss, Walker Todd, Bill Patterson, Erica Payne, Lance Lindblom, Katherine McFate, Leonardo Burlamaqui, George McCarthy, and Frank DeGiovanni.

As always, I am grateful to my colleagues at *The American Prospect* and at Demos, including Ben Taylor, Paul Starr, Mark Schmitt, Harold Meyerson, George Slowik, Miles Rapoport, Stephen Heintz, Tamara Draut, Tim Rusch, Gennady Kolker, Jinny Khanduja, Heather McGhee, Jim Lardner, Michael Lipsky, David Callahan, Kalin Drzewiecki-Sezer, and my other colleagues at the Demos project on regulation. Some short portions of this book are adapted from articles that appeared in the *Prospect*.

A special thank-you once again to the amazing Daphne Hunt, for heroic research assistance.

The Chelsea Green team has been extraordinary. It is a challenge to publish a book that is partly about a story that is still unfolding. The people at Chelsea Green went to great lengths to make sure that the book would not be overtaken by events. Particular thanks to Margo Baldwin, Joni Praded, Pati Stone, Laura Jorstad, Emily Foote, Allison Goodwin, and to Kevin Ellis.

I also gratefully acknowledge various courtesies by Arianna Huffington, Bill Moyers, Sara Bershtel, John Brockman, and Katinka Matson. All or parts of drafts of the book were read by Miles Rapoport, Rob Johnson, Damon Silvers, Michael Greenberger, Richard Parker, Daphne Hunt, and Joan Fitzgerald, all of whom saved me from errors small and large. Any remaining errors are my responsibility.

Particular thanks are owed to my family for indulging long periods of obsessive focus on this book, and especially to my constant editor and best friend, Joan. The book is dedicated to our five grandchildren, and not just for sentimental reasons; their life-chances will be enhanced if our president rises to the occasion. With this project completed, I am looking forward to spending more time with them.

INDEX

the politics and practice of sustainable living

CHELSEA GREEN PUBLISHING

Chelsea Green Publishing sees books as tools for effecting positive change and empowering citizens. If you liked *A Presidency in Peril*, consider these other books at the forefront of progressive politics.

OBAMA'S CHALLENGE
America's Economic Crisis and the Power of a Transformative Presidency
ROBERT KUTTNER
ISBN 9781603580793
Paperback • $14.95
A New York Times bestseller

THE LOOTING OF AMERICA
How Wall Street's Game of Fantasy Finance Destroyed Our Jobs, Pensions, and Prosperity—and What We Can Do About It
LES LEOPOLD
ISBN 9781603582056
Paperback • $14.95
One of Library Journal's *Best Business Books of 2009*

THE END OF MONEY AND THE FUTURE OF CIVILIZATION
THOMAS H. GRECO, JR.
ISBN 9781603580786
Paperback • $19.95
One of P2P Foundation's Best Books of 2009

WAITING ON A TRAIN
The Embattled Future of Passenger Rail Service—A Year Spent Riding Across America
JAMES MCCOMMONS
Foreword by JAMES HOWARD KUNSTLER
ISBN 9781603580649
Paperback • $17.95
One of Library Journal's *Best Books of 2009*

the politics and practice of sustainable living

For more information or to request a catalog, visit **www.chelseagreen.com** or call toll-free **(800) 639-4099**.

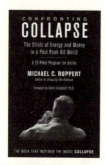
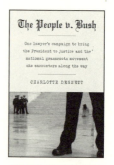
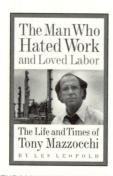
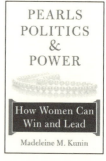